FOR THE PEOPLE?

The Berkeley Tanner Lectures

The Tanner Lectures on Human Values were established by the American scholar, industrialist, and philanthropist Obert Clark Tanner; they are presented annually at nine universities in the United States and England. The University of California, Berkeley, became a permanent host of annual Tanner Lectures in the academic year 2000–2001. This work is the fifteenth in a series of books based on the Berkeley Tanner Lectures. The volume includes a revised version of the lectures that Charles Beitz presented at Berkeley in October 2022, together with commentaries by Martin Gilens, Pamela S. Karlan, and Jane Mansbridge. The volume is edited by Henry E. Brady, who also contributes an introduction. The Berkeley Tanner Lecture Series was established in the belief that these distinguished lectures, together with the lively debates stimulated by their presentation in Berkeley, deserve to be made available to a wider audience. Additional volumes are in preparation.

KINCH HOEKSTRA
R. JAY WALLACE
Series Editors

Selected Volumes in the Series

DEREK PARFIT, *On What Matters: Volumes 1 & 2*
Edited by SAMUEL SCHEFFLER
With T. M. SCANLON, SUSAN WOLF, ALLEN WOOD, AND BARBARA HERMAN

JEREMY WALDRON, *Dignity, Rank, and Rights*
Edited by MEIR DAN-COHEN
With WAI CHEE DIMOCK, DON HERZOG, AND MICHAEL ROSEN

SAMUEL SCHEFFLER, *Death and the Afterlife*
Edited by NIKO KOLODNY
With SUSAN WOLF, HARRY G. FRANKFURT, AND SEANA VALENTINE SHIFFRIN

F. M. KAMM, *The Trolley Problem Mysteries*
Edited by NIKO KOLODNY
With JUDITH JARVIS THOMSON, THOMAS HURKA, AND SHELLY KAGAN

PHILIP PETTIT, *The Birth of Ethics*
Edited by KINCH HOEKSTRA
With MICHAEL TOMASELLO

ARTHUR RIPSTEIN, *Rules for Wrongdoers*
Edited by SAIRA MOHAMED
With OONA HATHAWAY, CHRISTOPHER KUTZ, AND JEFF MCMAHAN

SEANA VALENTINE SHIFFRIN, *Democratic Law*
Edited by HANNAH GINSBORG
With NIKO KOLODNY, RICHARD R. W. BROOKS, AND ANNA STILZ

FOR THE PEOPLE?

Democratic Representation in America

Charles R. Beitz

With Commentaries by
Martin Gilens
Pamela S. Karlan
Jane Mansbridge

Edited and Introduced by
Henry E. Brady

OXFORD
UNIVERSITY PRESS

Oxford University Press is a department of the University of Oxford.
It furthers the University's objective of excellence in research, scholarship,
and education by publishing worldwide. Oxford is a registered trade mark of
Oxford University Press in the UK and in certain other countries.

Published in the United States of America by Oxford University Press
198 Madison Avenue, New York, NY 10016, United States of America.

© Regents of the University of California 2024

All rights reserved. No part of this publication may be reproduced, stored in
a retrieval system, or transmitted, in any form or by any means, without the prior
permission in writing of Oxford University Press, or as expressly permitted
by law, by license or under terms agreed with the appropriate reprographics
rights organization. Inquiries concerning reproduction outside the scope of the
above should be sent to the Rights Department, Oxford University Press, at the
address above.

You must not circulate this work in any other form
and you must impose this same condition on any acquirer

CIP data is on file at the Library of Congress

ISBN 9780197780435

DOI: 10.1093/9780197780466.001.0001

Printed by Integrated Books International, United States of America

CONTENTS

Acknowledgments vii
List of Contributors ix

Introduction 1
   Henry E. Brady

FOR THE PEOPLE? DEMOCRATIC REPRESENTATION IN AMERICA

Preface and Overview 13

Lecture I: Intimations of Failure 17
   Charles R. Beitz

Lecture II: Regulating Rivalry 66
   Charles R. Beitz

CONTENTS

COMMENTARIES

The Preference-Policy Link and Representation — 119
Martin Gilens

Systems, Dyads, and a Contingency Theory of Competition: A Citizen's View — 139
Jane Mansbridge

Unrepresentative Democracy in America — 159
Pamela S. Karlan

RESPONSE

Reply to Commentators: Preferences and Policy, Legitimacy, and Countermajoritarianism — 173
Charles R. Beitz

References — 199
Index — 225

ACKNOWLEDGMENTS

I am grateful to the Tanner Lectures Committee of the University of California, Berkeley for inviting me to give these lectures; to Chancellor Carol T. Christ, the committee's chair, for her interest in the lectures and her hospitality; to the committee's vice-chair, R. Jay Wallace, for superintending the long road from invitation to visit and beyond so graciously; and to Henry E. Brady for deftly bringing this volume together. My warmest thanks to Martin Gilens, Pamela Karlan, and Jane Mansbridge, who commented when I gave the lectures at Berkeley. I could not have hoped for more expert and constructive interlocutors, or ones who could make the occasion of the lectures more stimulating.

Because I composed the lectures over a period prolonged by the pandemic, I relied on advice and help from more people than I can confidently recall. For suggestions and comments that helped me to improve the lectures I owe thanks to Christopher Achen, Arthur Barsky, Henry Brady, Daniel Browning, Atticus Carnell, Joshua Cohen, Gregory Conti, Samuel Freeman, Nannerl Keohane, Niko Kolodny, Frances Lee, Stephen Macedo, Nolan McCarty, Erin Miller, Jan-Werner Müller, Alan Patten, Nancy Rosenblum, T. M. Scanlon,

ACKNOWLEDGMENTS

Anna Stilz, Rob Tempio, Dennis Thompson, James Lindley Wilson, and two reviewers for the Oxford University Press. The members of a memorable Princeton graduate seminar on democratic representation in the Covid-constrained fall of 2020, appearing in Zoom boxes from California to Spain, and of an undergraduate seminar in the fall of 2022, helped me to digest both empirical and theoretical materials. I am grateful to both groups. My apologies to those I've missed.

Charles R. Beitz
May 5, 2024

CONTRIBUTORS

Charles R. Beitz is Edwards S. Sanford Professor of Politics at Princeton University. He taught at Swarthmore and Bowdoin colleges before coming to Princeton. He is a former editor of *Philosophy & Public Affairs* and director of Princeton's University Center for Human Values. He has written on global justice, democratic theory, the theory of human rights, and other topics in political philosophy. He is a member of the American Academy of Arts and Sciences and has held fellowships from the Guggenheim, Macarthur, and Rockefeller foundations, the American Council of Learned Societies, and the American Council of Education. His book, *The Idea of Human Rights* (OUP, 2009) won the Estoril Global Issues Book Award.

Martin Gilens is Professor of Public Policy, Political Science, and Social Welfare at UCLA. He has published widely on political inequality, mass media, race, gender, and welfare politics. Professor Gilens has held fellowships at the Institute for Advanced Study, the Center for Advanced Study in the Behavioral Sciences, and the Russell Sage Foundation. He is a member of the American Academy

CONTRIBUTORS

of Arts and Sciences, and taught at Yale and Princeton universities before joining UCLA in 2018.

Jane Mansbridge is Charles F. Adams Professor, Emerita, at Harvard University's Kennedy School of Government, and a past president of the American Political Science Association. Her work has received the APSA's Lippincott, Madison, Schuck, and Kammerer awards, the International Political Science Association's Deutsch award, and the International Johan Skytte Prize. She is a member of the American Academy of Arts and Sciences. She has written on feminism, adversary democracy, mutual collective deafness, oppositional consciousness, enclave deliberation, everyday activism, a selection model of representation, deliberative systems, representative systems, recursive representation, legislative negotiation, and the contingency theory of ideals.

Pamela S. Karlan is the Kenneth and Harle Montgomery Professor of Public Interest Law and co-director of the Supreme Court Litigation Clinic at Stanford Law School. Her scholarship focuses on constitutional litigation, particularly with respect to voting rights and the law of democracy. She has published dozens of scholarly articles and is the co-author of three leading casebooks. Karlan is a member of the American Academy of Arts and Sciences and Council of the American Law Institute. In 2021, she received the American Bar Association's Margaret Brent Award. In 2016, she was named one of the *Politico 50*—a group of "thinkers, doers, and visionaries transforming American politics."

Henry E. Brady is Class of 1941 Monroe Deutsch Distinguished Professor of Political Science and Public Policy at the University of California Berkeley. He has served as president of the American Political Science Association and dean of the Goldman School of Public Policy at UC Berkeley. He is a member of the American

CONTRIBUTORS

Academy of Arts and Sciences and a fellow of the American Association for the Advancement of Science. He has written on public opinion and political participation, political methodology, Canadian and American elections, the collapse of the Soviet Union, and topics in public policy including higher education, social welfare, and voting systems.

Introduction

HENRY E. BRADY

The Greeks' ideas about democracy may have led us astray. When we think of democracy, we envision the demos assembled in the agora participating in impassioned debates and formulating historic actions. There are Pericles's speeches urging Athenians forward during the early years of the Peloponnesian War (431–429 BCE) and Cicero's orations almost four hundred years later in the Roman Senate (63 BCE) defending the Republic against the Catilinarian Conspiracy. In these examples, since the link between oratory and action is immediate, it is not surprising that democratic theorists often concentrate on the role of deliberation in politics and how deliberation leads to decisions. Because there was not much activity in Greek democracy in between individual orations in the agora and the precipitation of community action, modern political theorists—with a few exceptions—do not say much about this interstitial area except sometimes offering theoretical reflections on "rational communicative action." This narrow focus persists when political theorists move on to the study of representative democracy, where they often study the dyadic relationship between individual citizens and their representatives, shorn of all institutional detail. Yet as Charles

Beitz tells us in *For the People? Democratic Representation in America*, modern representative democracy is much more than this.

Too seldom do political theorists consider the political parties, interest groups, and media that are the major "in-between" features of modern representative democracies. Through their intense competition and reverberating criticisms of one another, these institutions go a long way toward shaping, aggregating, and determining political outcomes in today's world. Omitting these organizations is as foolhardy as if someone tried to understand modern capitalism by studying commerce among small merchants and their customers in the medieval marketplace before the rise of large industries and corporations. Of course, something would be learned about individual acquisitiveness, the role of prices and exchange, and consumer needs and wants, but major features of the modern capitalist system such as large corporations, oligopolistic market-power, and the possibility of extreme exploitation would be missed. So it is with the American political system with its parties, interest groups, and mass media.

Beitz's focus on the competition among parties and interest groups—he omits the media to keep the scope of his project manageable—demonstrates that in order to design a healthy democracy we must investigate what defines good and bad political competition between parties and among groups. He pursues questions about political competition carefully, thoroughly, and revealingly. Unlike many political theorists who avoid the word "competition" because they seem to find it unseemly in any discussion of democracy where deliberation should be paramount, the word appears almost two hundred times in Beitz's two lectures.

There is a long history of underestimating and even ignoring competition among parties and interest groups in America. Almost 250 years ago, the Founding Fathers hoped to avoid the problems of competitive factions through the peculiar alchemy of a large nation, representative democracy, checks and balances among branches of the government, and institutions such as the Electoral College composed of upstanding citizens. Perhaps, as the first to create a large representative democracy, the Founders can be forgiven for their naiveté. At least they knew that competitive factions presented perils for the new republic, and they anticipated that they might cause problems, but they did not fully comprehend what factions would produce in the way of parties, interest groups, and the media.

At the transition from the nineteenth to the twentieth century a hundred years ago as the American frontier disappeared and the nation became urbanized and industrialized, the Progressives had little excuse for ignoring powerful institutions such as interest groups and parties. They had witnessed the rise of powerful corporations and had a century of party strife on which to reflect. In the economic sphere, they recognized the need to create countervailing powers such as trade unions, government regulations, and laws against monopoly to rein in oligopolistic corporations. Their solutions for ensuring a competitive economy were tailored to the task at hand.

While they were prescient in the economic sphere, the Progressives did not think about how to foster better competition among political parties (Rosenblum 2008, chap. 4). Even though they recognized flaws in American democracy, they evidently did not think it was very important to foster fruitful competition. Instead they developed ways to work around and to sanitize parties so as to decrease their competitiveness. They advocated political reforms such as the recall, referendum, and initiative that produced more populist democracy—more appeal to the demos—as ways to work around the political parties. They also tried to tame and reform one important intermediary institution, the urban political machine, through antiseptic "good government" managerial methods such as Civil Service laws, unified budgets, anticorruption laws, better auditing systems, and "nonpartisan" elections. Although these goo-goo "good government" reforms might have cleaned up governments and made them look prettier and perform more efficiently, they did little to ensure the productive functioning of political competition. Indeed the Progressives' solutions to political ills demonstrated virtually no understanding of the virtues or perils of political competition, and their favorite populist nostrums, the referendum, initiative, and recall, have arguably fallen prey to the dangers of allowing unbridled competition through political donations.

In the late 1960s and early 1970s, political reformers again failed to address the competitive implications of their proposals while adding still more populist institutions to American politics that weakened political parties. In the wake of the disastrous 1968 Democratic Convention in Chicago that led to what the National Commission on the Causes and Prevention of Violence called a "police riot" directed against antiwar demonstrators, the Democratic Party's McGovern-Fraser Commission established candidate selection rules that led to the replacement of caucuses and "party insiders" for selecting presidential candidates with primary elections first suggested by the Progressives. These elections opened up the presidential and other nomination processes to the party rank-and-file—typically the ideologically most intense members of the party who turn out in primary elections and who place ideological purity over winning. The net result has been the nomination of more and more extreme candidates on the left (for the Democrats) and on the right (for the Republicans) who are popular among the ideologically intense groups within their parties. These candidates, unlike those chosen by party professionals, who want above all else to win general elections, are not very electable in competitive general elections because they do not appeal to the preponderant center of the electorate, and they tend to take more extreme positions once gaining offices. If party reformers had thought harder about the importance of competition between the parties, they would have recognized that their reforms would weaken and polarize the parties and their candidates (Polsby 1983).

INTRODUCTION

The primary process has been made even more problematic on the Republican side by allowing winner-take-all victories in most of their primary states where all or most of the delegates go to the plurality winner instead of proportional allocation. Consequently, an early set of adventitious wins by a candidate driven by the peculiarities of the order of the states amasses an insurmountable number of delegates. More than any other feature of the 2016 Republican nomination process, this winner-take-all setup allowed Donald Trump with his uniquely intense but not overwhelmingly large base to overcome his many opponents, who split up the remaining Republican primary electorate. Although the advent of the modern primary season has allowed for greater participation and transparency, it has also made it possible for long-shot candidates (e.g., George McGovern and Donald Trump) to get nominated and, in Trump's case, even elected, and it has contributed to the polarization of American politics.

It is time for political theorists to take seriously the quality of political competition produced by parties and interest groups. Empirical political scientists already have a long history of studying parties and interest groups, although they have seldom taken the important step of thinking hard about how to improve the quality of competition. Empirical studies go back to Lord Bryce's *American Commonwealth* (1888) and Moise Ostrogorski's *Democracy and the Organization of Political Parties* (1902). These authors—like Tocqueville before them—were fascinated with the role of groups in American democracy and the way that they expressed people's interests and needs. Other political scientists shared this fascination, and more and more studies of interest groups were published in the early twentieth century. As time went on, the term "pressure" increasingly appeared in their titles, indicating their power but also hinting that something might be amiss with their influence. Some examples are Peter Odegard (1928), *Pressure Politics: The Story of the Anti-Saloon*

League, E. E. Schattschneider (1935), *Politics, Pressures, and the Tariff*, and V. O. Key (1942), *Politics, Parties and Pressure Groups*.

Despite these concerns, there was an undercurrent of recognition that in a large industrial republic, interest groups and political parties were the only way that most people could be represented in political affairs. Several authors made this explicit. In 1908 Arthur F. Bentley extolled the role of groups in his book entitled *The Process of Government: A Study of Social Pressures*. In 1918, Mary Parker Follett argued that *The New State* identified in the title of her book could be organized and controlled according to the process identified in her subtitle, *Group Organization the Solution of Popular Government*. One of the most influential political science books of the middle of the twentieth century, David Truman's (1951) *The Governmental Process: Political Interests and Public Opinion* defined government as the expression of group political interests and opinions. And finally, in a series of books (Dahl and Lindbloom 1953; Dahl 1956, 1961, 1967) Robert Dahl found the essence of democracy—which he called "polyarchy"—in competition among many groups, institutions, and parties.

Political scientists have been superb at cataloging the competition between parties and among interest groups. They also made a strong case, in the theory of political pluralism put forth in Truman's and Dahl's work, for the importance of these institutions as intermediaries between individuals and government, but they could not quite pin down the conditions for effective competition. The literature on pluralism grew to be enormous, but it foundered on the facile analogy between the virtues of the hidden hand of economic competition that economists claimed (according to mathematical theorems no less!) produced economic efficiency and the pluralist competition of interests that supposedly represented all groups effectively (Bauer, Pool, and Dexter 1963). Although critics pointed out the many flaws in the "pluralist heaven" (Schattschneider 1960;

INTRODUCTION

Bacharach and Baratz 1962; Parenti 1970; Garson 1974; Manley 1983; LaVaque-Manty 2006), there were few attempts to develop a deep-seated analysis of exactly what kind of competition democracy needed to be successful (but see Miller 1983). Charles Beitz asks political theorists to do that deeper analysis with a greater concern for the multidimensional role of competition.

To do that, Beitz examines the common wisdom about what is currently not working in American democracy. From those worries he distills a set of fundamental concerns, and then he develops some maxims about how we should approach the competitive political system. With these concerns and guidelines in hand, he examines three issue areas.

In the first part of this book, Beitz lays out the commonly mentioned maladies of our current political system to see if they really pose problems. He lists legislative gridlock, partisan polarization, unequal responsiveness by class, unequal responsiveness by race, and partisan bias in legislative districting. He finds that they lead to failures of effectiveness where pressing problems such as immigration fail to get addressed, failures of representational congruence and responsiveness where solutions bear little resemblance to people's preferences or needs—especially for lower- and middle-income citizens—and failures of fairness where some citizens such as ethnic minorities are consistently shortchanged in the results. If we were critiquing the political system in terms taken from economics, we would say that good products are not being produced, they do not match people's desires, and they are unfairly priced for some people. These are shocking flaws that seem to put America's political system at a disadvantage compared to its economic system. Although a discerning observer would probably only want to provide *Two Cheers for Capitalism*, as in the title of neoconservative Irving Kristol's 1978 book, it still seems likely that American business is performing better than American politics, especially given the fact that Gallup reports that only eight percent of the American public trusts Congress "a great deal" or "quite a lot" (Gallup 2023).

Perhaps we have done a better job of finding ways to harness competition in capitalism than to make it work for us in representative government. Perhaps we need to think harder about the conditions for successful competitive democracy. That is the task undertaken by Beitz.

Beitz begins by noting that an examination of parties and interest groups moves us away from the dyadic perspective of "citizen and representative" that dominates a great deal of democratic theory. Instead, we recognize that representative democracy is "more than democracy scaled up." Understanding its workings requires a systemic perspective that recognizes how parties animate political competition and make it comprehensible to citizens and how interest groups provide representation for many, but not all, of them. Although a political party and interest group system should not be equated in a simplistic Downsian (Downs 1957) fashion with the way that entrepreneurs compete in a marketplace, political and economic systems are similar in the sense that their operations are more than the sum of their parts—they are complete games with pieces, rules, and strategies. Competitive economies require property rights, a finance system, numerous competing entrepreneurs, receptive consumers, and a government to regulate the system to control its excesses and to make sure it does not devolve into monopoly capitalism. The problem confronting political theorists, which they have not solved, is to clearly say what those parts should be and how the sum of them should operate. Just as economists have stipulated a set of conditions under which markets work and conditions that lead to failure, political theorists need to determine the conditions that make competitive representative systems work—and the conditions that lead to failures.

Beitz starts by listing some general conditions, including responsivity to durable majorities, protecting citizens from systematic disregard of their concerns, ensuring that the system can make decisions and solve problems, and alerting citizens to a range of alternative policy options. He then applies them to three areas, political districting, ballot access, and campaign finance. I will not recount the rest of that fascinating story here since Beitz tells it very well. But I will end by mentioning a festering question behind Beitz's work. Can political competition get "off the rails" in the same way that a capitalist economic system can lose its competitive vitality or become a tired and inefficient set of monopolies? One possibility, as old as Aristotle's *Politics*, is that political competition can become performative—merely demagoguery playing to the fears and hopes of the crowd—instead of problem oriented with the intention of solving society's problems.

As I write this, the Republican-controlled House of Representatives of the United States is about to vote on the first articles of impeachment of a Cabinet member since 1876 for the supposed crime of not enforcing the laws. The secretary of Homeland Security, Alejandro Mayorkas, is being blamed for the problems at America's southern border, where most observers agree that there are insufficient resources to handle the crisis and to adequately enforce the laws. At the same time, the House of Representatives is said to be rejecting a bipartisan piece of legislation being drafted by the Senate that would provide at least some policy solutions to the problem. The impeachment is purely performative. There appears to be little evidence for "high crimes and misdemeanors," and in any case the Democratic-controlled Senate will almost surely not vote to convict Mayorkas. The legislation is solution oriented, but it may not pass. There is no indication that American voters will rise up in disgust because they are repelled by this concern with the performative over an effort to solve problems.

In a kind if Gresham's law of politics, can bad performative competition drive out good problem-oriented competition? Bad money drives out good money because it casts doubt on all money. Does performativity cast doubt on solution-oriented debates? Or are there limits to the harm that can be done? For most material products, people eventually tire of low quality or poor items. Even advertising cannot save them. An Edsel is, after all, an Edsel, a Pinto is a Pinto, and New Coke is New Coke. And businesses ultimately respond by working hard to demonstrate the worth of their products. But when the product is ideas, as with politics, is it possible that there is no limit to performativity and misleading communications from a clever source? And is it possible that there is no way to drive bad competition out of a political system once it has seeped in, especially when there is a media system that thrives on fears and emotions?

FOR THE PEOPLE? DEMOCRATIC REPRESENTATION IN AMERICA

Preface and Overview

The following chapters revise and extend Tanner Lectures on Human Values given at the University of California, Berkeley in October 2022. In preparing the text for publication I have tried to retain the style and structure of lectures while elaborating portions that were excessively compressed, elucidating some claims that were obscure or incomplete, and providing more satisfactory references to my sources. I have placed many details in footnotes that can be skipped without missing anything essential. Retaining the exploratory style of lectures has also meant preserving an order of presentation that one reader generously described as following a logic of discovery rather than of justification. Because this might be puzzling for others as well, I begin with an overview of the terrain ahead.

It has become a commonplace that democracy in the United States faces existential threats. This belief gained popular currency in the wake of Donald Trump's presidency, nourished by his conduct in office, the attempt to overturn the 2020 election, and continuing efforts to subvert the electoral process.

Whether the threats are genuinely existential, only time will tell. But a common narrative among scholars of American government holds that representative democracy is failing more systematically than the Trump phenomenon suggests. Unprecedented levels of elite polarization, extreme partisan gerrymandering, weakened party institutions, easing of restrictions on campaign finance, fragmentation of the public sphere, and other forces—all in the context of rising levels of economic inequality and the stubborn persistence of racial resentment—have produced dysfunction that subverts healthy political competition. A gridlocked Congress has not offered solutions to broadly recognized public problems. Legislation appears to favor the interests of wealthy elites when they conflict with those of the majority and to be insufficiently attentive to those of ethnoracial minorities. In this perspective, the Trump phenomenon concealed a deeper malfunction, or series of malfunctions, of democratic representation.

For those interested in the moral basis of representative democracy, the narrative of malfunction raises two questions. First, are the symptoms documented by professional observers of American politics really *failures*? What norms of democratic representation do they infringe? This is a problem of diagnosis. Second, approaching the subject more constructively, what would successful democratic representation look like? If we grant that democratic politics is unavoidably a form of regulated competition, what would it mean for its regulation to be fair and effective? This is a problem of prescription. The first lecture addresses the diagnostic problem. The second explores the problem of prescription.

In the first lecture, we examine several stylized facts drawn from political science that describe conditions that constitute or bring about what are purported to be failures of democratic representation. I call these "intimations of failure" because it is not always clear in what the purported failures consist. The most troubling failures, though not the only ones, can be interpreted as failures of effectiveness, failures of congruence and responsiveness, and failures of fairness. But these are only labels, and in each case we must examine the reasons for believing that the purported malfunction is actually a failure of institutional (or extra-institutional) processes to conform to democratic norms. The main conclusion is in a way negative: although there are good reasons to regard each of the failures as troubling, there is no single standard of success for democratic representation by which judgments of failure can be justified. This is because the aims or justifying purposes of democratic representation are plural. They are not easily reduced to a univocal overarching value such as that of political equality, as some understand it.

The second lecture begins by trying to draw lessons about the idea of democratic representation from the intimations of failure canvassed in the first lecture. Of the many lessons that might be learned, I pick out four: democratic representation is better understood as a system rather than as a collection of distinct, dyadic relationships; it is not simply democracy "scaled up" but rather an institutional structure embodying a morally consequential division of labor; it is fundamentally competitive; and political parties play an ineliminable if not always a salutary role in organizing political competition. These lessons—which will be truisms for many political scientists—should inform an attempt to articulate standards of fair and effective democratic representation.

I go on to sketch a normative conception of democratic representation as a competitive system—in Rawls's possibly surprising phrase, as a system of "regulated rivalry."[1] The basic idea is that competition is a distinctive means of solving problems that depends on its participants conducting themselves as adversaries. We rely on competition to produce social values as externalities. However, adversarial conduct can run off the rails, defeating its social purposes. This is one reason why rivalrous processes require regulation by rules and social norms. A central problem for a theory of democratic representation is to identify the social values we rely on political competition to produce and the arenas in which competition can produce them if it is appropriately regulated. Without claiming to be comprehensive,

---

1. Rawls 1999, 199. We return to the passage in which the phrase occurs in the second lecture.

I note four such values, which I refer to as "purposes" of democratic competition. Democratic representation should aim to produce policy responsive to the settled will of the majority; avoid predictable forms of substantive injustice; effectively resolve conflict about the content and direction of public policy, at least insofar as it pertains to achieving broadly valued public functions; and maintain deliberative environments in both the institutional and public spheres conducive to epistemically responsible judgment. The purposes can be realized in different ways and to different extents in competitive processes in various arenas within the system. The standards of fairness and effectiveness that apply to these processes derive from the basic purposes that democratic competition should serve, interpreted for the functional characteristics of each arena. To illustrate, I consider three arenas of competition—electoral competition, party competition, and interest competition—and try to articulate norms of fairness and effectiveness applicable to each. There are also, of course, other arenas of competition in the system of representation that I cannot consider here; the most important from a democratic perspective is the public communicative environment, whose competitive architecture has transformed in the last few decades.

In resisting the temptation to fill out the sketch, I yielded to a constraint imposed by the lecture form. I hope the compensation will be a sharpened appreciation of the challenge to democratic theory of working out the normative consequences of recognizing that representation can be fair only when democratic political competition is appropriately regulated.

Lecture I

Intimations of Failure

CHARLES R. BEITZ

Not very long ago, it was hard to find a political scientist who feared for the resilience of democracy in America. Nancy Rosenblum observed in 2014—accurately, at the time—that although there was an "acute sense of democratic failing," few worried that it would lead to "fascism or civil unrest."[1] Four years later, stimulated by Donald Trump's unexpectedly successful campaign for the presidency and his contempt for democratic norms, two of Rosenblum's colleagues published a book titled *How Democracies Die*.[2] It became a bestseller.

I share the anxiety about the resilience of American democratic institutions, more acutely now than when I chose the topic of these lectures before the insurrection of January 2021. But that existential anxiety is not my subject here, though it is a provocation. I shall not, for example, take up the threat posed by election denialism and other repudiations of common standards of constitutional democracy. I shall ask us, instead, to consider the "acute sense" of institutional failure that Rosenblum identified among professional observers of

---

1. Rosenblum 2014, 652–53.
2. Levitsky and Ziblatt 2018.

American politics well before Trump.[3] In addition to first-order concerns about the health of American democracy, their observations implicate problems for political theory about the nature, aims, and standards of democratic representation. The problems deserve systematic attention.

These lectures are an exercise by a political theorist reading political science as democratic theory. I ask two main questions. First, what are the arguments that our representative institutions are failing? We shall review some evidence from political science, but this is not mainly a matter of settling the facts. The question involves their normative significance—it is diagnostic. Second, what might we learn about successful democratic representation from a critical look at the diagnoses of failure? Taking the phrase, for the moment, as a placeholder: What do these diagnoses suggest about the requirements of fair and effective representation?[4] This question is prescriptive. We consider the diagnostic question in this lecture and the prescriptive question in the next.

The intimations of failure I shall describe are not products of the Trump years. If what many political scientists say is correct, democratic representation in the United States faces enduring challenges. The urgent practical question is whether the challenges are amenable to any feasible repair. A fully satisfying answer is beyond my competence, though I hope to shed some light by asking how we should judge whether representative institutions are failing and how we might recognize improvement. Democratic theory should be able to answer these questions. Yet the ideas of good representation that we find in contemporary political theory often seem too detached from

---

3. By "professional observers" I mean primarily political scientists but also other social scientists, scholars of public law, and some journalistic commentators attentive to American politics. For simplicity I sometimes say merely "political scientists," but I mean the phrase in this more inclusive sense.
4. "Fair and effective": *Reynolds v. Sims* 377 U.S. 533 (1964), 565.

ordinary politics to inform practical criticism of existing institutions.[5] I am gambling that a critical reading of political science might be a stimulus to take seriously aspects of democratic representation that too easily fall below the analytical horizon of many of its theorists.

A final preliminary note. In the last few decades political theorists have elaborated conceptions of political representation whose scope extends well beyond conventional understandings of the subject in political science.[6] Since my aim is to engage with political science, I leave those conceptions aside. Omitting some refinements, I shall understand political representation more conventionally as a process in which individuals are selected, typically by popular election, to occupy offices defined primarily by duties to participate in making law and policy and to oversee its execution. Contestation in the law and policymaking processes takes place within a larger environment in which individuals and groups seek to influence these processes by participating in various forms of public deliberation.[7] As Nadia Urbinati observes, "For political representation to work, societal deliberation must take place alongside that of the legislature: advocacy in the representative assembly requires and stimulates advocacy in society."[8] I refer to the domain of public deliberation as the

5. Of course, there are exceptions, including, for example, Mansbridge 2003 and many other studies; Rehfeld 2005; Rosenblum 2008; McCormick 2011; Muirhead 2014; Sabl 2015; and Disch 2021.
6. Perhaps most prominently Saward 2010. Also see Rehfeld 2018 and earlier papers cited there, and Urbinati and Warren 2008's review of literature, comprehensive at the time of publication.
7. Shapiro distinguishes deliberation from argument on the grounds that the first but not necessarily the second aims ideally to produce agreement (2017, 77). He argues that a competitive model of democracy, properly understood, anticipates argument rather than deliberation. I am not sure the distinction is accurate if taken as a report of ordinary usage. In any case, in these lectures I understand democratic political deliberation broadly as embracing forms of advocacy, debate, and public disagreement as well as Shapiro's more idealized deliberation. Shapiro is surely right that there is no realistic alternative.
8. Urbinati 2006, 48; compare her more recent account of democratic "diarchy" (2014, chap. 1). In the recent literature the juxtaposition of a political public sphere with the institutional political system traces to Habermas [1964] 1974, reformulated in Habermas

"public sphere," but I recognize that the phrase is open to a broader interpretation as well.[9] The important point is that we must conceive of democratic representation as having both institutional and extra-institutional deliberative elements.

There are important borderline cases for the conventional understanding (e.g., administrative officers with delegated rule-making responsibilities and, perhaps, elected judges). Beyond the borderlines, we can imagine non-electoral supplements to democratic representation as I understand it here (e.g., deliberative assemblies chosen by sortition). But the main idea is that political representation is a process for making authoritative public policy by individuals who are chosen in competitive elections to do so within a larger public deliberative environment. For some purposes this would be too narrow.[10] I hope not for mine.

IS REPRESENTATION FAILING? FIVE STYLIZED FACTS

The catalog of putative failures of representation in the literature of American politics is long. I cannot rehearse them all. I begin with

---

1996, esp. chap. 8, and subsequently Pettit 2000. Of course, the idea that democratic self-rule incorporates both components has a longer history in social thought about public opinion; see, for example, Lindsay 1935, 73–74. Without using the phrase, Manin notes that the idea of a free public sphere was made explicit in the American founders' endorsement of freedom of expression and of the press (1997, 167–75).

9. The possibility of a broader interpretation arises from the fact that the extra-institutional domain of representative politics is not a unitary subject. On one plausible view it includes, for example, the vast expanse of interest-centered lobbying and public advocacy as well as political parties, the press and public media, and labor and civil society organizations devoted to informing, organizing, and mobilizing for political action. Such a view is suggested, for example, by Saward 2010.

10. For example, in the context of systemic reform, in which representation by lot should not be excluded ab initio (as Guerrero 2014 and Landemore 2020 argue).

five facts drawn from the literature about democratic representation in the United States. It is an incomplete selection and I shall not try to defend it except to say that people who report these facts usually consider them to be signs, reflections, or causes of troubling failures.

To start, some caveats. First, versions of these facts are widely accepted in political science but there is obviously no consensus. Since I shall have to leave aside most of the obligatory qualifications, I should say that these facts are "stylized."[11] Second, things may be changing. For example, we might be at an inflection point, with trends in the partisan division of opinion shifting with changes in the composition of the Republican electorate.[12] Political science is retrospective and scholarship needs time to update. Finally, there is a difficult question about whether apparent failures are institutional dysfunctions or refractions of exogenous change. These can be hard to distinguish. Institutions that are unproblematic in some circumstances can become problematic in others. Institutions do not determine outcomes on their own. I shall offer a speculation about this later, but for the most part I must leave this question to social theory.

This last point suggests a further observation. The idea of a failure of representation may seem enigmatic. It suggests a failure to accomplish a purpose that we expect representative institutions to serve, or perhaps to realize an ideal. But the idea will be empty until we give the purpose or ideal normative content. One aim in beginning with

---

11. Kaldor, who evidently coined the phrase "stylized fact," wrote that the theorist who begins with "stylized facts" need not commit "himself on the historical accuracy, or sufficiency, of the facts or tendencies thus summarized" (1961, 188). So stylized facts need not be *facts*, in the ordinary sense. Elgin classifies them as "felicitous falsehoods"—felicitous because they focus attention on regularities that beg to be explained (2017, 26–27).
12. Carnes and Lupu 2021 show that white working-class voters have been shifting slowly to the Republican Party in recent decades. See also Riley 2020 and reflections on the impact of Donald Trump's presidency on the attitudes of Republican identifiers in Sides, Tausanovitch, and Vavreck 2022.

diagnoses of failure found in political science is to identify some candidate contents for these normative notions.

Let me list the five stylized facts and gesture at some reasons why some diagnose them as signs of failure. Then we can examine the diagnoses more carefully.

Gridlock

The first fact concerns the productivity of the Congress. By some measures, it has been declining for decades. Let us say, but only tentatively, that gridlock is a failure to make or change policy on important issues.[13] The poster child of gridlock is fiscal brinksmanship leading to government shutdown. But the more serious concern is that Congress is not responding to problems that need a response. Familiar examples include immigration reform, gun regulation, and climate policy. Sarah Binder finds that gridlock has been increasing since the 1970s: "Stalemate," she says, "at times now reaches across three-quarters of the salient issues on Washington's agenda."[14]

This is a long-standing concern of observers of congressional politics. James Macgregor Burns wrote in 1963 that

> as a nation we have lost control of our politics. We cannot collectively settle the elementary question of who may vote in national elections and hence we cannot extend the vote to millions of our fellow Americans, especially Negroes. We cannot exercise the primitive right of controlling congressional and presidential election arrangements, especially gerrymandering, rural overrepresentation, and one-party districts. We have lost control of political money and its misuse.[15]

---

13. I paraphrase Binder 2003, 3.
14. Binder 2015, 97. For updated data see Binder 2021.
15. Burns 1963, 324.

Those concerns, evident to Burns sixty years ago, of course remain familiar today.

James Curry and Frances Lee, in partial contrast, find that although congressional procedures have changed dramatically in the last few decades and polarization among members has increased, there has been surprisingly little impact on legislative output. On the one hand, more ideologically consistent parties have not been more successful in enacting partisan agendas. They have not succeeded at "party government." On the other hand, notwithstanding the increase in votes staged to underscore partisan divisions, the parties have managed to continue a pattern of bipartisan legislation despite changes that have centralized the legislative process and reduced the influence of committees.[16] Of course, even if we accept this understanding of the facts, the centralization of control of the agenda and increased partisan messaging have plainly had an adverse impact on the quality of congressional debate, particularly at the committee level, where substantive deliberation that might be most consequential for the quality of legislation has virtually disappeared.[17] And nobody who considers gridlock a failure of representation will take comfort in the fact, if it is a fact, that the phenomenon is even more long-standing than many believe.

Gridlock looks bad for effective representation. It reinforces the status quo bias in the constitutional system of checks and balances.[18] It interferes with the updating of policy, producing what Jacob

---

16. "Madisonian limits to party influence remain as robust in today's era of party polarization as they were in eras when parties were more internally divided and weakly organized. The American policy making system—characterized by constitutional checks and balances, separation of powers, and the decentralizing force of individualized elections for members of Congress—frustrates and moderates efforts at partisan lawmaking" (Curry and Lee 2020, 180).
17. Sinclair 2016, chap. 10.
18. A "harmonious system of mutual frustration," according to Hofstadter (1948, 323). See Gilens 2012, 70–77.

Hacker and Paul Pierson call "policy drift."[19] It obstructs oversight of administrative agencies and complicates their work applying policy to changing circumstances.[20] In an environment of increasing income inequality, it blocks changes in policy aimed at reducing it: gridlock is not distributionally neutral.[21] At the structural level, gridlock shifts influence to the executive branch and the courts and reduces the effectiveness of congressional oversight.[22]

Polarization

The second fact consists of a set of phenomena traveling under the common though possibly misleading heading of "polarization." The subject has at least three aspects.

First, ideological divergence among members of Congress, and more generally among party officials and activists ("elites"), has increased dramatically over the last four or five decades.[23] There is no longer overlap of ideological positions between Republicans and Democrats in the Congress. Elite polarization has been asymmetric, with Republicans moving farther to the right than Democrats have moved to the left.[24]

---

19. Hacker and Pierson 2014, 651, prefigured in Hacker 2004.
20. Mettler and Leavitt 2019; Spence 2019.
21. Kelly 2019, chap. 6.
22. Issacharoff 2018, 497–504. McCarty 2019, 141–45 summarizes the political science.
23. For surveys see McCarty 2019; Klein 2020. What is referred to in the literature as "ideological" divergence may not be *ideological* in the ordinary sense of that word. A member's votes would be ideological in the "ordinary sense" if the member regarded them as justified by some higher-order principles of political theory. But the standard measure of "ideological" polarization in the Congress is constructed from members' roll-call votes (McCarty, Poole, and Rosenthal 2016, chap. 2). It cannot detect a member's reasons or motives for voting as she does (see Lee 2009, 41–44, 50–53 on "ideology" as distinguished from team play).
24. "Movement" is a term of art. Much of the polarization, particularly before the mid-1990s, resulted from replacement of more moderate by more extreme members. More recently "ideological migration" has been more significant (Bonica and Cox 2018). On the asymmetry of ideological polarization and the reasons for it, see Hacker and Pierson 2015 and Grossman and Hopkins 2016.

From one perspective this observation might seem tendentious.[25] Over the long haul, the ideological center of gravity in the United States has obviously become more progressive. Early in the last century, a program like Social Security was ideologically extreme; today it is centrist. Relative to the baseline of, say, 1920, Republicans, too, have moved to the left. But this fact does nothing to undermine the concern articulated in political science, which starts from a more recent baseline.

According to what seems to be the majority view, increasing elite polarization has not been matched by either issue or ideological polarization in the mass electorate.[26] And to the extent that the electorate has polarized, it has followed rather than preceded elites. Those who take this view believe it shows a failure of representation. In Morris Fiorina's influential formulation, "[T]here is a disconnect between an unrepresentative political class and the citizenry it purports to represent."[27] Similarly, Seth Hill and Chris Tausanovitch

---

25. Glock 2022.
26. Fiorina 2017, chap. 2. Castle and Stepp 2021 reach a compatible position using a measure of policy polarization, while observing that social identities play a more significant role in driving policy polarization in the electorate (particularly on cultural issues) than is sometimes acknowledged. The most prominent dissenter from the majority view is Abramowitz (2010, 2018), who argues that there is a significant and evidently increasing degree of issue polarization among voters. For reviews of the disagreement see Benkler, Faris, and Roberts 2018, chap. 10 and McCarty 2019, chap. 4. It should be noted that a substantial portion of the public appears to hold views about individual policy issues that do not correspond to their ideological self-identification. Kinder and Kalmoe report that "genuine ideological identification—an abiding dispositional commitment to an ideological point of view—turns out to be rare. Real liberals and real conservatives are found in impressive numbers only among the comparatively few who are deeply and seriously engaged in political life" (2017, 7).
27. Fiorina and Abrams 2009, xix. We might wonder, however, whether the "disconnect" as conventionally measured accurately describes the kind of failure of representation often alleged. The question involves the relationship between a person's positions on a set of individual issues and the interpretation of her location on a postulated single dimension. When individuals' issue positions vary idiosyncratically, a representative who seeks to vote with the constituency majority on every issue may measure as more ideologically extreme than the majority. This means that the appearance of "disconnect" may be agnostic about

write: "If voters have not polarized, then Congress may not reflect the underlying views it is supposed to represent. Fundamental questions of democratic representation are at stake."[28]

One might disagree about this first aspect of polarization yet agree about a second: at both the elite and mass levels, people have sorted themselves into ideologically more homogeneous parties.[29] There are fewer moderate Republicans and conservative Democrats. (This is compatible with what I have just said about polarization: people do not need to change their beliefs about policy to change their partisan affiliation.) The deep source of this is the southern realignment—a racially driven response to the civil rights revolution—though it has a prehistory and the process is complex.[30]

Partisan sorting is not itself a failure of representation. But its consequences might contribute to failures. Sorting can encourage gridlock by making legislation more difficult.[31] It can create incentives for more extreme elite polarization as politicians compete for position within their own already sorted parties.[32] In a system of candidate selection using primary elections, it can produce candidates whose ideological positions are more extreme than their district (or even party) medians.

---

the actual quality of representation (Ahler and Broockman 2018, 1131; but also see Graham and Orr 2020; Fowler et al. 2023).

28. Hill and Tausanovitch 2015, 1059. In contrast to some other writers, however, they do not find that the "disconnect" is a recent development, at least in the Senate: "[O]ur results show that a weak aggregate electoral link is the norm over the past 60 years, not the exception.... If this is a breakdown of representation or government more broadly, then government has always been broken" (1060, 1074).
29. "Sorting" can occur in two ways. Voters can change their party identification to conform to their policy views, or they can change their policy views to conform to their party. In a study of sorting in the 1990s, Levendusky 2009 finds that the second way predominated, demonstrating inter alia the importance of party identification as a determinant of issue positions.
30. Schickler 2016.
31. Binder 2015, 98; Lee 2016, chap. 9.
32. Fiorina 2017, chap. 4.

INTIMATIONS OF FAILURE

Sorting may also be a source (and perhaps a result) of a third aspect of polarization: "affective" (or "negative") polarization or "partisan animosity." Here the dimension of interest is partisan affect rather than issue position or ideology. Two political scientists reported in 2021 that "Republicans and Democrats loathe each other more than ever previously measured in surveys."[33] Negative partisan polarization has been accompanied by a decrease in cross-cutting social identities in a process Lilliana Mason describes as "social sorting."[34] The sources of affective polarization are obscure, but I note that two of its closest students argue that "the single most important factor . . . has been the growing racial divide between supporters of the two parties."[35]

Like sorting, affective polarization is not itself a failure of representative institutions. But its consequences may be damaging to their proper functioning. It can motivate voters to change their previous policy or ideological positions unreflectively and destabilize the system's capacity to hold elected officials to account. Mason writes: "When individuals participate in politics driven by team spirit or anger, the responsiveness of the electorate is impaired. If their own party—linked with their race and religion—does something undesirable, they are less likely to seriously consider changing their vote in the ballot booth."[36] This can incentivize elite resistance to compromise, contributing to gridlock.[37] There is evidence

---

33. Dias and Lelkes 2021, 775. See Iyengar et al. 2019 for a survey of the literature.
34. Mason 2018, 32–34, for example. Compare Dias and Lelkes 2021.
35. Abramowitz and Webster 2018, 123.
36. Mason 2018, 126. Or, as Dias and Lelkes put it: "Affective polarization threatens citizens' ability to come together, fairly weigh political outcomes, hold elected leaders accountable, and ultimately self-govern. Nothing could strike closer to the core of the democratic enterprise" (2021, 789). But also see Brockman, Kalla, and Westwood 2023, which reports results from experiments suggesting that affective polarization among citizens does not affect their political judgments in the way it affects judgments about interpersonal relations.
37. "Political sectarianism compromises the core government function of representation. Because sectarian partisans almost never vote for the opposition, politicians lack the incentive to represent all of their constituents" (Finkel et al. 2020, 535).

that negative affect increases the chances that people will share false political news on social networks, degrading the deliberative environment.[38] Together with widespread perceptions of gridlock, increasing affective polarization may also contribute to a growing polarization of confidence in a wide array of institutions.[39] The most harmful result may be the motivated erosion of norms of forbearance and loyal opposition that are critical to the functioning of representative institutions.[40]

Unequal Responsiveness by Class

Our third and fourth facts involve disparities in policy responsiveness by wealth or income class (the third fact) and by race (the fourth).

The third, and perhaps the most remarked-upon, fact ("[t]he new stylized fact of American politics," according to Jeffrey Lax and colleagues)[41] is the tendency of policy to track the preferences of the affluent minority even when these diverge from those of the middle class or the median voter. Martin Gilens's pathbreaking book documents this fact. He notes that differences in policy responsiveness to different income groups vary by policy area, but policy responsiveness is "always strongest for Americans with the highest incomes."[42] These

---

38. Osmundsen et al. 2021. They report an asymmetry: Republicans are more likely than Democrats to share false political news (1013).
39. In recent decades average levels of trust have declined almost across the board, but there are significant partisan differences. Democrats tend to trust information-producing institutions and labor unions more than Republicans, who trust norm-enforcing institutions and business more than Democrats (H. E. Brady and Kent 2022).
40. Drutman 2020b, 27–29, citing Levitsky and Ziblatt 2018. I put the possible consequences tentatively because the underlying causal judgments are complex and not well understood. See Broockman, Kalla, and Westwood 2023 for some reasons for caution.
41. Lax, Phillips, and Zelizer 2019, 917.
42. Gilens 2012, 97 and, generally, chap. 4. Others report similar findings; for example, Bartels 2016, chap. 8; Ellis 2017; Rhodes and Schaffner 2017; Maks-Solomon and Rigby 2020. Schlozman and colleagues report compatible findings of differential degrees of policy influence by class and race for a range of modes of participation (2012, 2018).

findings are not uncontroversial, but they represent a preponderant view.[43] In a later paper, Gilens and Benjamin Page conclude, starkly, that "In the United States . . . the majority does not rule—at least not in the causal sense of actually determining policy outcomes."[44] This certainly sounds like a democratic failure. Like gridlock, it contributes to a further failure: to stop the growth of inequality of wealth since the Reagan years. Conventional models of democratic politics, of course, predict the opposite.[45]

A more recent stream of research might qualify these findings. Lax and colleagues find that affluent influence is conditioned by partisan differences. Democratic senators are more responsive to home-state opinion in aggregate than Republicans. Republicans are more responsive to their home-state wealthiest partisans. Their study concludes that "Republican senators, not Democrats . . . are primarily responsible for the overall pattern of affluent influence." Still, the diagnosis of failure is similar: "[P]artisan distortion in representation violates norms of equal voice."[46]

43. For doubts about these findings see Wlezien and Soroka 2011; Enns 2015 (and Gilens's 2015 reply); Bashir 2015; Tausanovitch 2016; and Branham, Soroka, and Wlezien 2017. Elkjaer and Klitgaard 2021 offer a comprehensive review of comparative studies of inequality and responsiveness in the United States and Europe. They find that "published research collectively suggests that the preferences of the rich are vastly better represented than those of the poor" (8–9) while noting a striking divergence among results (6–8).
44. Gilens and Page 2014, 576.
45. Bonica et al. 2013. Grossmann et al. offer a more circumstantial conclusion: "The parties do not compete to follow the wishes of the median income citizen, enabling the public to easily transfer income from the rich to the middle class when inequality rises. But they also do not uniformly follow the opinions of the rich, colluding to pass policy or avoid change. Instead, parties represent different public constituencies, different interest group sectors, and their own ideologies; they seek to influence policy adoption, but they face competition and usually end up seeing the status quo maintained" (2021, 1719; compare Grossmann and Hopkins 2016, chap. 6). This might suggest a refinement of the view taken by Gilens and Page 2014, though it should be said that they do not consider the intermediary role played by parties.
46. Lax, Phillips, and Zelizer 2019, 918, 917.

Unequal Responsiveness by Race

The study of policy responsiveness to racial and ethnic groups—the subject of our fourth fact—is less advanced, though it is developing.[47] In an ambitious study of race and responsiveness, Zoltan Hajnal argues that race, even more than wealth, is the most important demographic feature that "determines who wins and who loses in American democracy."[48] He reports that this is true of African-Americans' probability of winning in races for office, of voting for candidates who succeed, and of getting policy outcomes they favor. The measure of policy outcomes is limited to policies involving government spending, so it excludes a good deal. Still, Hajnal can identify no other group that loses—that is, whose preferences fail to correspond to outcomes—more often than African-Americans. He argues that the influence of race cannot be explained by any of the other factors we might think related, like class, education, political orientation, and partisanship. "Blacks lose by a larger margin than any demographic group, they lose more regularly over time, and they lose more consistently across issues."[49]

Here, again, there is partisan asymmetry: during periods when Democrats control the Congress and the presidency, the correspondence gap virtually disappears. Hajnal takes this to be a sign of fair representation ("Under Democrats, African Americans receive a full and fair say in the policies that our government

---

47. Harris and Rivera-Burgos 2021 provide a review of the literature. A related literature about the political influence of racial resentment and racism is more substantial; see, for example, Tesler 2016.
48. Hajnal 2020, 6. His more detailed findings qualify the broadly similar view taken in Griffin and Newman 2008, an earlier study of the relative policy success of distinct racial and ethnic groups. For example, Hajnal is less confident that Blacks are significantly more likely to win on policy measures that most interest them, although he acknowledges a positive relationship (chap. 4; compare Griffin and Newman 2008, chap. 6).
49. Hajnal 2020, 139–40, and more generally 128–33.

pursues"), whereas the racial gap in correspondence at other times is a failure.[50]

Partisan Bias in Legislative Districting

A fifth and possibly the most complex intimation of failure in representation is partisan bias in districting for the House of Representatives and many state legislatures. Partisan bias is a function of the way that single-member territorial districts have been drawn within a jurisdiction. As a first approximation, it is a condition in which a party that wins fewer votes than its rival can win more seats.[51]

Gerrymandering is one source of partisan bias. But it has emerged—though it is not a new discovery—that gerrymandering is not the only source of bias in districting.[52] In many parts of the United States, Democrats tend to be more geographically concentrated than Republicans, so even without deliberate manipulation, the districting system, taken nationally, would display partisan bias in favor of Republicans. In the South one must also take account of the interaction of these phenomena with racial gerrymandering mandated by the Voting Rights Act (to create majority-minority

---

50. Hajnal 2020, 215. Compare Frymer 1999, who argues that the structure of party competition has resulted in the interests of African-Americans being less well represented, even by Democrats, than those of whites. See also Abramowitz and Webster 2018, 123–27 on Republican efforts to capitalize on racial resentment among white voters in recent decades.
51. We owe this formula to D. E. Butler 1947, 285–86. He describes it as a "type of injustice." Today partisan bias is understood as a deviation from "neutrality," a condition in which "v percent of the vote results in s percent of the seats, and this holds for all parties and all vote percentages" (Niemi and Deegan 1978, 1304).
52. Schattschneider noted the importance of political geography in his seminal study of party government (the effect "seems incredible when first observed": 1942, 70). Butler noted it in 1947 while doubting that spatial variation in the distribution of the partisan vote was a significant contributor to partisan bias in the House of Commons (1947, 284–86). See also Gudgin and Taylor 1979. The most influential source in the recent literature is Rodden 2019. As he points out, there is also partisan bias in the definition of Senate constituencies, in that the median Senate constituency (or state) is more Republican leaning than the country as a whole (2019, 2). Obviously this bias isn't a product of gerrymandering.

districts), sometimes used by Republicans as a rationale for "packing" even larger numbers of minority voters into districts than the act requires and possibly diminishing the overall quality of representation of minority voters.[53]

Locke argued that officials charged with repairing malapportionment in the legislature should follow the maxim *salus populi suprema lex*.[54] Accepting that maxim, one might think that those who intentionally manipulate district lines for partisan advantage fail in their duties as public officials. But most political scientists believe the more basic failure is the *result* of partisan gerrymandering: it distorts the representation of parties in legislatures.[55]

If gerrymandering is objectionable because it distorts the representation of parties then, presumably, bias produced by political geography—"unintentional" or "accidental" gerrymandering—is objectionable for the same reason.[56] This is why I describe the source of failure as partisan bias rather than intentional manipulation. The purported failure is the asymmetry in the terms of party competition.

Another purported failure results from the division of geographically based communities of interest among multiple constituencies produced by the gerrymandering techniques of "packing" and "cracking." The apparent failure is the dilution of the capacity of

---

53. Rodden 2019, 173–74.
54. Locke [1689] 1988, II:158.
55. "The most commonly accepted standard for fairness of voting in a legislature is statewide partisan symmetry" (Katz, King, and Rosenblatt 2020, 166; they cite King and Browning 1987. Compare Rodden 2019, 267). Some disagree; Lessig, for example, writes that the asymmetries in representation produced by gerrymandering are objectionable in a way that other asymmetries are not because the former are produced by "rules crafted by the state" (2019, 30). Of course, partisan bias that reflects differences in the geographic concentration of the partisan vote might also be said to be produced by the state's rules establishing single-member territorial districts.
56. "Accidental": Erikson 1972, 1237; "unintentional": Chen and Rodden 2013, 239. If one regards partisan bias in districting as objectionable for its effects, then, as Rodden correctly observes, under many circumstances, to redress it would seem to require drawing districts "in a way that most would consider a form of gerrymandering" (2019, 267).

members of the communities of interest to secure representation of their shared interests.[57]

This may not be the worst of it. Although it need not do so, partisan gerrymandering also tends to increase the number of "safe" seats, making the system less responsive to changes in the partisan division of the vote. It can reduce electoral competitiveness. It is important to see that this is a distinct failure from partisan bias, even though both failures may have a common cause.[58]

TAKING STOCK

I have listed five purported failures, or sources of failure, in representation in the United States: (1) increasing gridlock in Congress; (2) ideological polarization among elites, sorting of voters into more ideologically consistent parties, and growing partisan animosity; greater responsiveness of policy to the preferences of (3) affluent and (4) non-Black voters than to the non-affluent and Blacks; and (5) partisan bias in districting for Congress and state legislatures.

This, of course, is not a comprehensive catalog of the intimations of democratic failure we find in political science. For example, I have not mentioned the reconstitution of the communications environment of the last twenty years, which, among other things, has stimulated what Nadia Urbinati describes as a "revolt against intermediary bodies" in the system of political representation.[59] And I have

57. Curiel and Steelman 2018; DeFord, Eubank, and Rodden 2021.
58. Tufte 1973 is the canonical source. In a recent paper Kenny et al. find that although the 2020 round of partisan gerrymandering produced little bias, on balance, at the national level, it significantly reduced overall responsiveness. "Partisan gerrymanders limit the voter's ability to hold politicians accountable because they decrease electoral competitiveness and responsiveness" (2022, 9).
59. Urbinati 2015, 477.

mentioned but not explored the important subject of representation in the states, where some of the pathologies I have identified at the national level are reproduced even more alarmingly.[60]

We have seen that some of these stylized facts are in some ways disputed. Still, it is enough that many political scientists accept them. Our question is whether and how these facts illustrate shortfalls from expectations of good representation that we might reasonably endorse. I do not doubt that we face failures. But we need to be clear about the normative considerations that justify the diagnoses.

To say that we shall consider "diagnoses" of failure may seem sloppy. We say that we diagnose an illness by proposing and testing hypotheses about the pathological mechanism that generates the history, symptoms, and physical findings that we observe. A diagnosis is a kind of causal explanation.[61] That is not quite my intention here. The political scientists who have documented the putative failures we shall consider often put forward accounts of the failures rooted in normative conceptions of representation. My aim is to consider whether these accounts offer plausible reasons for regarding the putative failures as matters to be regretted. When I refer to a "diagnosis," I intend it in this normative rather than the purely explanatory sense.

The stylized facts do not map neatly onto distinct diagnoses. Rather than examine the facts one by one, I shall organize the diagnoses under three headings: failures of effectiveness, failures of correspondence and responsiveness, and failures of fairness. I do not suggest that these categories encompass all of the ways that the facts

---

60. Within political science this has been a relatively neglected subject, though that is changing. In the recent literature see Hertel-Fernandez 2019 and Grumbach 2022.
61. This, anyway, is the aspiration. In some contexts (psychiatry, for example) the process of diagnosis does not always aim at identifying an underlying causal mechanism; it may simply seek to classify disorders by similarity of history and symptoms (for a critical discussion by a philosopher see Tabb 2015).

might suggest failures of democratic representation, but I believe they capture the most important elements.

DIAGNOSES (1): FAILURES OF EFFECTIVENESS

We might begin with failures of effectiveness. Notions of legislative effectiveness—tentatively, a capacity to legislate successfully—tend not to be prominent in democratic theory.[62] By contrast, the concern of many political scientists with what some believe is an increasing propensity for congressional gridlock suggests that congressional ineffectiveness is, for them, a troubling feature of democratic representation in the United States. Why is it something to worry about?

Modern scholarship on "congressional productivity" began when it was observed that a long period of unified party control of the executive and legislative branches came to an end in the 1950s.[63] This caused anxiety about representation. In a seminal paper in 1988, James Sundquist noted that the reigning theory of legislation in American politics had to do with party government. It held that parties coordinate the process of legislation with the leadership provided by a president elected by the whole people to advance a program. According to the theory of party government, this is only possible when there is unified party control of both branches. Sundquist recalls Key's observation that "for government to function, the obstructions of the

---

62. Perhaps effectiveness is simply presumed to be a virtue of legislatures. Or perhaps its disregard is a distinctive blind spot in American political thought. L. J. Sharpe observes in an influential critique of midcentury American political science that "the most important . . . of the aspects that are central to the notion of representative democracy . . . may be called functional effectiveness," but it "seems to be largely ignored in the American tradition" (Sharpe 1973, 130).
63. "Congressional productivity" is of course inaccurate in its implicit exclusion of the role of the president in the legislative process, both in supplying leadership and coordination and in control of the veto, but I shall retain the conventional phrase.

constitutional mechanism must be overcome, and it is the party that casts a web ... over the dispersed organs of government and gives them a semblance of unity."[64] The anxiety about divided government was that popular majorities would no longer be able to direct public policy: divided government would produce "ineffective compromise" for which "neither [party] could be held accountable."[65]

David Mayhew asked, in 1991, whether divided government really did render government less effective. He found, counterintuitively, that divided government was not less productive than unified government.[66] Those findings have been challenged more recently,[67] but the empirical dispute is orthogonal to our main interest. What matters here is the claim that, in the last several decades, there has been a trend toward more gridlock, with the moments of congressional productivity mostly occurring during periods of crisis (e.g., after 9/11, the 2008 financial crisis, Covid).[68]

Why is a propensity to gridlock a failure? As Jane Mansbridge reminds us, government's capacity to get something done is important, more so in a world confronted with challenging problems of collective action than in the world the constitutional system was designed for.[69] Gridlock obstructs solving collective action

---

64. Sundquist 1988, 618 n. 10, quoting Key 1952, 693. For Sundquist's (pessimistic) exploration of prospects for constitutional reform, see Sundquist 1992.
65. Sundquist 1988, 630.
66. Mayhew 2005 (first ed. 1991); compare Mayhew 2011, 78–79.
67. Most prominently by Binder (2003, esp. 40–44 and 2015, 91–98). For an early discussion, see Fiorina 1996, 88–89. Ansolabehere, Palmer, and Schneer (2018) offer an instructive review of the literature stemming from Mayhew's seminal work and an analysis of more comprehensive data.
68. "Congress appears to have retained the capacity to act swiftly when some crises occur, also evidenced by Congress's 2008 bailout of Wall Street after the Federal Reserve and Treasury allowed Lehman Brothers to go under. However, as we might expect, legislative unity dissipates when Congress turns its attention back to the regular policy agenda" (Binder 2015, 94).
69. Mansbridge 2012, 4–7.

problems: it prevents things from getting done that ought to get done. This might be enough to explain why we should consider it a failure.[70] But the persuasiveness of the diagnosis depends on how we identify the things that ought to get done. Binder quotes Bob Dole, who is supposed to have said, "If you're against something, you'd better hope there is a little gridlock."[71] Dole reminds us that views about "what ought to get done" are not likely to be politically neutral. People differ, for example, about which collective action problems should be solved by government action and how the costs of solving them should be distributed.

Dole's reminder suggests that to make a case that gridlock is an institutional failure, we need an idea of "what ought to get done" that is independent of political controversy. This is what Binder sought in her study. She constructed a list of issues that constitute the "policy agenda." By "policy agenda" she means "the range of policy ideas plausibly on the radar screens of policy making elite and active electorates."[72] She measured gridlock as a ratio of failures of Congress to act on those issues to the total number of issues on the agenda.

Leaving aside methodological concerns, the question is whether gridlock, on this understanding, is a normative failure. Perhaps the idea is that the agenda of issues "on the radar screens of the policy making elite" represents something like a consensus view of the issues facing the country. Is that idea plausible? We might doubt it. A proponent of "small government" conservatism, for example,

---

70. "If we care about whether and when our political system is able to respond to problems both new and endemic to our common social, economic, and political lives," we should want to understand the sources of gridlock (Binder 2003, 3); "[M]ost conservatives and liberals can agree that . . . government needs to take some sort of action in addressing the nation's major problems" (Howell and Moe 2016, xii).
71. Binder 2003, 3, citing Safire 1993, 305.
72. Binder 2003, 36; she cites Cobb and Elder 1983 as a source of this idea. The issues composing the "policy agenda" were drawn from an analysis of editorials published in the *New York Times* (Binder 2003, chap. 3).

could reasonably disagree that a lack of legislative productivity is a regrettable failure of the institutions of representation; it might be a sign that the Madisonian elements of the institutional structure are working properly.[73]

Neither of the somewhat contrived positions I have distinguished can be the whole truth. There clearly is a legislative agenda that we might regard as relatively detached from reasonable partisan controversy. On any responsible view, matters like extending the debt limit to pay for commitments already made and funding routine operations of government that serve common purposes belong on that agenda. When gridlock obstructs action on matters like these, we have reason for regret regardless of partisan commitments.[74] In this respect inaction might be thought to frustrate the public interest. To this extent, at least, legislative effectiveness does indeed appear to be a free-standing desideratum for democratic representation.

But the failure to act on genuinely controversial issues cannot plausibly be presented as a failure to act on a common public agenda. These include issues like climate change, gun control, anti-poverty policy, and so on. Even updating the minimum wage is a matter of partisan dispute.

The politically neutral idea of gridlock's failure stands in contrast to the view taken by Sundquist in the paper I mentioned earlier. His concern was that when partisan control of the government is divided,

---

73. As Justice Scalia said in a lecture at Princeton, describing the counter-majoritarian elements of the Constitution, "God bless gridlock! . . . It's the principal protection of minorities"' (Kennedy 2012). Someone might respond that gridlock also works against the political interests of conservatives, since it might obstruct efforts to reduce the size of government. Gridlock's main result is just to reinforce the system's status quo bias. This is true. But because status quo bias prevents updating of policy and facilitates policy drift, it is not obviously politically neutral.
74. Thus Rodden: "Divided government in the presence of partisan control over the legislative agenda produces drama and uncertainty even over votes that are clearly in the public interest, such as funding the government or avoiding default" (2015, 105).

"the normal tendency of the U.S. system toward deadlock becomes irresistible" and the president's program is frustrated.[75] On this account, the failure of representation lies in gridlock's obstruction of majority rule by undermining the operation of the party system.[76]

This yields a recognizably normative diagnosis of part of the failure of gridlock, and one that would survive Bob Dole's challenge. I will return later to the idea of responsiveness to the policy preferences of the majority as a kind of failure.

But first let us press the question whether gridlock is distinctively a failure *of representation*? This depends on how it is explained. The most common explanation is that gridlock arises from the combination of three factors, each a necessary condition: a system of checks and balances together with the Senate filibuster that create a "gridlock interval" in which policy change cannot occur, even if it is favored by a majority;[77] elite polarization that makes compromise difficult; and a closely divided electorate in which elections are often competitive, so that an out-party can regard itself as having a reasonable chance to win the next election.[78] In the absence of decisive control of both the executive and the legislature by one party, successful legislation requires compromise. But polarization narrows the space for compromise, and the prospect of winning the next close election decreases the incentive for it.[79]

---

75. Sundquist 1980, 192; cf. 189.
76. This suggests a notion captured in Brady and Volden's definition of "gridlock" as "a situation in which the status quo cannot be changed despite majority support in the country or the Congress for a specific policy change" (2006, 49).
77. For the idea of a "gridlock interval" (or "region") see Krehbiel 1998, chap. 2. The idea is a feature of Krehbiel's "pivotal politics" model of legislation. Parties are not analytically necessary for this model, yet there is evidence that the location of party medians influences the chances of gridlock (Binder 2015, 89–90).
78. Aldrich 2015, 17–19; Lee 2016, 198–200; Binder 2015, 97.
79. Anderson and colleagues observe a pattern of legislators at various levels rejecting "half-loaf compromises" that would, in fact, advance their legislative interests because they fear the political consequences within their own parties of doing so. They sacrifice their policy

Although elite polarization and close electoral divisions may be influenced by features of the system of representation,[80] they are fundamentally aspects of the political environment. If gridlock is a failure of the system itself, the reason must involve the effects of the institutional rules on congressional productivity. This means that we cannot avoid a judgment about those rules.

There is a familiar Madisonian account of the justification of the counter-majoritarian features of the constitutional structure. That account does not apply to the filibuster, but it is not hard to imagine a compatible justification. The gist is that the structure should restrain temporary majorities from precipitous action (Madison's "sudden or violent passions") or deception by "fractious leaders."[81] Without laboring the details, the underlying view is that political representation should be structured so as to produce policy that tracks something like the common interest over time—"the permanent and aggregate interests of the community"—while respecting everyone's rights. Durable majorities might plausibly be thought competent to identify these interests.[82] As a general matter, it is not far-fetched that on a reasonable interpretation of "the permanent and aggregate interests of the community," constitutional checks and balances might be justified by these aims.

---

interests for electoral interests. The authors point out that this phenomenon itself contributes to gridlock. "While not every compromise is normatively good, finding solutions to pressing issues is an important and desirable attribute of our governance institutions" (2020, 8).

80. For example, the system relies on private contributions to finance campaigns. Campaign donors tend to be more ideologically extreme than non-donors. This may create an incentive for candidates to move toward the extremes, increasing elite polarization (Hill and Huber 2017).
81. Madison [1788] 2001b, 322 (*Federalist* no. 62).
82. Madison [1787] 2001a, 43 (*Federalist* no. 10) and Kloppenberg's gloss (2016, 425–33). And note Madison [1788] 2001c, 327 (*Federalist* no. 63) on the role of the Senate in protecting against adoption of "measures which [the people] themselves will afterwards be the most ready to lament and condemn."

However, the Madisonian view depends on background assumptions about how the constitutional provisions are likely to operate under prevailing political circumstances. The case that the propensity for gridlock is a failure of representation, rather than an indication of success, would have to be that under contemporary circumstances, the Madisonian institutions are too obstructionist: they resist movements of policy that would track the majority's settled view of the common interest. Something like this case has been made recently by Paul Pierson and Eric Schickler, who emphasize the impact on political outcomes of the interplay of the institutional structure, growing partisan polarization, and asymmetrical changes in the behavior of the parties.[83] The case seems to me reasonable, though the details are beyond our scope. For our purposes, the point is that we cannot explain why the propensity for gridlock is a failure of representation without a theory that connects the provisions of the political constitution that enable it with a view of the normative aims of democratic representation. It is not always (or only) a matter of falling below some neutral threshold of effectiveness or productivity.

A propensity to gridlock might be thought problematic for various other reasons as well. For example, as Suzanne Mettler and Claire Leavitt write, the expansion of the contemporary "policyscape" has transformed the nature and range of the tasks the Congress confronts. Policies need oversight, maintenance, review, and updating. Gridlock impedes the Congress in performing all these functions.[84] Gridlock may also have undesirable consequences for the legislative process: for example, it may diminish the effectiveness of deliberation,

83. Pierson and Schickler 2020.
84. Mettler and Leavitt 2019, 250–62. A diagnostic question arises when a party or faction uses the affordances of representative office to impede the administration of a law with which it disagrees. (Consider, e.g., Republican efforts to constrain the enforcement of tax law [Hacker and Pierson 2016, 305–11].) Is this a failure of effectiveness, or something else?

and occasionally even its possibility, in the Congress.[85] It may also have undesirable consequences for the legitimacy of public institutions, perhaps reflected in the substantial decline of trust in institutions of the last several decades.[86] And there may be implications for the accountability of the larger constitutional structure; as I noted earlier, gridlock can shift effective rule-making power to the executive branch and the courts. Under a reasonably broad understanding of the effectiveness of political representation, all of these consequential harms might plausibly be counted as failures of effectiveness.

DIAGNOSES (2): FAILURES OF CONGRUENCE AND RESPONSIVENESS

The idea that policy should bear some systematic relationship to citizens' preferences is ubiquitous in the empirical literature about political representation in the United States.[87] We see this in commentary about most of the putative failures I mentioned. As I observed, gridlock might be reckoned a failure of responsiveness if the legislature consistently fails to act on issues on which majorities prefer action. Elite polarization without corresponding polarization in the electorate might be a failure of responsiveness if the legislature produces more extreme policy than what electoral majorities favor. Durable tendencies to satisfy the political preferences of the wealthy rather than of the majority, and of non-Hispanic whites rather than Blacks,

---

85. For two views, see Sinclair 2016, chap. 10; Wallner 2019.
86. For pertinent speculations see H. E. Brady and Kent 2022, 55–58.
87. Sabl 2015, 346, and references cited there. The research tradition in which high congruence is associated with successful representation derives from the seminal Miller and Stokes 1963. As Eulau and Karps (1977) point out, their own view was more nuanced than some who were inspired by them. For important analytical refinements see Achen 1978. For other sources see Disch 2021, 611 n. 11. These writers do not always distinguish congruence and responsiveness as I do in the text below.

when these conflict, might also be seen as failures of responsiveness, though perhaps not of the same kind.[88]

These worries all involve claims about distortions in the relationship between the political preferences of some group and either the political positions taken by representatives or the policy outcomes they produce. The trouble is that the complaint of *un*responsiveness can be equivocal and, however interpreted, it is not clear why it should concern us.

Let me begin with two points of clarification. First, there is no generally agreed sense of "responsiveness" (though I believe the following remarks represent the preponderant view). The central ambiguity is a conflation of what are sometimes called "congruence" (or "correspondence") and "responsiveness" in what we might regard as a quasi-technical sense.

Bingham Powell describes congruence as a "fit between the preferences of the citizens and the committed policy positions of their representatives."[89] One might also speak of congruence as holding between citizens' preferences and policy outcomes. Either way, the idea is that when there is high congruence, citizens mostly get the outcomes they want; or, anyway, the median voter in the group of interest—at the limit, the entire electorate—gets the outcomes she wants. Understood this way, congruence is not a causal notion. It might come about for other reasons than that the legislature is responding to voters' preferences: for example, some exogenous factor might explain both preferences and policy.

---

88. Canes-Wrone observes that the literature on unequal responsiveness, and on responsiveness more generally, relies on data from public opinion surveys, but these surveys generally are limited to issues that are (or likely to be) on the public agenda. This means that issues that matter to groups that are unable to command public attention may not appear in the data, producing inflated estimates of responsiveness that do not register the lack of influence of those groups (2015, 156).

89. Sabl 2015, 346 quoting Powell 2013, 10 (his 2012 APSA Presidential Address).

Responsiveness (or, sometimes, "dynamic responsiveness")[90] in the quasi-technical sense is different: it implies a causal relationship. The most natural way to describe it is with a counterfactual: policy is responsive to a group—a constituency, say, or an income class—if it would change in response to a corresponding change in the policy preferences of the group. Alternatively, one might say that responsive representatives (or responsive representative bodies) are those whose positions can be explained, at least in part, by the positions of those whom they represent.[91] To the extent that responsiveness has normative interest, of course, the concern is *positive* responsiveness: the tendency of policy (or a representative's policy position) to change in the same direction as changes in constituency preferences.

Congruence and responsiveness can be related, but it is important to see that they are distinct ideas. High responsiveness is an indication of influence, whereas high congruence is not, or not necessarily. It is possible, for example, to combine relatively high responsiveness and low congruence. Although a responsive system might produce high congruence, it is a contingent matter whether it will do so.[92]

The second clarification is simpler. Congruence and responsiveness can be considered at two levels. At the "dyadic" level, our interest is the relationship between the policy preferences of a single constituency or group and the policy position or aggregated roll-call

---

90. Caughey and Warshaw 2018; they are clear about the difference with congruence.
91. See Achen 1978, 490, for a more careful formulation.
92. For example, in a study of responsiveness and congruence in the states, Lax and Phillips find that although policy tends to be highly responsive to changes in public opinion for policies of higher salience, it matches opinion less than half the time: "Limited congruence in the presence of responsiveness (which is what we typically observe) shows a limited degree of popular control—*influence without sovereignty*" (2012, 153). Matsusaka 2022 offers an accessible explanation of the theoretical independence of these concepts and shows empirically that responsiveness is not, in general, a good proxy for congruence.

votes of the group's representative. (This means that "dyadic" is literally inaccurate; constituency representation is a one-to-many—not a one-to-one—relationship, a significant fact because the "many" most likely disagree among themselves.) At the level of the system or jurisdiction, we consider the relationship between the preferences of the people or the electorate as a whole and either the legislature taken as a body or the set of policy outputs. The relationship is many-to-many.[93] Scholars have paid more attention to dyadic representation than to the performance of the system even though we might reasonably believe that the latter should be the more basic concern. If preferences matter at all for successful representation, we might think that what should finally concern us is not whether an individual representative does what the constituency wants but whether enacted policy tracks the people's preferences.[94]

Returning to the distinction between congruence and responsiveness: the difference matters because writers disagree about which is the better standard of successful democratic representation.[95] To adjudicate the disagreement, we should ask how, if at all, we might understand either feature as a normative standard of democratic self-government.

---

93. Golder and Stramski 2010 give a clearheaded analysis.
94. See Weissberg 1978 and Stimson, MacKuen, and Erikson 1995's analysis of "dynamic representation." I return to this subject in the next lecture.
95. Gilens 2012, for example, adopts a variation of the criterion of responsiveness—indeed, he uses "responsiveness" and "representation" interchangeably (2012, 47). Caughey and Warshaw write that "in a democracy, policy change should also be driven by citizens' policy preferences: elected officials should respond to public opinion by moving policy in its direction. Dynamic responsiveness of this kind can be thought of as a minimal standard for democratic representation" (2018, 249). In contrast, Rehfeld holds that "the presumption of democracy is that there be a close correspondence between the laws of a nation and the preferences of citizens who are ruled by them" (2009, 214). In a comparison of congruence and responsiveness, Matsusaka holds that congruence is the better measure of representation, whereas responsiveness has "shaky theoretical foundations" (Matsusaka 2022, 11). Hajnal measures good representation as congruence, though he seems to infer "responsiveness" from it (2020, 120–21).

Beginning with congruence, notwithstanding its prima facie plausibility, I doubt that high congruence of preferences and policy is a reliable sign of successful democratic representation. This is partly because we have familiar reasons to resist giving preferences, as such, much weight in judging the democratic credentials of policy. For example, policy preferences are often not good indicators of interests and, as usually measured, may not take account of the moral and material opportunity costs of satisfying them.[96] It is also partly because the idea that policy should satisfy preferences can be embarrassed by the fact that representatives often help to shape preferences. Preferences are not formed exogenously to the process of representation. Someone might therefore wonder why we should celebrate congruence between preferences and policy: "It cannot vindicate democracy to find legislators responding to preferences they helped to create."[97]

For now I leave aside both reasons for doubt because there are at least three more fundamental considerations. First, the concern for congruence is in tension with the fundamental idea of political representation, which is that the whole people delegate to a smaller number the responsibility of making law and policy. Political representation is a division of labor. Considerations of efficiency and effectiveness argue in its favor: it reduces the cost of decision-making and, if properly institutionalized, can improve its quality. But neither

---

96. Compare Sunstein 1991, 6–14.
97. Disch 2021, 35. Is this too strong? Preference formation is evidently a complex process, and we might want to understand the means by which legislators "helped to create" preferences before deciding what to make of evidence of high congruence or responsiveness. Mill, for example, argued in *Representative Government* that one of Parliament's "offices" is "to create and correct that public opinion whose mandates it is required to obey" ([1861] 1977a, 348; see Krouse's discussion [1982, 526 and 534]). If this were how people's judgments were formed, it would not, without more, undermine a vindication of representative democracy in terms of responsiveness to those judgments. Note, too, that empirical studies of elite efforts to manipulate preferences find limited success (e.g., Druckman and Jacobs 2015, chap. 6).

consideration suggests that the institutional structure should aim for outputs that track the first-order policy preferences of the people. And neither suggests that representatives should aim exclusively or even mainly to satisfy those preferences.[98]

The second consideration has to do with the broader values of constitutional government. Institutions of democratic representation are elements of a larger constitutional structure. A democratic constitution seeks to enable the people to govern themselves while protecting against various pathologies that elective representative institutions might be expected to exhibit. For example, as John Rawls argues, we might think that constitutional design should aim for policy outcomes that are compatible with the essentials of social justice. Or, as Christopher Eisgruber observes, we might hope that constitutional self-government would serve values of stability and effectiveness as well as popular control.[99] If either view is right, then we should not necessarily object if representative institutions embodied in a larger constitutional structure fail to achieve congruence of preferences and policy.

The third and perhaps the most basic consideration follows directly from the distinction between congruence and responsiveness. High congruence does not tell us how it was brought about. It does not tell us that preferences actually influence policy as we might think, operating at some level of abstraction, the value of democratic self-government requires. Of course, a pattern of congruence across issues and over time might be evidence that the system is responsive in the causal sense.[100] But if this is the reason we

---

98. Thus Mansbridge: "Constituents choose representatives not only to think more carefully than they about ends and means but also to negotiate more perceptively and fight more skillfully than constituents have either the time or the inclination to do" (2003, 515).
99. Rawls [1971] 1999, sec. 31; Eisgruber 2001, chap. 1.
100. This might be Powell's view ("competitive elections should *systematically create*" ideological congruence [2013, 10, my emphasis]).

should care about congruence, it is just to say that what really matters is responsiveness.

We might, of course, have reasons to care about congruence that are not inferences from the value of democratic self-government. We might believe that policy outputs should advance the common interest and that, as a contingent matter and, at least in favorable deliberative circumstances (a demanding condition!), high congruence with constituency preferences is an indicator that policy does so. Or we might think that persistently low congruence for some groups—the poor, or ethnoracial minorities—is evidence of systematic disregard of their political interests. Both are important considerations but, in each case, our reason to care about congruence derives from a further concern; it is not about satisfying preferences as such.[101]

It may follow that we should discount "delegate" conceptions of representation in favor of "trustee" conceptions, but I shall not pursue the point here. Preoccupation with the traditional contrast can deflect attention from more puzzling aspects of the role of representative. And neither conception, taken strictly, is morally appealing or practically realistic.[102]

Responsiveness of policy to preferences, considered as distinct from congruence, is a different matter. Congruence is a feature of political outputs. Responsiveness is a feature of political inputs. It is a fact about the extent of a constituency's (positive) influence over the policy process: a matter of realizing popular control of government. Responsiveness of policy to preferences matters for popular control—an input value—in a way that correspondence—an

---

101. See Kolodny 2023, sec. 25.2, for a more detailed examination of the (in)significance of interests in congruence ("correspondence," as he calls it).
102. For helpful discussion see Rehfeld 2009. Pitkin 1967, chap. 7, offers a fair-minded summary of what can be learned from the contrast of "mandate" and "independence" theories of representation. Mill's discussion of "pledges" in *Considerations on Representative Government* is instructive ([1861] 1977a, chap. 12).

output value—does not. This is true even if we grant that the formation of preferences is partly endogenous to the process of representation: that fact is not obviously relevant to the reasons we have to value our collective capacity for self-government.[103] The force of the point may be clearer if put negatively: taken to the limit, if policy were not responsive to preferences at all, we could hardly say that the people rule. Here I am channeling V. O. Key: "Unless mass views have some place in the shaping of policy, all the talk about democracy is nonsense."[104]

To say this much is not to say that we should expect policy to be perfectly, or highly, responsive to preferences, or that all failures of responsiveness are equally to be regretted. For example, high policy responsiveness might conflict with the values of stability and predictability of policy. And constitutional restrictions on the power of majorities to change electoral laws, while limiting responsiveness in one respect, might be necessary to protect responsiveness in another. There is no obvious way to say, in general, how the value of popular control bears on the optimal level of responsiveness.

So far we have been considering policy responsiveness as an aggregate feature of democratic representation. This follows the central tendency of the empirical literature, which treats some degree of aggregate policy responsiveness as a democratic desideratum. However, as disparities in policy responsiveness by class and race suggest, this can be shortsighted. Those differences raise a distinct question, not about aggregate responsiveness but about political fairness.

---

103. As Ingham argues, popular control might have normative significance even if many citizens are ignorant or suggestible: "So long as no group of elites has dominating control over the popular will, this popular control may be reasonably described as popular rule" (2016, 1084).
104. Key 1961, 7.

DIAGNOSES (3): FAILURES OF FAIRNESS

Fairness and Political Equality

The putative failures in our inventory might all seem to involve generic unfairness, but distinctive forms of unfairness arise for three of them. These are disparities in responsiveness of policy by class and race and partisan bias in legislative districting. The appearances of unfairness derive from what seems to be an inappropriate distribution of political influence—over policy, in the first and second cases, and over election outcomes, in the third.

This, in turn, might suggest that we should understand these failures as violations of a democratic ideal of political equality.[105] I have argued elsewhere that this is a complex ideal, not well presented in a single formula.[106] For the sake of this discussion, however, let us provisionally adopt a single formula, even though we may have second thoughts. Following Joshua Cohen, we might say that one component of political equality (in his view, there are also others) is that citizens should have "equal opportunities for effective political influence."[107] Following T. M. Scanlon, we might understand this abstract idea somewhat more concretely as requiring that each citizen have "equal access to the *means* for attaining office and, more generally, influencing policy through the electoral process."[108]

The question is whether disparities in responsiveness or partisan bias in districting are unfair because they fail to afford each individual

---

105. Lessig, for example, frames both gerrymandering and private campaign funding as corruptions of a "core principle of equality" (2019, 4–30, 56–66). Compare Hasen 2016, 72–83, on "equality of inputs" and campaign finance; Page and Gilens 2020, 161–62.
106. Beitz 1989, chap. 5. For a different analysis of the ideal's complexity see Wilson 2019, chap. 2.
107. Cohen 2009, 271.
108. Scanlon 2018, 80. Scanlon is here concerned with interpreting Rawls's view that justice requires political liberties to be guaranteed their "fair value" (Rawls 2001, sec. 45.1).

equal access to the means for influencing policy through the electoral process. To telegraph the point that will emerge: in all three cases, a diagnosis of unfairness depends on the mechanism that produces it. But once we identify a plausible mechanism, it is no longer clear that the problem is that individuals have unequal means of influence. Judgments of institutional unfairness also implicate other concerns.

Disparities by Income Class and Race

Let us begin with disparities in policy responsiveness by income class or race. If policy is consistently more responsive to the preferences of the wealthy, or of non-Hispanic whites, than to those of others, when their preferences conflict, then it might seem obvious that the advantaged groups enjoy greater access to the means for influencing policy. The disparity in responsiveness is objectionable because it results from a violation of equal access to the means of influence. This may be right but, before we agree, we should want to understand more clearly the mechanisms that produce differences in policy responsiveness. We must explore this question separately for class and race.

INCOME CLASS

Thinking first about affluence, we know that participation in political activity increases with income. The rich may get the policy they want because representatives know that they pay more attention to politics and are more likely to vote.[109] We also know that members of Congress are typically wealthier than their constituents; they may favor the interests of wealthy constituents because they identify

---

109. Leighley and Nagler observe that "the income bias of U.S. presidential voters is large, even huge" (2013, 46; compare K. L. Schlozman, Brady, and Verba 2018, 210–11). Do the rich pay more attention because they have more time (arguably a means of influence)? Possibly; but Schlozman et al. find no evidence of systematic inequalities in time available for political participation by income class (2018, 52–54).

with those interests personally or are more familiar with how policy affects them.[110] It may be objectionable for representatives to pay more attention to the politically active or to the interests of constituents with whom they identify; in either case we might complain that they have failed to show equal concern for the interests of all citizens.[111] But neither possibility is obviously a matter of inequality in the means of influence available to individual citizens unless we are willing to stretch the meaning of "means of influence" well beyond its ordinary sense.[112]

One might be tempted by the thought that the policy bias produced by these mechanisms shows that the non-rich have been deprived of equal means of influence. After all, if the non-rich had greater political resources, then presumably they could deploy them to offset the advantages of the rich.[113] But this would misunderstand the mechanisms in question. These mechanisms do not produce outcomes that favor the interests of the wealthy by increasing their capacity to exercise influence over either election or policy outcomes or by decreasing those capacities of the non-wealthy. The unfairness involved is not transactional; we might say that the greater influence of the wealthy is a case of structural unfairness or, perhaps better, what Peter Morriss calls "systemic bias."[114] To this one might respond

---

110. Carnes 2013; D. M. Butler 2014. Butler argues that this form of affluent influence would persist even if participation rates could somehow be equalized. This is because representatives are influenced by the information and attitudes they acquire before entering office and because this information creates an incentive to concentrate on issues of interest to those with whom they identify.
111. Scanlon 2018, 84.
112. There is, of course, a separate objection if differences in turnout are the result of efforts to suppress the vote of lower-income or minority ethnoracial groups.
113. Scanlon suggests a similar objection in a different context: that "poorer citizens are deprived of an opportunity that they should have to influence electoral outcomes and political decisions, and that, consequently, wealthy citizens have an unfair degree of influence" (2018, 82).
114. Morriss 2002, xxxviii, citing Dowding 1991, 137–38, who refers to "systematic luck." Morriss warns against identifying resources with power on the grounds that the amount

that the policy bias is produced by a kind of transactional unfairness at one remove from the election system: perhaps the means to contend for office are unfairly distributed, with the result that candidates tend to be selected from among those who can better afford to run. This may be true, but, again, it is a different kind of unfairness than what is supposed to be involved in voters having unequal opportunities to influence election outcomes and policy choices.

Still, money is a means of influence, and at least some of the skewed responsiveness plausibly reflects the fact that the rich control so much of it. Most of the scholarly attention devoted to the political influence of wealth has focused on two further mechanisms. The first is the system of campaign finance, which depends on voluntary, private contributions; the second is the system of lobbying and interest representation. I discuss the first of these here and the second in the next lecture.

Election campaigns are financed from multiple sources, but we know that the bulk of campaign contributions increasingly comes from wealthy individuals rather than organizations.[115] These contributors may seek to influence policy outputs by influencing the priorities of the candidates they support, but that influence is mediated by the election process itself: the candidate must win the election in order to be in a position to carry out their policy priorities.[116] The

    of power an agent is in a position to exercise by deploying a resource can depend on factors beyond an agent's control, such as the willingness of other agents to be incentivized to act in response to deployment of the resource.

115. One study showed that in the 2012 election cycle, 28 percent of all disclosed political contributions were made by the *top ten-thousandth* of the public—about thirty-one thousand people. "This pattern shows no sign of abating. In the 2014 cycle, the 100 biggest campaign donors contributed nearly as much, $323 million, as the $356 million from the 4.75 million people who donated in amounts no larger than $200" (K. L. Schlozman, Brady, and Verba 2018, 213–14).

116. According to a recent study of roll-call votes in the Senate, senators become more likely to take positions supported by the national donor pool of their party as the donors' support for the position increases. But, interestingly, the association virtually disappears when a senator is likely to face a competitive reelection (Canes-Wrone and Gibson 2019). This

"unequal means" diagnosis of unfairness holds that the campaign finance system allows the rich to exercise greater influence over policy outcomes by devoting greater means to supporting the campaigns of candidates who share their priorities.

However, I doubt that we can fully explain the appearance of unfairness as a violation of a principle of equal means of influence for individuals. The principle is hard to interpret in the scaled-up context of electoral competition. And it does not register all of our reasons for concern about fairness in the system of campaign finance.

The first problem, about interpreting the principle, emerges when we recognize that the value of money in political campaigns depends on who is spending it. Most studies show that, on average, contributions to incumbents do not make much difference to their chances of success, whereas comparable contributions to challengers can make a larger difference.[117] One reason is that incumbency is usually itself a kind of resource—it involves command of various non-monetary means to influence election outcomes.[118] This means that equalizing the capacity of individuals to contribute to election campaigns will not necessarily redress the unequal impact of contributions on election outcomes.[119] So we might wonder whether the point of the

---

illustrates that the value of money as a means of influence may depend on aspects of the political environment—in this case electoral competitiveness.

117. Incumbents typically receive far greater total campaign contributions than their opponents, so the marginal value of an additional contribution is less (Jacobson and Carson 2020, 67–76). Jacobson 2015, esp. 36–38, summarizes the earlier literature, which generally supports the claim that communicative activity in campaigns tends to help challengers more than incumbents when it is adequately resourced, more clearly in campaigns for non-presidential offices than for the presidency. The assumption that campaign activity, including campaign communication, has a significant impact on election outcomes may be open to question (Kalla and Broockman 2018) but for our immediate purposes we should accept it.

118. These include, for example, familiarity gained through media exposure, ability to perform constituent services, and so on. In most cases challengers lack comparable resources.

119. "If incumbent spending is ineffective in increasing their vote shares, while challenger spending is effective in reducing incumbents' vote shares, the argument of some reform

"equal means of influence" requirement is really to equalize means of influence or, instead, to equalize a more abstract capacity to affect election outcomes. The latter seems more basic but it might not be feasible to achieve and is certainly not easier to interpret.[120]

There is a deeper problem. If we think about a system of competitive elections as an institutional process with certain purposes, standards of fairness emerge at the level of the system that are not concerns about the distribution among individuals of the means to influence outcomes.[121]

Here is an example. Campaigns are partly exercises in communication among candidates and potential voters: campaign communication seeks to mobilize and educate. A central interest of citizens in this competitive context is deliberative: roughly speaking, it is to have an information environment conducive to making epistemically responsible judgments about how to vote. One complaint about large inequalities in resources available to candidates is that they can distort the deliberative environment for citizens in ways that undermine or obstruct their capacities for responsible judgment.[122] As a first

---

advocates that limits on spending level the playing field between advantaged incumbents and disadvantaged challengers does not apply" (Stratmann 2019, 140).

120. The critical point is broadly sympathetic to Pevnick 2016's critique of what he calls the "egalitarian rationale" of campaign finance reform. He argues that it is a mistake to regard all forms of influence over election outcomes as analogous to the vote. Campaign communication, for example, because it operates by persuasion whose results are mediated by voting, should be regulated by different norms.

121. In their discussion of measures to limit the influence of wealth on political campaigns, Page and Gilens write, "Even with the threat of outside spending, public funding has been shown to increase the competitiveness of elections and give otherwise poorly funded candidates a chance to compete" (2020, 195). As I suggest in the second lecture, the concern with fostering competitive elections (in general) and with enabling poorly funded candidates to be competitive (in particular) is critical in grasping the requirements of fairness in the context of elections. But it is not clear to me that we can infer a concern for competitiveness from a more fundamental concern to equalize either the voting power or the electoral influence of voters taken as individuals.

122. For example, Miller argues that unregulated, differential access to the means to "amplify speech" in order to reach larger audiences can cause "epistemic distortion" by preventing

approximation, what citizens need to deliberate and choose responsibly is access at reasonable cost to multiple, reliable sources of information and commentary and at least occasional opportunities to observe and perhaps participate in public debate about choices of candidates and policies. The deliberative interest of citizens seems to me critical, but satisfying it may not be compatible with satisfying the interest of voters in being equally able to influence the outcome of voting (the "equal means" requirement). For example, under some circumstances satisfying the "equal means" requirement might result in minority views failing to be adequately represented in the public sphere.[123]

The theoretical point is that there are multiple evaluative perspectives. The outcome-oriented perspective generates pressure to equalize the means of influence over election outcomes for individual citizens. This is the perspective of citizens as agents. But there is another perspective, that of citizens considered as the beneficiaries of political (in this case, epistemic) competition, who have interests in being enabled to make good judgments about how to vote. Looked at from that perspective, we might wish the system to promote competition between candidates or parties in a way that enables people to deliberate responsibly and make informed choices. This does not necessarily require that citizens have equal means of influence—indeed,

---

"a diverse range of views from being heard" (E. L. Miller 2021, 60). Whether resource inequalities among candidates actually have this effect is a further question. It may be, as Lessig (2019, 71–128) suggests, that the evolution of "post-broadcast" network communications has had a more profound impact on the epistemic environment. That view is supported by Benkler et al.'s detailed study of the recent development of what they call the "right-wing media ecosystem" (2018, 13).

123. There is also another objection. Communicative practices that are deceptive, or skew the selection of information presented in the public forum, or obscure the political interests or preferences of potential coalition partners, impose greater deliberative costs on those seeking to reach responsible political judgments. Citizens are not equally situated to bear these costs. As Wilson argues, this may be another kind of unfairness: a regime of equal democratic citizenship should seek a fair sharing of the deliberative costs of citizenship (2019, chap. 10).

it is not a matter of the distribution of influence among individuals at all. The perspectives of citizens considered as agents and as beneficiaries of political competition do not necessarily converge.[124]

There is an orthogonal consideration in the design of the campaign finance regime. There appears to be a relationship between the structure of the regime and ideological polarization. In brief: the more parties are restricted by federal and state law in raising funds and contributing to campaigns, the greater the incentives for candidates to solicit funds from private (individual and group) donors and to acquiesce in officially uncoordinated independent expenditures in support of their candidacies. Because individual donors and ideological non-party groups tend to be more extreme in their policy views than party leadership, this can result in the selection of more extreme candidates and greater polarization in the federal and state legislatures.[125] What this shows is that differences in the characteristics of donors of campaign resources can affect the quality of representation independently of differences in the quantity of resources available. A concentration on the distribution of the means of influence obscures this.

We have been concentrating on the influence of wealth on the election of representatives, but of course there are also other ways

---

124. This might be another way of putting Estlund's observation that the quality of public political deliberation may be impaired by attempts to enforce equality of opportunity for influence (2008, chap. 10). Or consider Christiano's discussion of what he calls "qualitative equality" in deliberative settings: "It would be wrong to allocate expressive resources equally to individuals because this would result in the more-widely-held view being expressed more frequently than other views. A citizen's interest is in being exposed to the range of 'ideas in the community' in roughly equal measure" (1996, 93). It is not clear that this is actually a kind of equality in any morally significant sense, partly because there is no obvious way to differentiate "ideas in the community."
125. As La Raja and Schaffner put it, "[T]he institutional flow of money affects the ideological direction of political parties" (2015, 105). We might see this as a perverse consequence of attempts at campaign finance reform that neglect the "hydraulics" of campaign finance (Issacharoff and Karlan 1998b). See also Gilens, Patterson, and Haines 2021.

that the system of campaign finance bears on policy. The most familiar and probably the most practically important is that it creates a need for representatives to attract and retain donor support. This can be an incentive for representatives to adopt their donors' policy positions even if the representatives do not judge those positions to be best on their merits.[126] As Scanlon observes, the failure here is that representatives are induced to be responsive to the wrong reasons—that is, reasons that would be excluded in the performance of their duties as representatives.[127] This seems to me clearly right. But we should note that the underlying objection of democratic principle is not, except incidentally, to a violation of equal means of influence. It is to the undermining of the representative's motivation to perform as the legislature's justifying purposes require. The structure of incentives induces a failure of official duty.

RACE

Let me turn more briefly to the problem of differential responsiveness by race. Zoltan Hajnal's study argues that policy is consistently more responsive to the preferences of non-Hispanic whites than to those of Blacks. This seems unfair on its face. Once again, the difficulty in diagnosing the unfairness is that it is unclear what mechanism produces it.

This is too large a topic to explore here, so I offer only a few speculative comments. The Hajnal study was not designed to identify a mechanism, but it might be read to rule some out. African-Americans, of course, are the paradigmatic "discrete and insular" minority, so one might think they lose disproportionately because their political interests are systematically opposed to those of the majority. But while they have some political interests in common, they also differ about

---

126. Lessig 2015, chap. 12; Canes-Wrone and Miller 2022.
127. Scanlon 2018, 84. See also Thompson 1993 on "mediated corruption."

INTIMATIONS OF FAILURE

some interests and share some interests with others. Whether there is agreement or disagreement, however, Hajnal finds that Black voters consistently lose more often.[128] Or perhaps the disparity is mediated by differences in wealth, education, political views, or partisanship. But the pattern remains even after these factors are controlled for.[129] Institutional rules are not enough to explain the pattern of outcomes, although changes in districting, for example, might improve the descriptive representation of Blacks and make policy more responsive.[130] And, because Black voters tend to live in more populated states, to the extent that they have shared political interests, the small-state bias of the Senate may contribute to the disadvantage.[131]

Hajnal's own data show that Black voters succeed less often in electing the representatives they want. They are also represented by Blacks less frequently than non-Hispanic whites are represented by whites. In these respects, one might say that Blacks are less well represented in legislatures. But this only pushes the mechanism question back a step. Now we need to know what skews rates of electoral success. Hajnal suggests that racial prejudice among non-Hispanic white voters, sometimes exploited in racialized stereotypes and increasingly aligned with partisanship, is a significant part of the mechanism that explains the relative lack of electoral success of Black voters, particularly in biracial contests.[132] He suggests further that discrimination

---

128. Hajnal 2020, 139.
129. Hajnal does not deny that class as well as race help to explain his results. But he argues that when race and class are considered together, race is the better predictor of differential responsiveness. This is partly because in his sample rich and poor disagree about policy less often than African-Americans and non-Hispanic whites (2020, 131–32).
130. Hajnal 2020, 112; compare Griffin and Newman 2008, chap. 7.
131. Griffin and Newman 2008, 13, 103–6.
132. Hajnal 2020, 93–95. The fact that campaign contributors are disproportionately white might play a role in explaining these outcomes (Grumbach and Sahn 2020). On racial attitudes and partisanship, see Tesler 2016, 193–95. Of the other factors Hajnal explores to explain the disparity in electoral success (e.g., gerrymandering, supply of candidates, relatively low minority turnout rates), only one—"meager financial resources for

by public officials contributes to the lack of policy responsiveness to Black preferences: "Perhaps politicians simply heed Black voices less."[133]

According to this analysis, the problem is not inequality in the means available to Blacks for taking advantage of political opportunities. The asymmetric failure of responsiveness to Black preferences does not obviously reflect an inequality of political means, even though an inequality no doubt exists. The failure might persist even if political means were equalized. The objection is that institutions allow discriminatory treatment to obstruct Black citizens' efforts to use their institutional opportunities to protect and advance their political interests. Without claiming that this fully diagnoses the failure, we might describe it as another case of structural injustice or "systemic bias." It counts as a failure of representation if, as some argue, institutions can be reformed to avoid or overcome the obstruction.[134]

Partisan Bias and "Vote Dilution"

The case of partisan bias in districting is in some ways more complicated. People sometimes say that the votes of those who are disadvantaged in a biased system are "diluted" or that they receive less

---

campaigns in minority communities"—is a matter of the "means" available to make use of the right to campaign for office (Hajnal 2020, 95). Although Hajnal does not explore the subject in detail, historical differences in turnout for non-Hispanic whites and minority voters are substantial and may account for some of the disparity in policy responsiveness (Fraga 2018, chap. 2).

133. Hajnal 2020, 140. Butler and Broockman 2011's field experiment finding that state legislators respond differently to requests for help from constituents with putatively African-American and white aliases is evidence in support of the suggestion.

134. See, e.g., Guinier 1994; Young 2000, chap. 3; E. Anderson 2010, 108–11. Anderson suggests that the failure to treat the political interests of Blacks as equally important as those of non-Blacks may be due to failures of understanding endemic to a segregated political culture as well as to more overt forms of racial prejudice.

"weight."[135] "Dilution" suggests a violation of equality. What is the violation?

Whatever else it requires, political equality requires formal opportunities for influence over election outcomes to be equal. Importing an idea from the study of voting power, we might say that voters have equal formal opportunities in an election system if they have equal a priori chances to cast a "decisive" vote—that is, a vote that would change the outcome of an election. Chances are "a priori" when they are calculated in ignorance of voters' actual political preferences.[136] The precept "one person, one vote" (OPOV) promises equal a priori decisiveness. But biased systems can satisfy OPOV. In this respect, there is no violation of political equality.[137]

A more substantial impression of inequality might seem to emerge when we consider voters as partisans. Abbreviating a longer discussion,[138] we can say that it is possible for voters to have equal a priori chances of influence while having unequal chances of influence, once we take account of the likely voting behavior of others in

---

135. Rawls, for example, writes that "the weight of the vote can be as much affected by feats of gerrymander as by districts of disproportionate size" (1999, 196).
136. That is: we assume that it is equally probable that each of the voters will vote for any of the candidates on the ballot (or, more technically, that all the possible profiles of votes are equally probable). See Morriss 2002, chap. 22; Laruelle and Valenciano 2008, chap. 3.
137. Sometimes the egalitarian objection is put in terms of violations of some technical properties of decision rules found in axiomatic social choice theory, such as the properties of neutrality or anonymity. But it is not obviously true that either condition is violated when there is partisan bias in a districting system as a whole. The objection turns on conflating the decision situation in a committee or a single-stage assembly with two-stage systems with multiple constituencies in the first stage: it confuses decision rules and seat allocation rules. When we take note of the difference, we see that partisan bias violates these properties, if at all, only at the level of the jurisdiction as a whole, but not at the level of individual constituencies. But the election of representatives takes place within constituencies, in local competitions; there is no point at which voters throughout the jurisdiction are asked to vote on jurisdiction-wide slates of candidates. The objection falls wide of the mark. For a more detailed discussion see Beitz 2018, 332–35. Compare Kolodny 2019, 1022.
138. Beitz 2018, 336–41.

the district—ex ante decisiveness, as some theorists of voting power say.[139]

The difference between the a priori and ex ante perspectives is this. My a priori chances of affecting the outcome of a vote—that is, of being decisive—depend only on the rules of the system. This is why, in theories of voting power, one calculates these chances by assuming that every other voter has an equal chance of voting either way on any issue. By contrast, my ex ante chances of being decisive depend on how others in my district are likely to vote. To calculate my ex ante chances, rather than assume that each possible profile of votes is equally likely to occur, one assigns probabilities to all the possible profiles of votes in a district except my own based on what is known about voters' past behavior. Since gerrymandering operates by changing the partisan division within districts by shifting district boundaries, it will affect voters' ex ante decisiveness while leaving equal a priori decisiveness untouched.[140]

So there seems to be a coherent way to understand the effects of bias on the weight or value of the vote. But this, unfortunately, is not much help. The "vote dilution" objection to partisan bias cannot be that it introduces inequalities in ex ante chances of decisiveness. This is because partisan bias does not affect the voting power of every member of the party it disadvantages in the same way. A voter for the disadvantaged party who is "cracked" (or separated) into a competitive district is more likely to be ex ante decisive than a voter for that party who is "packed" into a district with a large majority of co-partisans. This is not what the familiar objection to "vote dilution" intends.

139. "Ex ante" voting power: Laruelle and Valenciano 2008, 57–60. In Morriss's terminology, this is "ableness" as opposed to "ability" (2002, 80–85 and chaps. 22–23).
140. To be precise, gerrymandering (and, more generally, partisan bias) usually exacerbates ex ante inequalities. Ex ante decisiveness will be unequal in any district in which the partisan division is unequal, whether or not gerrymandered. For a doubt about the normative importance of ex ante decisiveness, see Kolodny's discussion of the "compossibility principle" (2023, sec. 29.1).

INTIMATIONS OF FAILURE

The lesson I draw is that, in spite of the usual framing, it is not plausible to understand the conventional concern about "vote dilution" as a matter of the value of votes taken one by one. It is better seen as a kind of systematic unfairness endemic to single-member districting. Its significance emerges at the level of the jurisdiction as a whole: avoidable partisan bias thwarts electoral competition between parties by setting one party at a disadvantage to the other.[141] It is a further question, to which we return in the next lecture, why we should regard this as unfair.

I observed earlier that partisan bias is not the only representational harm associated with gerrymandering. It can also reduce the competitiveness of elections by creating "safe" seats, making the electoral system less responsive.[142] An adverse impact on electoral responsiveness would be a distinct democratic harm, not to be confused with bias.[143] I shall say more about this, too, in the next lecture.

---

141. This is consistent with Issacharoff and Karlan: "Reapportionment is almost entirely about the collective, aggregative aspects of the political process" (1998a, 2292). We need the qualification "avoidable" because the geographic distribution of partisan voters may make eliminating partisan bias impossible. See, for example, Chen and Rodden's attempt to simulate nonpartisan districting maps for Florida constrained only by the requirement that districts be compact and contiguous. None of the simulated nonpartisan districting plans were either politically neutral or demonstrated a pro-Democratic bias (2013, 257).
142. This may seem counterintuitive, since partisan gerrymandering works partly by the gerrymandering party increasing the number of districts it can expect to win by spreading out its voters, making those districts more competitive than the districts the other party can expect to win. In practice, however, the gerrymandering party will try to avoid creating excessively competitive districts. We should remind ourselves that electoral responsiveness—the responsiveness of changes in partisan vote shares to seat shares—is only contingently connected to policy responsiveness. Highly competitive districts do not always produce more moderate representatives (McCarty et al. 2018).
143. "In the partisan gerrymandering context, the claimed victims of discrimination have ample recourse to political redress, even if not immediate satisfaction within the jurisdiction in question. But beyond the question of political redress, the magnitude of the risk of discriminatory partisan gerrymandering is overwhelmed by the fact of nondiscriminatory bipartisan gerrymandering that renders elections in the United States immune to voter preferences" (Issacharoff and Karlan 2004, 571; compare Pildes 2005). It is relevant here that parties disadvantaged by partisan bias appear to perform their basic competitive functions less effectively than others (Stephanopoulos and Warshaw 2020).

LOOKING AHEAD

Let me conclude for now with two observations.

First, perhaps not surprisingly, what emerges from these reflections is that there does not appear to be any single standard of success or failure of institutions of representative democracy. They can fail in multiple ways: for example, by failing to be decisive when there is conflict involving the means of attaining widely shared ends; by frustrating popular control of government by being unresponsive to changes in the majority's settled will; by producing consistently inequitable outcomes for politically vulnerable minorities; by failing to support or enable deliberative environments that make for constructive contestation among opposing views and epistemically responsible choice; and by undermining representatives' motivation to perform as a representative legislature's justifying purposes require. We might think of each kind of failure as a shortfall from achieving an aim or purpose that we reasonably expect democratic representation to satisfy. Part of the work of a theory of fair and effective representation is to identify those purposes and the rules that should govern the mechanisms we rely upon to achieve them.

The second observation follows from reflection about cases of failures of fairness. In those cases, what appears at the outset to be a matter of unequal influence turns out to mask a more complicated set of failures. Their dimensions only become clear when we think about representation as a system rather than only as a set of dyadic relationships. The preoccupation with constituency representation can obscure the critical role in determining policy outcomes played by the structure of political competition throughout a jurisdiction, the functions of parties within it, and the surrounding political environment. We see this especially clearly in connection with campaign resources and districting, in which forms of unfairness arise from aspects of the social and institutional structure. Another part of the work of a critical theory of political fairness is to grasp the normative implications of the fact that features of the system as a whole have such predictable effects on outcomes.

In the next lecture we explore the consequences of these observations.

Lecture II

Regulating Rivalry

CHARLES R. BEITZ

In the first lecture we considered some reasons from political science to believe that democratic representation in the United States is failing. I grouped the putative failures under three headings: of effectiveness, of congruence and responsiveness, and of fairness. Some disagree about the underlying facts. I did not try to adjudicate the disputes. My question was diagnostic: Taking the facts as presented, by what standards might we think that democratic representation is failing? I considered some standards implicit in the political science, resisting some and suggesting alternatives to others, but did not try to infer lessons for democratic theory. That is our first task in this lecture. The main theme that will emerge is that the normative theory of democratic representation should take its systematically competitive nature seriously. It should try to say what it would mean for democratic political competition to be fair and effective. After drawing some lessons, I offer an exploratory sketch of a proposal to do so.

FOUR LESSONS

To begin, I shall suggest four lessons for the theory of democratic representation that we might draw from reflection about the putative failures and their diagnoses. These will be truisms for many political scientists and some democratic theorists, but they are not commonplace and, in any case, they deserve to be made explicit.

Systemic Perspective

Much of the political science of democratic representation is devoted to examining the "dyadic" (actually, the one-to-many) relationship between individual elected representatives and their constituents. We find this concentration in many studies of congruence and responsiveness. It is inherent in the traditional contrast of delegate and trustee conceptions of representation. But the most consequential failures of democratic representation only become visible at the level of the system. Disparities in policy responsiveness by class and race, partisan bias, and legislative dysfunction are features of the system as a whole.

The first lesson is that democratic representation is primarily a jurisdiction-wide practice. Those elected to legislative office, each selected in her own constituency, constitute a group that purports to act for the whole people. The dyadic relationship plainly matters for both representatives and constituents, and a representative's performance will almost certainly be influenced by the extent and depth of her engagement with her constituents. But it is a mistake to think that either representatives' responsibilities or the consequences of their official conduct can be well understood within the representative-constituent relationship alone. Representatives also have responsibilities to others because the consequences of their choices can be felt throughout the system. We need this fact to make sense of the idea of "virtual representation," but its significance is more general: it explains why we think that representatives can have reasons to advance the programs of their parties, even if their own constituents disagree about parts of the program. (Indeed, the phenomenon of the legislative party would be difficult to comprehend if one were to regard the relationship of representation as entirely dyadic.) And it is necessary to grasp how we can say that members of legislative committees represent those whose interests fall under the committees' jurisdiction, regardless of their constituency.[1]

This first lesson recapitulates one of Hanna Pitkin's main conclusions about the concept of representation. In a passage in her seminal book that is sometimes overlooked, she writes: "Political representation is primarily a public, institutionalized arrangement involving many people and groups, and operating in the complex ways of large-scale social arrangements. What makes it representation is not any single action by any one participant, but the over-all structure and functioning of the system."[2] The implication is that in seeking normative standards for representation—not precisely Pitkin's project, but ours—we should consider the properties that would be desirable in the system.

More Than Democracy Scaled Up

A second lesson follows. There is a long-standing tendency to think of democratic representation as a second-best arrangement, adopted for polities that are too large for assembly democracy. This perspective can tempt us to think that the regulative norms of representative democracy derive from those of direct (or assembly) democracy. It

---

[1]. As Weissberg 1978 observes in an influential critique of the research tradition on dyadic representation.
[2]. Pitkin 1967, 221–22. Lisa Disch persuades me that this is Pitkin's considered view (2021, 36).

may, for example, explain why high congruence of policy preferences and legislative outcomes has seemed to many to be an attractive democratic norm.

Mill might be read to suggest something like this perspective in the conclusion of the third chapter of *Representative Government*. He devotes most of that chapter to commending the virtues of direct citizen participation in political decision-making. He writes that "the only government which can fully satisfy all the exigencies of the social state is one in which the whole people participate." He then observes that direct participation in government is not feasible in communities larger than small towns and concludes with a startling non sequitur: "It follows," he says, "that the *ideal type* of a *perfect* government must be representative."[3] The inference is that we should evaluate representative institutions according to standards that derive from those that apply to direct or assembly democracy: representative democracy should aspire to be direct democracy scaled up. It fails when it does not deliver outcomes that the people themselves would choose if they were in a position to do so. Many have criticized this perspective, but it persists in more or less sophisticated forms.[4]

"Democracy scaled up" is, however, too thin an evaluative standard to diagnose some apparent failures of democratic representation. (Mill himself seems to recognize this in some of his remarks about matters of institutional design—most notoriously, perhaps,

---

3. Mill [1861] 1977a, 412 (my emphases). Thompson remarks that the passage "intrudes almost as an afterthought" (1976, 13). Perhaps reflecting a similar thought to Mill's, James Wilson is reported to have told the Constitutional Convention, "The Legislature ought to be the most exact transcript of the whole Society. Representation is made necessary only because it is impossible for the people to act collectively" (Madison 1966, 74 [1840] [proceedings of June 6, 1787]). Thanks to Henry Brady for pointing out the passage.
4. For variations of this tendency: Singer 1974, 105–32; Barry 1965, 312–13; Fishkin 1995, 33–34; Dunn 2019, chap. 4. For resistance to it: Schattschneider 1942, 13–15; Kateb 1981; Manin 1997, chap. 5; Brennan and Hamlin 2000, chap. 11; Mansbridge 2003, 515; Urbinati 2006, chap. 1; Disch 2021, 76.

his proposal of a scheme of plural voting in the election of representatives.) Consider, for example, failures of legislative effectiveness, which cannot be explained as failures without some conception of the purposes that political representation should serve. We noted several such purposes in the first lecture. They include responding to durable changes in majority preferences, as "democracy scaled up" might suggest. But the role of representative requires its occupants to take decisions on matters beyond the scope of public preferences and to make judgments about their veracity, when they exist. It requires representatives to participate in negotiations about policy. And it requires them, at least occasionally, to participate in public deliberative activities that aim to inform and persuade constituents. For these requirements, "democracy scaled up" can offer no guidance.

The second lesson is that democratic representation is a compound idea: as Paine wrote of the Constitution, it is "representation ingrafted upon democracy."[5] A representative democracy is a complex institutional arrangement with a division of labor at its core. A subset of the people decides, on the whole people's behalf and in some way under their control, what law and policy should be. Representation shifts the question facing the people from "What should be law?" to "Who should decide?" Of course, in a well-functioning democracy, deliberation in the public sphere enables people to consider the choices put before them, and these deliberations shape the political agenda and influence the range of electoral choice. To reiterate, we must regard the affordances of the larger deliberative environment as elements of the system of representation. But this does not deny that the political responsibilities of citizens are different from those of their representatives. Representation simplifies the burdens of

---

5. Paine [1792] 2000, 180. That these ideas are distinct is clear in Victorian thought about political representation, where representation figured more often as an alternative to democracy than as a means of achieving it (documented in Conti 2019).

citizenship.[6] In doing so it renders the idea of "democracy scaled up" normatively inapt. We should expect the "democratic" and the "representative" elements of the compound idea to cast orthogonal normative shadows.

Pervasiveness of Competition

The third lesson concerns what we see when we take the perspective of the system. We see many things, of course, but the most prominent fact is that democratic representation is competitive. In Mansbridge's terms, it is primarily an instance of "adversary democracy."[7] The adversarial character of democratic representation is not only manifested in the fact that it must resolve conflicts of interests. It is also, and more importantly for our purposes, shown in the nature of the processes through which conflicts are resolved: people and groups contend for influence over authoritative decisions about policy. The most visible form of competition is for elective public office. But democratic political competition occurs in other arenas as well, and its broader scope matters in ways we shall consider.[8]

In the presence of regular disagreement about policy, political competition in a representative democracy is unavoidable; indeed, the system depends on it. Yet competition also seems to figure in several kinds of failures. For example, it might plausibly be said to generate congressional dysfunction and ineffectiveness, to motivate elite

---

6. I do not mean to endorse the common (and commonly underspecified) idea that representatives have an agency relationship with their constituents (Ansolabehere and Kuriwaki 2022, 123). Without qualification, that idea seems to me both empirically and morally inadequate. See Beerbohm 2012, chap. 7, for helpful discussion.
7. Mansbridge 1980.
8. I am agreeing here with Jeffrey Green's criticism of Schumpeter's view that the "competitive struggle" in representative politics is primarily electoral: "No matter what Schumpeter might claim, there is the fundamental fact that the central dynamic he thematizes—existential competition—is neither a binary nor a simple term: there are degrees of competitiveness and multiple domains within the political sphere in which it might be applied" (2010, 271).

efforts to promote affective polarization, and to incentivize partisan gerrymandering.

The idea that democratic politics is competitive, of course, is hardly new. In the last century Joseph Schumpeter, E. E. Schattschneider, and Anthony Downs presented influential theories of democratic politics in which competition is the chief dynamic. These theories differ in the forms of political competition they postulate and in the political values it is supposed to serve.[9] And none of these writers devotes much explicit attention to identifying conditions under which the structure of political competition might be regarded as compatible with the normative aspirations of democratic representation.

We might add Rawls to this list, though his view may be ambivalent. In a puzzling passage in *A Theory of Justice*, he observes that "the democratic political process is at best regulated rivalry."[10] But aside from some important remarks about ensuring the "fair value" of the political liberties and a comment about gerrymandering, he does not consider how democratic rivalry ought to be regulated in much detail. That is not unusual in democratic theory, but I shall suggest it is a mistake. (We return to the puzzling passage later.)

To avoid misunderstanding let me note here, what ought to be obvious, that to recognize the centrality of competitive mechanisms in democratic political life is not to approve of the results that competition can produce when inadequately regulated. To put it dogmatically, on the view we shall explore, the theoretical problem is not to devise ways to transform competitive institutions into noncompetitive forms of political cooperation, as the "democracy scaled up" view might tempt one to think. It is to frame normative standards for the

---

9. Schumpeter 1942; Schattschneider 1942, 1960; Downs 1957. For the contrast of Schumpeter and Downs as theorists of competition see Bartolini 1999, 446–49.
10. Rawls 1999, 199. In *Political Liberalism*, Rawls describes democratic procedures as aimed at "moderating political rivalry within society" between "classes and interests" as well as among citizens favoring different political principles ([1993] 2005, 158).

design and conduct of competitive democratic institutions and processes so that they yield results compatible with their justifying purposes. We turn to this problem shortly.

Functions of Parties

The final lesson, perhaps inherent in the last, is that political parties play an ineliminable functional role in democratic representation, though they do not always play that role constructively. Schattschneider is famous for the thesis that "political parties created democracy and . . . modern democracy is unthinkable save in terms of parties."[11] If democracy is unthinkable without parties, it is largely because parties make political competition intelligible to voters. In Schattschneider's view, parties are impelled by competitive pressure to build coalitions of interested groups by identifying policy programs on which a majority can agree. Their distinctively democratic function is to socialize conflict: to define salient political cleavages in a way that structures public deliberation and makes meaningful electoral choice possible.[12]

This should not need to be said but for another Schattschneiderian truth: that parties are "the orphans of political philosophy."[13] His

---

11. Schattschneider 1942, 1. One might plausibly argue that Schattschneider overstates the case. As Caughey (2018, 14) observes, there was a significant degree of contestation in the one-party South of the 1930s to 1950s, even though it was confined to primary elections of the white southern Democrats. He argues that political competition produced representation in Congress (though not in state legislatures) comparable in its responsiveness to "selectorate" opinion to that found in the two-party non-South (chap. 6). Of course, contestation in primaries for federal office depended on the fact that southern Democrats participated in the system of two-party competition within the Congress. For another view see Aldrich and Griffin 2018.
12. In a later, more theoretical, work, Schattschneider writes, "The people are involved in public affairs by the conflict system. Conflicts open up questions for public intervention. Out of conflict the alternatives of public policy arise. Conflict is the occasion for political organization and leadership" (1960, 135).
13. Schattschneider 1942, 10.

immediate point was that parties were not, at least not explicitly, part of the constitutional design of the framers.[14] But he also meant to criticize political theories of his own time for failing to register the democratic potential of well-functioning parties. With some important exceptions, the critique applies to much of democratic theory in our time as well.[15]

As with competition, so with parties, there is a danger of misunderstanding. To assert that parties play an ineliminable role in democratic representation is not to say that they play their role well or that the role that prevailing institutional incentives establish for party organizations and leaders is the role that democratic norms require them to play. Parties, as John Aldrich observes, are "endogenous institutions."[16] Their organizational form, operational norms, and political capacities relative to those of other organizations are importantly determined by the uses to which political actors put them within a regulatory framework that is itself subject to change.

Parties, of course, are not the only kind of intermediary organization whose competitive dynamic exerts influence in policymaking. Interest groups, for example, also play an empirically significant and probably an ineliminable role. I shall comment about fairness in interest representation later. For now, the point to stress involves the different roles of parties and interest groups. For reasons anticipated by Schattschneider, we must distinguish them. It is parties, or anyway well-functioning parties, that have the capacity to discipline

---

14. "Not explicitly" because, as Schattschneider observes, aspects of the constitutional design—in particular the freedoms of expression and association—made parties inevitable (1942, 7).
15. Exceptions include Muirhead and Rosenblum 2006; Rosenblum 2008; Muirhead 2014; and White and Ypi 2016. As Muirhead and Rosenblum (2006) point out, although Rawls might appear to understate the value of partisan competition in democratic politics, his political theory is compatible with according it a more robust role.
16. ". . . in fact, the most highly endogenous political institutions of any substantial and sustained importance" (Aldrich 2011, 17).

the interests, to engage them in broad coalitions, and to hold them to public account.[17] They are not unique in these respects; under some conditions, some civil society organizations might exercise some of the capacities of parties (labor organizations, for example). But the gatekeeping role of parties in electoral competition places them in an advantaged position for these other functions.

Parties should feature in a theory of democratic representation because distinctive questions arise about the fairness of the rules that structure party competition.[18] We see this, for example, in objections to "partisan bias" in districting plans. The same is true in thinking about the ballot access regime, the campaign finance regime, and the rules of procedure of the Congress. As I suggested in the first lecture, to make sense of those objections and disagreements we may need a notion of fairness to parties (or, perhaps, to partisans).

DEMOCRACY, RIVALRY, COMPETITION

Taking these lessons on board, let us return to Rawls's observation that the democratic process "is at best regulated rivalry." I remarked that this observation is puzzling. This is partly because it is unclear why political rivalry needs to be regulated and partly because it is unclear what to make of the phrase "at best." The latter is an exegetical matter I leave aside.[19] But we should ask why political rivalry needs to be regulated.

---

17. Schattschneider 1942, chap. 8; see also Schattschneider 1960, 20–35.
18. The legal regulatory regime is complex: the review of legal regulation of parties in Issacharoff and colleagues' authoritative casebook runs to more than one hundred pages (2022, chap. 4). The subject is further complicated by the fact that intraparty competition is also regulated by rules adopted by the parties themselves.
19. Notwithstanding the immediate context, Rawls does not appear to think that "regulated rivalry" is only a feature of nonideal democratic politics. In the following paragraph, he writes: "[A] just constitution sets up a form of fair rivalry for political office and authority. By

Rawls's source is Frank Knight's *The Ethics of Competition* (1935).[20] In his time, Knight was among the most influential contributors to economic thought about market competition.[21] In the passage Rawls cites, Knight describes democratic politics as a competitive "game" and compares it with economic competition—also a "game."[22] He worries that rivalrous conduct in both realms produces a "cumulative tendency to inequality and consequent disruption of the system" as differences in natural talents and abilities express themselves in unequal outcomes. If the process goes on too long, unregulated, the game will stop serving its purposes as the losers come to see it as unfair. Knight says that the "main problems" to be solved to keep a game fair are "to prevent continued concentration of power in the hands of individuals or organizations; to assure to all a really equal start, or at least one as fair as possible, through an 'equitable' sharing of the material and cultural inheritance; to arrange such 'handicaps' as would give everyone a 'chance'; and to provide the best distribution of prizes for making the contest interesting to participants and spectators."[23]

presenting conceptions of the public good and policies designed to promote social ends, rival parties seek the citizens' approval in accordance with just procedural rules against a background of freedom of thought and assembly in which the fair value of political liberty is assured" (1999, 199, my emphasis; and see Cohen 2003, 100–103).

20. Rawls's citation is actually to Knight's American Economic Association paper "Economic Theory and Nationalism" (1934), one of several essays collected in Knight 1935. As a historical matter, we know that Rawls took Knight's ideas very seriously; Forrester reports that he annotated his copy of the book containing Knight's essay in three colors (2019, 13).
21. Stigler 1957, 11. Knight is rightly considered to be a founder of the "Chicago school" of economic thought, but it is a mistake to associate him with the most distinctive ideas of the generation that succeeded him (Emmett 2009).
22. "[A]s it has worked out in practice in the modern world, *democracy is competitive politics*, somewhat as free enterprise is competitive economics (though inherently a competition for monopolistic position), and shows the same weaknesses as the latter" (Knight 1935, 295). The metaphor of the game for market behavior first appears in Knight's *Risk, Uncertainty and Profit* (1921, 53, 89, 360–61). He explores it in "The Ethics of Competition" (1923, reprinted in Knight 1935, 40–75). Emmett speculates that he adopted it from Veblen (Emmett 2009, 193 n. 4).
23. Knight 1935, 303n.

In trying to take a systemic perspective on democratic representation, I propose to follow Knight and Rawls and consider how political rivalry should be regulated if it is to function fairly and effectively over time.[24] The question is whether we can understand at least some prominent failures of democratic representation as shortfalls from fair democratic competition. The question needs to be unpacked, but simply formulating the problem in this way suggests two respects in which a system-level conception of fair political competition departs from a common view in political theory and constitutional law. First, in seeking conditions of a fair system of political competition, we do not commit ourselves to thinking that the basic problem is to reconcile equal individual rights with aggregate public interests.[25] Judgments of systemic unfairness might also have other grounds than offenses to the political equality of individuals as this is conventionally understood. Second, we do not take dyadic representation to be the focal concern. We accept Pitkin's considered view that good representation is an emergent property of a jurisdiction-wide system and ask what features a competitive system of democratic representation should display if we are to regard it as fair and effective.

As I noted, social scientists have long associated democratic politics with partisan competition for control of government. The idea is also prominent in "law of democracy" jurisprudence.[26] Indeed, many would agree with Sartori that the association is analytic: if institutions

---

24. Rawls's position is more complicated than my language suggests. Notwithstanding his view that the democratic process is "at best regulated rivalry," he also holds, in relation to contrasts between the ideal market and ideal legislative process, that "[t]here seems to be no way of allowing [ideal legislators] to take a narrow or group-interested standpoint and then regulating the process so that it leads to a just outcome" (1999, 317). This raises the question what role regulation is supposed to play in the "rivalry" of democratic politics at its "best."
25. On this view in election law jurisprudence, see Pildes 2014 and Pildes 2018.
26. Formative works include Issacharoff and Pildes 1998; Issacharoff and Karlan 1998b; Pildes 1999; and Issacharoff 2001.

make political competition impossible, they are authoritarian—not even minimally democratic.[27] So it might be surprising that political competition and its regulation have not featured more prominently in democratic theory.[28]

One reason may be that competitive models arose historically from an analogy with competition in economic markets and, as most agree today, that analogy can mislead. For example, there is no political analog of the price system, and political competition is inevitably, although to varying extents, oligopolistic.[29] Knight himself notes some differences. He thinks that the tendency to inequality and disorder is greater in politics than in markets because political rivalry lacks a material foundation; it is not disciplined by the forces that moderate the influence of the desire for market power.[30] But competition is a more general social phenomenon than market rivalry. We need not abandon the idea that democratic politics is competitive simply because the analogy to markets is defective.

Competitive conceptions might also seem to fit uncomfortably with an ideal of democratic public deliberation, which is sometimes

---

27. Sartori 1976, 217–18.
28. Not that the subject is altogether missing. See, for example, Shapiro's sympathetic interpretation of Schumpeterian competition as a normative conception (2003, chap. 3) and Pettit's illuminating discussion of "dual-aspect democracy," making explicit the role of various forms of competition in the "short haul" of democratic politics, producing in the "long haul" policy satisfying the public interest (as if by an "invisible hand") (2012, chap. 5; "invisible hand," 275; see also Pettit 2000).
29. For some criticisms of market analogies for democratic politics see Miller 1983; Strom 1992; Bartolini 1999 and 2000; Thompson 2002, 7–8, 176; and, again, Shapiro 2003, 58–64.
30. Knight says, strikingly, that in political rivalry "equal suffrage... provides little or no guarantee of equality" (1935, 297). The priority that Rawls accords to provisions guaranteeing the "fair value" of the political liberties draws the inference (Rawls 1999, 197–99). So, too, does his later contention that the capitalist welfare state, in contrast to "property-owning democracy," is not compatible with the fair value requirement (1999, xiv–xv; 2001, secs. 41–42; for illuminating discussion see Edmundson 2020).

presented as a cooperative enterprise.[31] But this is naive. Public deliberation in its modern, democratic form is essentially contestatory.[32] Consider, for example, Mill's account of "the real morality of public discussion" in *On Liberty*. He argues that only the vigorous public presentation of opposing views can satisfy the educative aims of public deliberation. Political debate achieves its social aims by setting participants at odds with one another. To be sure, Mill believes that to be socially beneficial, discursive contestation should be regulated by norms that promote honesty and tolerance. But the competitive structure of the public deliberative environment is essential to its serving its purposes.[33] (It is also essential to explaining its dysfunctions, as concern about the "epistemic crisis" of the contemporary networked public sphere illustrates.)[34]

For our purposes, the problem is that social scientists typically deploy competitive models for positive purposes rather than to advance normative principles. This is no criticism, but it means there is less to go on than we might have hoped in framing regulative norms for democratic political competition. To pursue the subject, I shall ask what competition is; suggest two reasons why democratic competition needs to be regulated if it is to contribute to fair and effective

---

31. This thought traces at least to Pateman 1970's critique of Schumpeter and those influenced by him. As Manin observes, parliamentary discussion was commonly understood as a collaborative effort in later nineteenth-century thought about representation even though its actual practice could be sharply contestatory (1997, chap. 5).
32. This fact is prominent in the literature about complex deliberative systems (e.g., Dryzek 2010; Parkinson and Mansbridge 2012; and, for a summary of findings and possible applications, Dryzek et al. 2019).
33. Mill [1859] 1977b, 257–59. Goodin offers a sympathetic account of policy choice in a representative system as an activity that takes place in a sequence of deliberative steps, in each of which it takes a different and occasionally a contestatory form (2008, chap. 9). And see Miller's distinction between "laissez-faire" and "process" models of "epistemic competition" implicit in First Amendment doctrine (E. L. Miller 2021, 30–39).
34. Benkler, Faris, and Roberts 2018, chap. 1; Lessig 2019, 79–98. On differences in the competitive structure of old and new media in comparative perspective, see Nielsen and Fletcher 2020.

democratic representation; identify some purposes we rely on political competition to serve; and then consider, mainly as illustrations, three arenas of competition in the system of democratic representation. What I shall propose is at best an exploratory sketch.

WELL-REGULATED COMPETITION: A PROPOSAL

What, then, are the elements of a conception of well-regulated democratic competition? We should begin at the beginning, with the idea of rivalry.[35] The idea is ambiguous because rivalry in its ordinary sense need not be regulated at all. Let us say that rivalry, considered generically, is a kind of interaction in which two or more agents seek a good under conditions in which only one can succeed in securing it (or, more accurately, conditions in which not all agents can succeed in securing it). And let us say, semi-stipulatively, that competition is a form of rivalrous interaction structured by rules or social norms. Under the rules, one agent can succeed only if others do not.[36] Competition sets agents against each other. In this abstract sense, it is adversarial. Competition stands in contrast to non-adversarial mechanisms for resolving conflict—for example, by command or lottery.[37]

---

35. Philosophers have had less to say about the nature and value of competition than one might expect, a fact lamented by MacCallum 1993, who offers interesting speculation about the reasons why. Here and below I am indebted to Strom 1992; Bartolini 1999 and 2000; Heath 2014, chap. 4; and Hussain 2020. For comprehensive references to the relevant philosophical, economic, and legal literatures see Agmon 2022. Black 2005, chap. 1, provides a clear-headed and instructive analysis of the difficulties in conceptualizing competition and distinguishing it from rivalry.
36. In Hussain's terms, competition is a "rivalry-defining arrangement" (2020, 83).
37. In works I mentioned earlier (note 15, above), Muirhead and Rosenblum, writing alone and together, have called attention to the "regulated rivalry" of political parties. They refer to it as a "discipline": "Electoral politics and policy making as usual—where intentions are not questioned in their democratic essentials—are constraints, and are experienced as such. There is temptation to throw them off" (2016, 24). That temptation leads to what, below, I call competition running off the rails.

Competition can be adversarial in a less abstract sense as well: it can be structured so that an agent can increase her chances of success by taking steps to thwart the efforts of other agents to succeed. Many competitive sports are of this kind: to play defense in a competitive sport is to try to thwart the offense's attempts to score. But not all competitive sports are like this: golf, for example, is adversarial in the more but not the less abstract sense. Its rules do not license individual players to take actions that aim to thwart others' play of the game, even though, by making it the case that one player can win only if others do not, they induce players to regard each other as adversaries.[38] For the most part we shall be concerned with competition in its more concretely adversarial sense.

Without meaning to be comprehensive, I shall be interested here in competitive processes that share three features: they can produce social value; they can do so even if, and sometimes because, the competitors are not motivated by that fact; and they are regulated by rules and norms.

The first point is that, considered as a social phenomenon, competition can affect people who are not themselves competitors. It can produce positive externalities—or social value—for non-competitors. The prospect of desirable outcomes for third parties is one reason why we approve of various kinds of competitive processes—public games of sport and criminal trials are obvious examples—even though their adversarial character might otherwise be troubling.

Second, in order to succeed in a competition, competitors need not be motivated by an interest in the social value whose production justifies it. They may recognize the social value, of course, but

---

38. Agmon 2022, 6–7, therefore distinguishes between "friction" and "parallel" kinds of competition. And see Hussain 2020, 85, on the difference between "rivalry-defining arrangements" and other types of competition. These distinctions are not sharp.

they are usually motivated by a desire for the payoff the game offers to the victor. Indeed, this is typically necessary for competition to succeed: competition can be costly and the social value may not be enough to motivate it.[39] This was clear to Schumpeter in the political case: "[T]he social meaning or function of parliamentary activity is no doubt to turn out legislation and, in part, administrative measures. But in order to understand how democratic politics serve this social end, we must start from the competitive struggle for power and office and realize that the social function is fulfilled, as it were, incidentally—in the same sense as production is incidental to the making of profits."[40]

We should not, however, overstate the motivational point or mistake its significance. When they are effective, norms of fair play regulate competitive struggle, in part, by being internalized by the competitors. Knight recognizes that competitors share an interest to "keep up the game" while noting that it can conflict with the interest in winning.[41] Joseph Heath adds: "Moral judgment [of the conduct of competitors] is always guided by a sense of what the overall 'point' of the competition is, what the beneficial consequences of the activity are, and how the competition serves to generate them."[42]

---

39. Heath 2014, 95–98, gives a perspicuous account. I do not mean to deny that in actual games, there can be and often is a payoff to the players from aspects of the experience of play itself—for example, the pleasure of achieving excellence in exercising the skills required for the game or perhaps simply the pleasure of becoming fully immersed in the play, to the exclusion of other concerns. See Nguyen 2020, chap. 3, for illuminating discussion. There is obviously much room for variation in generalizing from the pleasures of actual games to those of other forms of competition.
40. Schumpeter 1942, 282.
41. The "interest in winning and the interest in the game tend to run into conflict; too much interest in winning first spoils a game and then breaks it up altogether, converting it into a quarrel, or beyond this into a fight. Unless people are more interested in having the game go on than they are in winning it, no game is possible. And the social interest, which is the concern of the social scientist, is precisely the interest in keeping up the game, preventing it from deteriorating, and beyond that in making it a still better game" (Knight 1935, 302).
42. Heath 2014, 106.

Third, as I have stipulated, competitive interaction occurs in a regulated environment. It is guided by more or less enforceable rules and informal norms. Some rules are constitutive of competition, like rules defining what it means to win—for example, the rule of chess defining checkmate. Others are more precisely regulative; they constrain the manner of competition—for example, the rule of chess prohibiting deliberately distracting behavior.

Combining these three points, one reason why competition needs regulative rules is that the adversarial motivations it depends upon to produce social value can induce competitors to do things that undermine the production of that value. Knight's worry that political competition would produce a "cumulative tendency to inequality and consequent disruption of the system" is an instance of this general tendency. Competition can run off the rails.[43] Adherence to the appropriate regulative rules and background norms distinguishes between competitive behavior that advances a practice's justifying purposes and behavior that undermines them—that is, between what we might call "healthy" and "unhealthy" competition. Often we describe unhealthy behaviors as unfair. What we are saying is that the behaviors undermine the competition's capacity to produce the social values for which we rely on it.[44]

Running off the rails is an "internal" pathology. But competition can also be pathological in other ways—not by undermining itself but by violating other moral constraints. For example, the design

---

43. "Off the rails": Heath 2014, 101. For simplicity I describe competition in a pure form, as noncooperative interaction. But we know that competition can be impure, with its motives combining elements of cooperation as well as competition. Whether the cooperative elements are substantial enough to resist the tendency of competition to run off the rails is obviously a contingent matter, but even in mixed cases that is a possibility.
44. On fairness and the purposes of competition, see MacCallum 1993, 215, 216, 218–19. I am not persuaded—and MacCallum may not have been either—that his "title" and "possession" models of competition are fully distinct types (219–21).

of democratic institutions is subject to a norm I once described as equal recognition: institutions should define the public status of citizenship in a way that conveys a communal acknowledgment of the equal worth of citizens.[45] This norm is not internal to political competition: we do not depend on the competitive dynamic to satisfy it. Equal recognition is an external constraint on institutional design required by democratic commitment. Yet the competitive dynamic can defeat it if it is not appropriately regulated. For example, institutions that are systematically unresponsive to the interests of ethnoracial minorities may be objectionable because they manifest a pattern of (failures of) interest satisfaction that undermines the equal public status of citizens. For the same reason one might object to a campaign finance regime that manifestly allows the wealthy to exert more influence than others.[46] (In both cases, of course, there are also other reasons to object.)

Competition is sometimes regarded as an alternative to cooperation. The distinction might be suggested by my earlier observation that competition stands in contrast to non-adversarial mechanisms for resolving conflict like command or lottery. This, however, is in one respect too simple. It is true that competitive processes might be distinguished from cooperative ones by the primary motives of their participants and by the internal standards by which we judge their conduct. But competitive processes as we understand them here require regulation by rules and norms in order to protect against both internal and external pathologies. Although the regulative rules might be embedded in law, in cases of social consequence

---

45. Beitz 1989, 110. Compare Dworkin 2000, 200–201.
46. This objection does not depend on a violation of a principle of equal opportunity for influence over election outcomes. Some inequalities of influence arising from inequalities of wealth might be compatible with equal recognition if, for example, they did not systematically produce policy outcomes that treat some citizens' interests unfairly.

they are unlikely to be effective in the long run unless they are broadly recognized as legitimate by those to whom they apply. We might see such a recognition, where it exists, as a form of second-order normative cooperation within which a competitive dynamic is nested. And its absence may explain cases in which competition turns pathological.

Let me attempt an interim summary of the notion of fair and effective representation that I have sketched. The main idea is that representative democracy consists of a set of competitive processes—for example, for selecting representatives, making policy in the legislature, influencing administrative agencies, contesting in the public sphere. We might call these sites or arenas of competition. Democratic representation relies on competition in these arenas, among others, to serve functions that enable the system as a whole to satisfy its justifying purposes by producing various kinds of social value. But competition is subject to both internal and external pathologies; it requires regulation by rules and norms to protect against them. Regulative standards for these arenas of competition derive from the more general purposes, interpreted for the characteristic functions of each particular arena. The proposal, in short, is that fair and effective democratic representation is representation conducted according to the regulative norms that should apply to the various arenas of competition that compose the system.[47]

---

47. Sometimes I refer to these regulative norms as norms of fairness, or of fair competition, taking "norms" to include both institutional rules and social norms and "fairness" to summarize the normative considerations that determine when competition is well regulated in view of its purposes. On the view I explore, these considerations vary from one arena of competition to another. One might wish for a more parsimonious account of fairness in competitions, but I suspect that any such account would be too abstract to be practically illuminating or interesting.

JUSTIFYING PURPOSES

What I have said so far is abstract. I shall offer some illustrations in a moment. But first let me say more about the idea of fair and effective representation that is emerging. Central to this idea is the thought that regulative norms of political competition derive from the general purposes we believe that democratic representation should satisfy. Ideally we should motivate these purposes by showing how they express an integrated normative conception of democratic self-government among free and equal citizens. But that idea is morally complex, and even a minimally illuminating account is beyond the scope of these lectures. So I shall settle for a list of four purposes, taken from our review of putative failures of representation. The first two purposes relate to the fairness of democratic representation and the second two, to its effectiveness. I state these purposes briefly, understanding that they need elucidation, and without claiming that they constitute a complete list.[48]

1. The system should be responsive to the people in the sense that policy would change when durable electoral majorities favor change. This embeds one dimension of political equality: it is a condition of fairness to citizens considered as the agents of government.[49] I observed in the first lecture that there is no obvious way to specify an optimal degree of policy responsiveness, so the imprecision of this formulation seems to be unavoidable.

---

[48] The idea that democratic representation should be understood to serve multiple and possibly conflicting functional purposes can be found in Birch 1971, 106–23, which offers a more capacious list than I suggest here.

[49] I do not suggest—and do not believe—that the majority principle in its familiar form can be reached by a straightforward inference from considerations of political equality. For discussion, see Beitz 1989, 58–67; Kolodny 2023, sec. 29.2.

2. The system should resolve conflict in a way that takes fair account of the substantive political interests of each citizen. This might more realistically be put negatively: the system should protect citizens from systematic neglect of their interests.[50] This condition embodies another kind of political equality: it requires fairness to citizens considered as the beneficiaries of government. If the negative formulation seems insufficiently demanding, consider that, whereas it is unrealistic and perhaps morally overreaching to expect that institutions can induce any particular distribution of interest satisfaction, it may be possible to design institutions so as to avoid or compensate for various predicable and serious threats to particularly urgent interests. One justification of special provisions for minority representation takes this form.[51]

I referred to "political equality" in both of these formulations. To elaborate: I think of this as a kind of blanket term that incorporates multiple dimensions of political fairness. It is a mistake to think of political equality as a univocal notion. This is a familiar point but bears restating. Fairness does not always require giving equal weight either to everyone's preferences or to their substantive interests. Some interests are more urgent than others, and some people are more vulnerable than others to having their interests overlooked. Standards of political fairness should be sensitive to these differences. A distinctively democratic idea of equal treatment occurs at a more fundamental level, in the requirement that political institutions should treat citizens as free and equal members of political society.[52]

---

50. This is Scanlon's formulation (2018, 86–87).
51. For example, Williams 1998, chap. 7.
52. I argue for this way of thinking about political equality as an ideal in Beitz 1989, esp. chaps. 1 and 5. Dworkin 2000, chap. 4, adopts a broadly similar view, holding that "political equality" is in principle compatible with various institutional forms of unequal treatment

The first two purposes rely on a distinction I drew in the first lecture between two evaluative perspectives associated with democratic citizenship. On the one hand, citizens are the agents of democratic self-government and the ultimate arbiters of democratic law. In this capacity they have interests in having a share of control over lawmaking. On the other hand, they are also the law's subjects or beneficiaries. They have interests in how policy affects them.[53] When we say that democracy is government "by" and "for" the people, we invoke distinct evaluative interests.

3. The third purpose is that the system should be decisive in this sense: it should be capable of resolving conflict about the content and direction of public policy, at least insofar as conflict pertains to achieving broadly valued public functions. This is a condition of effective government: it should be able to solve what are widely regarded as problems requiring public resolution in the face of disagreement about alternative solutions.[54] Citizens have an interest in the effectiveness of political institutions in their capacities as beneficiaries of government whatever their substantive interests in particular policies. In this respect it is distinct from any interest in responsiveness.

---

provided they are justified by the more abstract requirement that political institutions treat citizens with "equal concern and respect."

53. This distinction tracks Hobbes's distinction between the perspectives of subjects as the "makers" and "matter" of government (Hobbes [1651] 1994, Introduction, ¶2; chap. 29, ¶1, discussed further in Beitz 1989, chap. 5).
54. Waldron puts a similar point more generally: "the felt need among the members of a certain group for a common policy or decision or course of action on some matter, even in the face of disagreement about what that policy, decision, or action should be" is among the "circumstances of politics" we must accept as a condition of democratic political life (2008, 200).

4. Finally, the various deliberative environments that comprise the representative system should enable their participants to advance and be exposed to a reasonable range of alternatives and to deliberate responsibly about them. This condition applies in the environments of electoral and interest competition and in the broader public sphere. We have interests in epistemic conditions of responsible deliberation both as agents of democratic government and as its beneficiaries. As agents, we have interests in having opportunities to participate in deliberative environments conducive to our making well-informed, responsible political choices. As beneficiaries, we have interests that others charged with making choices—both policymakers and other citizens—have similar opportunities so that the policies to which we are subjected are more likely to be epistemically well grounded. We would have such an interest even if we were entirely uninterested in participating in political activity.[55]

It seems to me plausible that a system of democratic representation should seek to satisfy (at least) these four purposes, though it is perhaps not beyond debate. But I will have to leave this list undefended for purposes of this lecture. The main points are that the requirements of fair and effective democratic representation are plural and they need to be interpreted for the institutional contexts in which competition seeks to satisfy them. In this latter sense, institutional norms of fair and effective representation are context sensitive or, as we might say, local.[56]

55. This will recall Meiklejohn's dictum: "The point of ultimate interest is not the words of the speakers, but the minds of the hearers. The final aim . . . is the voting of wise decisions" (1948, 25).
56. Macedo (2010, 1030–31) stresses this point. Cain's account of fair contestation among intermediary bodies is suggestive (2015, 25–29, 142–43, 210–15).

The fact that democratic representation must serve a plurality of purposes means that we may face conflicts among the purposes when we approach questions of institutional design. For example, as I mentioned earlier, special provisions for the representation of ethnoracial minorities are sometimes justified as means to reduce predictable threats to their most urgent interests by empowering minority voters. These provisions might also be justified as means to ensure that these minorities can achieve some degree of "descriptive" representation in the legislature, which might enrich the deliberative environment.[57] Yet it is by now a familiar observation that the aims of empowering minority voters and enhancing their descriptive representation may be in conflict.[58] It is not clear that there is any more abstract perspective in which conflicts of purposes can be reconciled, and in any case that question is beyond us here. But it is worth observing that when conflicts of this kind arise in connection with institutional design, one ordinarily looks in two directions: to the underlying reasons for concern about the purposes in question and to the possibility that the purposes can be satisfied by alternative institutional strategies. The hope is that a clearer understanding of the underlying reasons and a more discriminating appreciation of the institutional alternatives might suggest ways of reconciling the conflict. In the case of minority representation, for example, one might ask if the deliberative aims of measures to improve the descriptive representation of minority voters can be achieved in ways that do not conflict with measures to empower them.

When I say that competitive institutions should seek to satisfy the purposes listed, I am not suggesting that these aims can

---

57. Influentially advocated by Mansbridge 1999b.
58. Drutman 2021, 1005–14, reviews the literature in the context of a larger argument about the defects of single-member-district election systems. On the conflict of purposes, see also Pildes 2018, 225–28.

be satisfied simply by getting institutions right. As I said earlier, competition can fail when institutional rules are not adequately supported by suitable social norms—the obvious example is norms of sportsmanship in games of sport. The practical possibility of healthy competition depends on a supporting normative environment that institutions may not be able to guarantee by themselves.[59]

ARENAS OF COMPETITION

To make this idea of fair and effective competition more concrete, I shall consider briefly, and mainly for purposes of illustration, three arenas of competition that ought to be subject to norms of fairness according to the proposal I have sketched. These are electoral competition, competition between parties, and competition among interests. In each case I focus on one element in the larger phenomenon. The question is how we might understand norms of competitive fairness local to each arena and how they might help us to identify failures of fair representation.

Electoral Competition

The first arena is the most familiar: it is the process of election to legislative and executive office. Questions about regulating competition arise most prominently in connection with legislative districting, the conditions of ballot access, and the regulation of campaign finance.

---

59. This is a theme of Levitsky and Ziblatt 2018. We might add that, although institutional rules may not be able to substitute for a supportive normative environment, they might help. For example, in an account of the idea of loyal opposition in British politics, Waldron observes that its norms are reinforced by creation "of an official recognized role for oppositional practice within the constitutional fabric" (2016, 106).

I focus on the first two topics and comment briefly about the third. How competitive should elections be?

The idea of competitiveness is ambiguous. In one sense, a competitive system is simply one in which the rules define an adversarial process for attaining some good. Let us say that such a system has a competitive structure. Nothing follows about whether agents within the structure are all-things-considered likely to conduct themselves as adversaries—that is, to be competitive. Resources might be so unequally distributed that it makes more sense for the less advantaged to take what they can get by cooperating. This points to a second sense of "competitive": it might refer to a situation in which there is some doubt about which of the competitors will prevail, perhaps because resources are not too unequally distributed. Adopting a term from Kaare Strom, we might say that such a system is "situationally" competitive.[60] Situational competitiveness (henceforth simply "competitiveness") is variable: some competitive situations are more competitive, in this sense, than others. This is true, for example, of election districts. However, it would be myopic to say that even a highly competitive situation is necessarily competitive in another sense that might interest us. In this third sense, a competitive system is one that is open to participation by anyone willing and able to compete. Again following Strom, we might say that such a system is "politically contestable"; all willing competitors face comparable barriers to entry that are not unduly restrictive (a condition that requires clarification in context).

These distinctions matter for political competition. Politics in the old South had a competitive structure but general elections were not situationally competitive; Democrats almost always won. When there were primary elections for Democratic nominations, those elections might have been (situationally) competitive, but they were

---

60. Strom 1992, 384–86.

not very contestable because barriers to entry prevented some who might have wanted to compete from participating.[61]

We should consider competitiveness and contestability separately.

Competitiveness. Many people believe that competitiveness is a desirable feature of election systems. To be more precise, they believe that some significant proportion of constituencies should satisfy some threshold of competitiveness. (Interpretations of significance and the threshold can vary.) Some think a degree of competitiveness is a requirement of democracy. Edward Tufte, for example, writes in a seminal paper that a system of representation should satisfy a condition of electoral responsiveness in order to be "minimally democratic."[62]

What Tufte calls responsiveness is situational competitiveness. It is not the same as policy responsiveness, of course. But these ideas may be related; at least when the partisan division is fairly close, electoral competitiveness can be a condition of policy responsiveness. This is because it can incentivize incumbent representatives to take account of constituency preferences in the conduct of office.[63] If one

---

61. On the structure of political competition in the one-party South see Caughey 2018. He reconsiders the wisdom received from Key 1949 about the lack of competition in southern politics.
62. Tufte 1973, 553. He also identified a second condition: that the system "should be relatively *unbiased* with respect to political party; [it] should treat Democrats and Republicans alike" (1973, 553). Tufte associated the two conditions—absence of partisan bias and reasonable responsiveness—with "fair and effective representation," respectively. I turn to the concern about partisan bias below.
63. This a priori suggestion gives rise to the empirical "marginality hypothesis": that an incumbent elected by a narrow margin is more likely to be responsive to constituency interests than an incumbent elected by a wider margin. Griffin describes the hypothesis as an "important claim going to the heart of the democratic process" (2006a, 912). His analysis of thirty years of data ending in 2000 offers considerable support for the hypothesis. On the other hand, evidence from state legislatures suggests that when competitive districts are also highly polarized (if district ideology is multi-peaked), incumbents may be uncertain about the location of the district median and take more extreme positions. This could reduce incentives for accountability (Masket 2019; see also McCarty et al. 2018). The lesson is that it can matter how competitive districts are composed, complicating reform efforts to encourage responsiveness-inducing competitiveness.

of the social purposes a competitive system of representation should serve is to be responsive to durable changes in the majority's political preferences as they express them in elections, then we should agree that some degree of competitiveness is a desirable feature of election systems.

The value of policy responsiveness is not the only reason why we might value electoral competitiveness. We expect competing candidates and parties to define the choices open to voters and to make them subjects of public deliberation. But if a district is uncompetitive, the candidate of the majority party has less incentive to articulate a program that takes account of voter interests or to advocate for such a program within the party. In addition, the challenger may have fewer resources to communicate her views to the electorate. The quality of the epistemic environment would suffer, and, as we know from social science, the level of voter engagement would likely be suppressed.[64] If another purpose of electoral competition is to enable voters to deliberate responsibly about the alternatives on offer, then features of the system that subvert the exercise of this responsibility are independently objectionable.[65]

So we have at least two reasons to regard electoral competitiveness as a virtue.[66] But just as there is no clear basis for judging some

---

64. Lipsitz 2011, chap. 3; Seabrook 2017, chap. 5. There is evidence that a lack of competitiveness in Senate elections can result in less voter attention paid to senators' policy records, reducing the system's capacity to hold incumbents accountable (Jones 2013).
65. Here I am agreeing with Richard Hasen, who argues in an early critique of Issacharoff and Pildes's analysis of anti-competitive partisan "lock-ups" (1998) that we can only judge whether the system is sufficiently competitive by asking whether, at a given level of competitiveness, the system serves the valuable purposes it ought to serve (Hasen 1998, 727). I would not agree (and Hasen may not have meant to suggest) that these purposes are primarily concerned with protection of individual rights such as freedom of expression and association.
66. Some argue that a third reason is that more competitive districts might attract less extreme candidates (e.g., Page and Gilens 2020, 220–21). This may be right but, as I observed above (n. 63), the way that competitive districts are composed matters: it will influence the extent to which the districts promote responsiveness by incumbents and challengers.

level of policy responsiveness to be optimal, there is also no clear basis for judging some degree of electoral responsiveness or district competitiveness to be optimal—though it is clear that the optimum is not typically the maximum.[67] Still, as Tufte suggests, we might think that a democratic system of election should display some reasonable degree of responsiveness, where we interpret "reasonable" in terms of the capacity of the system to produce a change in representation when a majority in the jurisdiction as a whole prefers it.

What I have described is a familiar, pro-competitiveness view. There are some reasons to resist it. I mention one and explain why I am not persuaded by it. The objection involves the satisfaction of members of a constituency with the incumbent's job performance. In a Downsian world, under ideal conditions, incumbents will act in ways aimed at satisfying the median voter in the issue space. This would minimize the aggregate dissatisfaction with her performance in office. But aggregate dissatisfaction depends on the voters' relative locations in the issue space. The more concentrated the voters—that is, the more homogeneous the constituency—the less the aggregate dissatisfaction. So, someone might argue that it is better to make districts as politically homogeneous as possible so as to minimize aggregate dissatisfaction.[68] But this could reduce their competitiveness.[69]

The response to this objection invokes our doubts about the importance of congruence. For reasons we considered earlier, it is not

---

67. As Thompson remarks, the aim in institutional design should not be to maximize competitiveness "but to find the optimal level for sustaining a just democratic process" (2002, 8). For contrasting views about optimal responsiveness, see McGann et al. 2016, chap. 3, and Nagle 2017. To put the issue into perspective, consider that, as many (including Nagle 2017, 197) have pointed out, a maximally competitive district map could produce a winner-take-all result (the majority party winning all the seats).
68. A view suggested in different ways by Brunell 2008 and Buchler 2011.
69. Party primaries complicate this argument. Because an increasing number of congressional districts are uncompetitive at the general election stage, effective competition in primaries has become more important for competitiveness within districts (Thomsen 2023). The subject deserves closer attention than I can give it here.

clear why the prospect of dissatisfaction of voters with the conduct of their representatives in the legislature should matter in assessing the institutional structure of democratic representation. Dissatisfied voters can always vote to replace their representatives. A more competitive system, assuming it would be more responsive, increases the chances that they can succeed. A less competitive system, although it might produce a higher aggregate level of voter satisfaction when looked at synchronically, reduces the chances of voters to hold representatives accountable when looked at in time. This is incompatible with the aim that political competition should foster responsiveness to changes in the popular will.[70]

Contestability. A generic notion of competitiveness includes the dimensions of both situational competitiveness and contestability. We can have one without the other. In the United States, districts vary in their situational competitiveness, but there is much less variance in contestability. Barriers to entry for third parties and independent candidacies are high almost everywhere.

These barriers might seem unfair for two reasons. First, they are very likely the result of the two major parties taking advantage of a natural duopoly to avoid competition—a case of "partisan lockup."[71] Second, the reasoning that led us, earlier, to a pro-competitiveness view of districting systems also seems to lead us to value greater contestability. A system that excludes participation by representatives of

---

70. Another reason to resist the pro-competitiveness view follows from the fact that the more competitive the district, the less certain the incumbent can be of re-election. In response she will feel greater pressure to devote time to preparing for the next campaign (e.g., by fundraising) rather than to acting as a legislator in ways that would advance the political interests of her constituents or her party. Offhand this suggests a decrease in the quality of representation, presumably a bad thing. But this is not best seen as a dysfunction of competitiveness. The underlying problem in the case imagined is the system of private campaign finance. Repair campaign finance and the problem would be significantly diminished. We have ample independent reason to do so.
71. Issacharoff and Pildes 1998. The duopoly is "natural" for reasons familiar from Duverger 1954.

some minority positions cannot promise to be responsive to them even if it is situationally competitive. On reflection, however, these two reasons reduce to one. The "partisan lockup" concern arises from skepticism that partisan efforts to avoid competition have the appropriate kind of justification. The skepticism may be warranted, but it does not rule out that there might be a good justification after all. That is why the second reason is important: it argues that the lockup treats those excluded unfairly. If this is right, then ballot access restrictions are internal pathologies of competition: cases in which competition undermines the social value that justifies it.

Before reaching that conclusion, however, we should remember that, with a first-past-the-post plurality decision rule, an election with three (or more) candidates can produce a winner who ranks lower in the preference orderings of a majority of voters than another candidate. The decision rule allows "spoilers." One solution to this problem is to allow "fusion" candidacies—candidates whose names appear on the ballot for more than one party.[72] Another is to use a rule for aggregating votes that is sensitive to voters' preference orderings—perhaps ranked choice voting (RCV).[73] On the face of it, these are attractive solutions. But if neither possibility is available, then the force of the prima facie preference for greater openness seems to me substantially reduced, because it can produce minority winners.

I put the point tentatively because there is a difference between the argument that we need a competitive election system to promote policy responsiveness and the analogous argument for broad contestability and thus openness to third parties and independent

---

72. "Fusion bans" are ubiquitous in the United States. They seem to me to be pure cases of misuse of the advantages of two-party duopoly. For a detailed discussion of the competing considerations, see Thompson 2002, 70–80; also Disch 2002, Conclusion.
73. For the case in favor of RCV in some US elections, see Drutman 2020a, 177–83; for some doubts, Fiorina 2021.

candidates. Some think that contestability can be achieved in other ways.[74] In the traditional view, this is the role of party primaries: they allow many candidates to compete in a process that winnows the pool to a small number among whom voters can make informed choices at the general election. Primaries are hardly a perfect substitute for greater openness, but it is hard to see how the values of fairness and effectiveness can adjudicate the choice because they may be in conflict. This may be a point where even local normative considerations must be agnostic.

Campaign resources and competitiveness. We have been considering legislative districting and regulations governing access to the ballot because they can affect the competitiveness and contestability of elections. Both are aspects of the institutional structure of electoral competition and therefore, in principle, open to regulation. If we continue to think of ("situational") competitiveness as related to the extent of doubt about which competitor will prevail, then we might think that competitiveness, if not contestability, can also be affected by the balance of campaign resources available to the competitors—money, campaign services, and so on. To some extent this, too, is in principle open to regulation.

Without repeating our earlier discussion of fairness in the context of campaign finance, let me note briefly the inference to be drawn about electoral competitiveness. This follows from the differential value of campaign resources for incumbents and (anyway high-quality) challengers. Although there is some empirical uncertainty, it seems very likely that the marginal value of a unit of campaign resources is greater (perhaps considerably greater) for challengers than for incumbents because incumbency status itself confers a competitive advantage. If one were to think electoral

---

74. For example, by fostering intraparty competition. Bagg and Bhatia 2022 provide a helpful, critical survey and discussion.

competitiveness desirable for reasons we considered earlier, then one might think that the design of a fair campaign finance system should aim to reduce the electoral impact of the incumbent advantage (e.g., by subsidizing challengers). We should note that if this is indeed a matter of fairness in electoral competition, its normative significance is to be found in the desirability of competitiveness at the level of the system as a whole; it is not, even indirectly, a means of reducing inequalities in the electoral influence of individual voters.

Party Competition

Earlier I said that parties play an ineliminable role in democratic representation. At the most abstract level, they matter because they have practically unique capacities to organize political conflict and public deliberation.[75] In one helpful, though not much less abstract, formulation, Daniel Schlozman and Sam Rosenfeld write that the parties' functions include "aggregating and integrating preferences and actors into ordered conflict, . . . mobilizing participation and linking the governed with the government."[76] Parties serve these intermediary functions both in the electoral arena and in legislatures, where, in both cases, they have institutional advantages over other agents. Party candidates have privileged access to positions on the election ballot, and parties enjoy a license to choose their candidates, subject to state regulation. In the Congress, their caucuses control significant aspects of the legislative process, including the distribution of committee positions and the floor agenda. We should regard parties as

---

75. Rosenblum emphasizes the role of a competitive dynamic in serving these ends: "The benefits of party conflict can be the un-aimed-for result of what partisans do half-thinkingly, and what will not be done without them" (2008, 307).
76. D. Schlozman and Rosenfeld 2019, 120; see 122–26 on the prevailing academic controversy about defining parties.

competing entities even though, as empirical phenomena, they may be difficult to conceive of as collective agents.

Party competition can be regulated in various ways. One is through the laws that define conditions of ballot access and candidate selection. Another is through the campaign finance regime's rules that structure the flow of resources to campaigns and affect the parties' capacity to influence the selection of candidates.[77]

I want to consider a third way that institutions influence party competition. It involves the impact of legislative districting on the transformation of votes into seats in elections to Congress and the state legislatures. As I said in the first lecture, a combination of the geographical distribution of partisan voters and partisan gerrymandering can produce partisan bias, making it possible for one party to elect more members of the legislature with a given share of the vote than the other party could if it attracted the same share of the vote. As I observed, many argue that partisan bias in districting is unfair.[78]

There is one obvious way that partisan gerrymandering might seem to be a failure of fair competition. It is a use of power by the majority party to entrench itself, aiming to block competitive threats in the future—another case of "partisan lockup." So we might think of it as a matter of competition going off the rails. But that is a difficult position to sustain without some notion of the social value that party competition is supposed to produce. The problem cannot simply be that gerrymandering fails to offer partisan voters equal formal (or a priori) opportunities for electoral influence; as we know, gerrymandering (and more generally partisan bias) is compatible with that.

---

77. There is, however, disagreement about the wisdom of attempting to empower parties by directing the flow of privately provided campaign resources to them: doing so might simply strengthen another channel of elite influence. Compare Persily 2015 and McCarty 2015 with Mann and Dionne 2015 and Schlozman and Rosenfeld 2019.
78. See note 55 in chapter 1 above.

The question is whether we can make sense of the distinct idea, broached but not explored in the first lecture, that partisan bias is unfair to political parties or to their partisan voters. Here is one attempt at a reply.[79]

What responsible partisan voters aim for when they vote is not (only) election of the candidate they favor but also advancement in the legislature of the candidate's political commitments which they endorse. They want to contribute to the election of a candidate who will contribute to the movement of public policy in the direction of their policy preferences. Unlike parties in the electorate, parties in legislatures are relatively coherent organizations. Their leaders participate in managing the agenda, coordinate the framing of legislation, organize coalition-building, and (try to) provide the discipline to enact (or obstruct) legislation. Ordinarily a member wishing to advance her political aims in the legislature will have to rely on the leadership and other members of her party for help in doing so.[80] One factor that determines a member's capacity to get the legislative outcomes she wants is the voting strength and organizational discipline of her party in the legislature. Partisan bias diminishes the capacity of voters for candidates of the disadvantaged party to get the legislative outcomes they want by diminishing their party's representation in the legislature in relation to what it would be in the absence of bias.

Why should we regard this as objectionable? Partisan bias is made possible by the use of single-member territorial district systems of representation (SMD). It is best seen as a pathology of these systems. Presumably SMD systems are chosen because they are supposed to have certain advantages. Some think, for example, that they produce more stable governments and make policy choices more

---

79. This revises Beitz 2018, 346–50.
80. McGann et al. 2016, 208–9.

transparent.[81] But they come with what might seem to be the disadvantage, at least in comparison with some kinds of proportional systems, that the majority party ordinarily wins a larger share of the seats than its share of the votes. (In technical terms, the "swing ratio" is typically greater than one.)[82] The minority party's influence in the legislature is correspondingly smaller than its share of the vote would suggest. It is important that this can (and usually does) occur even in the absence of partisan bias, but partisan bias can make it worse. This suggests that the unfairness of partisan bias is its differential impact on the capacity of partisan voters to attain their political ends through participation in a party. In contrast to the disproportionality more or less unavoidably produced in an SMD system, no reasonable democratic purpose is served by the avoidable difference in partisan political capacity due to bias.

A view that is both simpler and more radical is that the failure of partisan bias is just the failure to represent parties in proportion to their shares of the jurisdiction-wide vote. If it takes more minority-party votes, on average, to elect a representative than it takes majority-party votes, the majority party will be unfairly overrepresented.[83] This more radical view is attractive, but from one perspective it proves too much. As I noted, deviations from seats/votes proportionality are common in SMD systems. For that reason there might be at least a pro tanto objection to any such system. But if we take the system as fixed in its main elements, either because it has

---

81. Powell 2000 provides an extended comparative analysis of the advantages of SMD versus proportional systems. For a discussion of the comparison from an explicitly normative perspective, see Wilson 2019, chap. 8.
82. This means, roughly, that the percentage change in the winning party's share of seats is greater than the change in its share of votes (Tufte 1973, 542). The losing party's seat share is smaller.
83. A view of this kind is suggested by Urbinati's remarks on democracy and proportionality (2006, 40–44). Christiano holds that considerations of political equality argue for a principle of proportionality for partisan votes and seats (1996, chap. 6).

offsetting advantages or because it is practically beyond reform, we might still object to partisan bias because it exacerbates differences in partisan voters' capacities to attain their political ends in the legislature without a compensating democratic benefit.

Beyond partisan unfairness, bias can also produce consequential damage for groups that participate in a party's coalition. For example, as we noted earlier, in some states, Black voters, who are overwhelmingly Democratic, tend to be concentrated geographically in urban areas in districts with large Democratic majorities. In some states in the South, where Black voters are more dispersed, the Voting Rights Act's requirement to construct majority-minority districts has been used to justify gerrymandering to create a comparable degree of concentration.[84] Under these circumstances, the Black vote is relatively inefficient in influencing the election of representatives (even though more Black representatives might be elected). This can contribute to partisan bias at the level of the jurisdiction that advantages Republicans.[85] Other things equal, the effect is to relatively disempower Black voters as contributors to the party coalition.

The argument I have sketched may be needlessly indirect. I am not sure, in any case, that I can defend its details. But it seems to me to offer a plausible interpretation of the intuitive idea that, in view of the functions of parties in organizing competition for influence over legislation, partisans can object when electoral institutions differentially affect their parties' capacities to secure their legislative ends without an appropriate justification.

Earlier I observed that partisan gerrymandering might seem to be a case of competition running off the rails because it involves a

---

84. Rodden 2019, 192.
85. On race, gerrymandering, and Republican bias in the states see Keena et al. 2021, chap. 5. They argue that satisfying the requirements of the Voting Rights Act need not increase Republican bias, although it often does in Republican-led states.

party's use of a competitive advantage to entrench itself. That seems true. But the objection to partisan bias that we have arrived at is different (though not incompatible). It holds that partisan bias offends an external constraint on districting—that the system should not impose on partisan voters a larger competitive disadvantage than what is necessary to attain the social values that SMD systems (are supposed to) produce. We might say that the opportunity costs of the choice of institutional design have been unfairly shared. It is a failure of regulation, by law and the courts, not to rectify the unfairness.

The subject of the role of parties in electoral competition is part of a larger understanding of their functions as organizers of political conflict. This includes their roles in congressional procedures and in the public sphere. In both realms, one focus of normative attention is the impact of institutional rules on the capacity of parties to shape interest conflicts.

At the moment, the capacity of American parties to play these roles seems to be significantly diminished. It is not clear to what extent we should consider this to be an institutional failure. To reach a view about this we would need a better grasp of the reasons for the diminished capacities and the prospects of reforms that could strengthen them. This is beyond us here, though it seems likely that aspects of the campaign finance regime as well as the procedural rules and organizational structures of the parties themselves are implicated.[86] But even if the parties were to become more capable of integrating interests, there would be a further problem about the representation of interests in the modern policy state, one that carries us beyond partisan electoral competition.

---

86. D. Schlozman and Rosenfeld 2019 offer one plausible account, emphasizing prospects for renewal of the parties as mass membership organizations under contemporary circumstances of sorting and increased partisanship. Compare Rosenbluth and Shapiro 2018, chap. 5.

Interest Competition

Interest representation—particularly as it occurs in lobbying—is our third arena of political competition. Notwithstanding the attention given to interest representation in political science and to some extent in law, it is strikingly absent from democratic theory even though its institutional structure and conduct present clear issues of political morality.[87] The question we should consider is whether conceiving of interest group lobbying as a competitive activity in democratic representation would influence our thinking about the norms by which it should be regulated.

Lee Drutman defines lobbying generically as "activity oriented towards shaping public policy outcomes."[88] The subject may seem esoteric for political theory, so let me place it in context. One way that inequality of wealth can threaten democratic politics is by shifting the boundary between public and private power. When government is unable to assert control over concentrations of private economic power that threaten the people's capacity for self-rule, then the scope of democratic government has been constrained. The failure is not only one of process—for example, a failure to ensure that individual citizens have equal opportunities to influence outcomes. It is a structural failure. Even if the means of electoral influence were somehow to be equally distributed, in the presence of sufficient inequality of wealth there could still be a tendency to produce outcomes that democratic government exists to avoid—namely, those in which private concentrations of economic power become politically hegemonic. This, we should recall, was Knight's concern: he worried

---

87. As always there are exceptions, though they are relatively few. The canonical study of interest representation in the administrative state is Stewart 1975. More recent works attentive to normative issues include Richardson 2002; Warren 2014; Emerson 2019.
88. Drutman 2015, 15.

that the natural tendency of political competition was to aggravate background inequalities of private wealth and power.

The lobbying system presents this phenomenon in microcosm. But it is hard to describe the normative problem accurately. I begin with some observations about the nature of interest representation, the role of competition within it, and its place in the policymaking process. Then we can ask how, as now constituted, the system can manifest a form of political unfairness.

Four observations frame the problem. First, the organized representation of interests in the processes of legislation and administrative regulation seems to be inevitable in the modern policy state. In some form, moreover—at least in the absence of large structural changes— it is most likely desirable as a means of providing information and expertise to those charged with making policy.[89] Second, interest representation is competitive: interests conflict in policymaking, and their conflicts are resolved by public officials in a system that has a good deal of structure (e.g., in the system of agency rule-making). Third and relatedly, the system is capable of regulation, and is in fact regulated, by law and administrative rules.[90] Finally, although lobbying has long been a conspicuous feature of democratic representation, it has grown strikingly in the last forty years.[91] It commands very substantial resources. An anecdotal indication is that interest groups spend more on lobbying than the entire congressional budget. Most

---

89. "[O]rganized interests are not merely to be tolerated in a democracy; they also have a central part to play in its functioning. Representatives of organized interests perform a crucial role in providing information in the policy making process: they call attention to issues, furnish evidence about how problems are being experienced on the ground, and provide expertise about the anticipated consequences—both substantive and political—of proposed solutions. Furthermore, by making possible a two-way process of communication, organized interests facilitate the acceptance and legitimation of policies by interested stakeholders" (K. L. Schlozman, Brady, and Verba 2018, 149).
90. Hasen 2012, pt. 1, offers a detailed overview.
91. The growth is documented by Drutman 2015. See Charnock 2020 for evidence of the expansion of interest group activity from lobbying to electioneering in the last few decades.

of this derives from business and professional organizations.[92] Thus, for example, any attempt to explain Gilens's findings about the class bias of public policy should therefore take account of lobbying as a mechanism.[93]

Forty years ago, Robert Dahl observed that the role of organizational activity in democratic politics raises a question of fairness. He treats the question as an extension of the problem of political equality. He argues that in an ideally democratic state—that is, a state in which the conditions of political equality among individuals had been fully satisfied—it would still be necessary to regulate organized interests to ensure that their activity does not distort the equality that had been realized among individuals. As Dahl puts it, political equality can only be realized if "the political resources of all organizations are effectively regulated so that resources are proportional to the number of members."[94]

Dahl is right that there is a distinctive problem of fairness in the organization of interest representation. But his formulation of the appropriate regulative aim is inadequate, even in the perspective of its own theoretical motivation. (For example, since different individuals are likely to have interests represented by different numbers of organizations, making each organization's resources proportional to its membership will not necessarily equalize the all-things-considered influence of individuals.)[95] It also betrays an unrealistic conception of organizational activity: in that conception, all organizations have

---

92. Drutman and Mahoney 2017, 291.
93. As Gilens himself emphasizes (2012, chap. 5). See also Hacker and Pierson 2010, chaps. 4–6.
94. Dahl 1982, 84.
95. Kay Schlozman therefore suggests a more abstract principle: "[E]ach citizen's total share of group-based input—whether as a member of one or several groups and whether on one or several issues—must be equal to that of every other citizen" (1984, 1009–10). She is skeptical that inequalities of this kind can be measured with any imaginable data (1011). In any case, she and Dahl seem to recognize that such a standard could never be met. The idea that a norm of political equality applies to interest groups survives in recent work; for example, Drutman and LaPira write that a criterion of congressional representativeness

memberships consisting of individuals with common interests and all politically salient shared interests are represented by organizations. But, in fact, most organized interest groups are not membership organizations in the ordinary sense; if they have members at all, the "members" are more likely other organizations like business firms or universities than individuals.[96] And, of course, it is clearly untrue that all salient interests are equally well organized (or organized at all).

Another and, for our purposes, a more important misperception is that lobbying operates primarily by exerting pressure on policymakers (perhaps by offering quid pro quos). Views like Dahl's (indeed, the idea of lobbying as a "pressure system") might seem to suppose that the primary function of lobbying is to transmit pressure from individuals and groups to those who make decisions about policy (the metaphor may be the idea of a force vector).[97] However, while lobbying relationships plainly involve transactional elements, a more comprehensive view would also understand them as part of a deliberative system.[98] Lobbyists belong to professional communities of experts, their expertise has value, and policymakers can benefit from it. This explains the form of competition we observe in the arena of lobbying. Lobbyists compete for policymakers' attention by offering information and points of view, facilitating relations with other interests, and coordinating the building of coalitions. Policymakers

---

should ask how well Congress represents "the diversity of interests in society and ensure[s] their equal opportunities to influence in the policy process" (2020, 14).

96. For documentation see K. L. Schlozman et al. 2015. They argue that "each of the representational inequalities characteristic of membership associations of individuals is exacerbated when politically active organizations are organizations without members" (1018).
97. Kolodny 2023, sec. 24.2, citing Goldman 1999.
98. See Mansbridge 1992, 36–39, for the idea that interest representation might be considered as part of deliberative policymaking. On the idea of a deliberative system more generally, see Mansbridge 1999a and Mansbridge et al. 2012 and, for helpful critical discussion, Owen and Smith 2015.

depend on this competitive process for resources they need to make policy. Properly organized, competition among lobbyists for attention might generate a valuable externality for policymaking.[99]

Schattschneider describes the main normative problem in the "pressure system" by saying that its chorus sings with an upper-class accent.[100] This is plausible only if we understand "class" broadly. It is true that there is extreme imbalance in the system, but the imbalance is not best described in terms of social or income class. The imbalance is primarily reflected in the fact that business and professional interests are represented by groups with far greater resources than the organizations we might classify as representing other interest-sharing groups in the public (by one calculation the ratio in spending is 34:1).[101] But it is too simple to assume that the groups that dispose greater resources work to advance some set of substantive interests shared by the "upper class." The interests of business firms and professional groups are diverse and often in conflict even though in some cases they may coincide to form the basis of coalitions.[102]

Putting these last two points together, the concern about unfairness in the system of interest representation is not only about class bias in the capacity to control what policymakers do by apportioning rewards and punishments. In some circumstances that concern is plainly justified,[103] but if so it is an application of the generic objection

---

99. The most detailed study is Baumgartner et al. 2009; on the organization of lobbying see chapter 3 and, more recently, Drutman and Mahoney 2017. Also see Hall and Deardorff 2006, who propose a theory of lobbying as "legislative subsidy."
100. Schattschneider 1960, 34–35.
101. Drutman and Mahoney 2017, 291.
102. Baumgartner et al. (2009), chap. 3, find that most issues that become subjects of lobbying are multidimensional in the sense that they implicate several standards of evaluation and produce lobbying coalitions that shift from issue to issue. Drutman 2015, chap. 5, emphasizes the increasing extent of intraindustry competition among lobbyists to shape policy for the interests of individual firms.
103. It is suggested, for example, by Kalla and Broockman 2016's finding that policymakers grant preferential access to their contributors.

we identified earlier to features of the institutional structure that create incentives for officials to violate their official duties by responding to the wrong kinds of reasons.

An objection that is more distinctive to lobbying arises from the ability of well-resourced lobbyists to overwhelm the epistemic capacities of policymakers to process and evaluate the information the lobbying system makes available to them. Those capacities are limited by time, attention, and staff support.[104] Substantial differences in resources exploit these deliberative limitations.

If we understand the social value of competition in the system of interest representation as providing policymakers with the resources they need to make good policy, then the basis of the objection is this. Under contemporary circumstances of policymaking, the imbalance of resources skews the epistemic environment in which deliberation about policy takes place. This can create an advantage for the better-resourced interests, although it does not always do so.[105] The imbalance is a kind of unfairness, but it is not a simple matter of inequality of opportunity for influence among individuals. The unfairness lies in the subversion of an epistemic environment conducive to responsible policy judgments to which citizens are entitled. Sufficiently imbalanced resources undermine the capacity

---

104. For example, Drutman describes efforts by well-resourced interests to saturate the policymakers' "intellectual environment" to elevate some arguments to "top-of-mind status" in the professional community (2015, 36). On the (substantial) decline in Congress's institutional capacity to manage policymaking and the shift of staff resources from policy to political messaging, see Reynolds 2020.
105. The relationship between the resources an organization devotes to lobbying activities and its success in attaining its aims is not straightforward. In their comprehensive study, Baumgartner et al. are unable to find a systematic relationship between resources and policy success. They argue that success depends on building coalitions of interests, typically with varying amounts and kinds of resources, and establishing partnerships with like-minded government officials. They also note that in the competitive structure of lobbying, mobilization on one "side" of an issue usually elicits an offsetting mobilization on the other (2009, chap. 10).

of the competitive process to secure the social value that justifies it. This is the sense in which the unfairness is structural rather than only transactional. Repairing it does not necessarily require equalizing individual resources (assuming that the idea is coherent in this context). It requires creating conditions for effective contestation of opposing views within the deliberative system of which lobbying is a part.[106]

The distortions at issue do not only occur in the context of deliberation about potential policy changes already on the legislative or agency agendas. They can also occur in the process of setting those agendas. The policy agendas of lobbyists are systematically different from those found in other parts of the system of representation (e.g., in congressional hearings, presidential policy programs, and public opinion).[107] This means that deliberative distortions arising from differences in lobbying resources may not only affect the way contested policy changes are resolved but also the selection from among potential changes of those that become contested.

Other views of the problem are possible. For example, Richard Hasen dismisses "platitudes about 'undue influence'" in favor of a view that would regulate lobbying so as to obstruct its potential to reduce national economic welfare by contributing to rent-seeking and other inefficiencies.[108] His interest is the constitutional basis of regulation, and he may be correct that objections to "undue influence" lack an adequate foundation in constitutional jurisprudence. As a first-order normative matter, however, if, as it appears, the lobbying system skews the epistemic environment of policymaking in favor of interests that can devote greater resources to the process,

---

106. For example, Cain argues for a "rule of two": "[I]n interest group lobbying, the critical question is whether the dominant position or interest can be contested. The evidence of contestation is the presence of a second viewpoint" (2015, 11).
107. Baumgartner et al. 2009, 15–19.
108. Hasen 2012, 253.

then concern about "undue influence" should not be platitudinous, even if it is also true that lobbying encourages the kinds of undesirable policy choices that Hasen describes.[109]

My remarks about these three arenas of competition are at best sketches: gestures at a larger project of articulating norms of fairly regulated competition in each arena. In a more comprehensive inquiry one would also try to elaborate the idea of fairly regulated competition in other arenas, including the organization of the public sphere, perhaps the most important omission here and a challenging subject in its own right.[110] But I hope to have illustrated a general idea about standards of fair competition in various arenas where it takes place: they derive from a conception of the justifying purposes of democratic representation interpreted for the functions we should expect competition to serve in each arena. I do not suggest that these standards can be "read off" features of the context: the view I have suggested is normative from top to bottom while trying to be sensitive to the varying functional roles of competition at different points in the system.

---

109. It is not my aim to recommend policy changes. But if we were to understand lobbying as part of a deliberative system undermined by economic inequality, we might consider measures to reduce the advantages of private-sector lobbies in the deliberative system and to improve the diminished capabilities of Congress. Some measures that have been proposed include subsidizing public interest groups (a "public defender" model), improving the transparency of lobbying activities so that they can be monitored by public interest lobbies and the press, and enlarging the analytical capacities of Congress to reduce the imbalance of information resources. See, e.g., Cain 2015, 142, 158; Drutman and Mahoney 2017; LaPira, Drutman, and Kosar 2020.
110. For an analysis of the contemporary public sphere as a competitive arena, see Balkin 2021. He argues that social media companies are the principal information intermediaries in the digital public sphere, that as the competitive environment is now constituted competition among them undermines rather than serves democratic purposes, and that regulation is required to bring the structure of the environment and the incentives facing participants into alignment with these purposes.

REVIEW AND CONCLUSION

In the last few decades many professional observers of American politics have worried that the constitutional system of democratic representation is failing. The convergence on intimations of failure was my starting point. It raises first-order normative concerns about the health of democratic representation in America that should worry all of us. The convergence also raises more theoretical questions about the nature and aims of democratic representation or, as I have put it here, about standards of fair and effective representation. Both sets of questions have preoccupied us in these lectures.

In the first lecture, after noting some stylized facts that purport to describe shortfalls from democratic representation, I distinguished among failures of effectiveness, failures of congruence and responsiveness, and failures of fairness. In each case my aim was to grasp the normative grounds of judgments of failure explicit or implicit in the empirical literatures. On inspection, we saw that the judgments of failure appeal to several distinct considerations of democratic political morality. It was difficult to see how these considerations might be brought within a single perspective that could make sense of them all.

In this second lecture I have tried, in an exploratory spirit, to sketch one way we might construct such a perspective. The perspective I suggested conceives of democratic representation as a competitive system. The system serves multiple democratic purposes by organizing competitive activity in several functionally differentiated arenas. Electoral competition between or among candidates for office is central. But it is myopic to limit ourselves to it; parties compete both within and beyond elections, interests compete for attention and influence in legislatures and executive agencies, and speakers compete for attention in a structurally complex public sphere. In each of these arenas, competition can go well or badly (or be healthy or unhealthy), depending on how effectively it is regulated by rules and shared background norms. To illustrate, we considered three arenas of competition within the system of representation—electoral competition, party competition, and interest competition—and asked how competition in each arena should be regulated to serve its justifying purposes. Taken together, these cases show that the requirements of fair and effective democratic representation are plural and need to be articulated within the competitive arenas in which questions of fairness and effectiveness arise. This perspective may also enable us to see how the stylized facts canvassed in the first lecture might be seen to describe failures (or the results of failures) of fair and effective representation.

I have only gestured at a response to a question I raised in the first lecture about whether the intimations of failure are signs of institutional dysfunction or, instead, expressions of exogenous changes in the political environment. That is primarily a question for social theory, but what seems clear, offhand, is that different forms of failure are brought about by different combinations of causes within and beyond institutions. For example, to the extent that problems of ineffectiveness due to gridlock are growing worse, failure appears to be a result of exogenous changes in political society (in particular, growing elite polarization, negative partisan affect, and a closely divided electorate) acting through institutions with an inbuilt bias for the status quo. Partisan bias in districting, on the other hand, is largely a result of choices in institutional design that might have been otherwise, even though resistance to reform may be explained by developments in political society. In general, the most troubling failures seem to me to result from a recalcitrant combination: changes in the political environment have been refracted through institutions that may have functioned well enough under different circumstances but do not do so today. If this is right, then our institutions, including their associated norms, are ill-suited to meet the contemporary challenges of a changing polity. Yet the exogenous changes that explain contemporary forms of dysfunction also suggest that institutional reforms on a scale required to render government more responsive and effective are unlikely to be made without a shift in the partisan balance in the electorate.

This observation leads me, finally, to what must seem to many readers to be the elephant in the room. In the framework I have described, there is no more troubling case of political competition in the United States running off the rails than the erosion of healthy party competition that has been in progress for at least thirty years (or, arguably, longer). The erosion has many sources but has been propelled primarily by a Republican Party whose leadership's strategic choices have destabilized democratic norms that are essential for effective political competition in a process that now appears to have escaped the party leadership's control.[111]

The Trump phenomenon is the main contemporary expression of this competitive failure. At this writing it is still a focus of the existential anxiety I mentioned at the beginning, only to put it aside. In the perspective we have arrived at, however, the Trump phenomenon now appears less as an idiosyncratic episode than as an opportunistic effort to exploit long-standing failures of competitive fairness.

This is a deeply disturbing prospect. I do not believe that democratic theory can say more to illuminate it than to recognize it and identify its sources in forms of competition that have evaded effective regulation by law and social norms. I do believe that restoring healthy party competition is among the most critical challenges facing representative democracy in the United States today. It is a prerequisite, even if it will not be sufficient, for fair and effective representation.

---

111. See Hacker and Pierson 2020 for a perceptive analysis of the structural roots of this transition and Grossmann and Hopkins 2016 for an account of differences in the development and contemporary character of the parties. Among journalistic accounts of the trajectory of the Republican Party see Milbank 2022.

COMMENTARIES

The Preference-Policy Link and Representation

MARTIN GILENS

It is an honor to be invited to reflect on Professor Beitz's Tanner Lectures on democracy in America. I'm an empirical political scientist, not a political theorist, but my attempts to understand the "facts" of American politics are motivated by the same concern Professor Beitz addresses: Is our political system providing fair and effective representation?

In my comments on Professor Beitz's lectures I'll share some facts about representation in the United States derived from my research, and then describe what I take the normative significance of those facts to be. My argument, in a nutshell, is that policymakers in America respond weakly and unequally to the preferences of our citizens, that this link between citizens' preferences and government policy is essential to fair and effective representation, and that our normative evaluations of systemic features of American politics rest largely, although not exclusively, on the impact of those features on this link between citizens' desires and government policy.

For the People? Charles R. Beitz, Oxford University Press. © Regents of the University of California 2024.
DOI: 10.1093/9780197780466.003.0005

REPRESENTATION

"Representation" is typically understood to refer to the actions of elected officials in shaping policy and interacting with constituents. That will be my focus too, but it is worth noting that citizens' lives are shaped by government actions in other ways as well. The "administrative state" of government agencies implements the policies that representatives adopt and determines many of the details of those policies as well; law enforcement directly impacts citizens and communities in myriad ways; courts determine the impact of government on citizens by ruling on individual cases, by defining the meaning of indeterminant laws and by constraining government action through constitutional review. Although these government functions are not typically understood as "representation," fairness and effectiveness of government are powerfully shaped by these mechanisms and institutions as well.

Within the narrower realm of representation, scholars frequently distinguish between "descriptive representation" (the extent to which a legislator or body of legislators reflects the characteristics of their constituents along racial, gender, religious, or other demographic lines) and "substantive representation" (the extent to which a legislator or body of legislators work to advance the policy interests and preferences of their constituents). Descriptive representation might be desired in part because it may make substantive representation more likely: Black legislators might be more likely to advance the interests of Black voters, female legislators those of female voters, and so on. But descriptive representation might also be valued in its own right. A legislature that "looks like" the body of citizens it represents might be viewed with greater trust and legitimacy by a wider range of constituents than one that produces the same policy outcomes but leaves many citizens feeling disconnected from the legislators that represent them. I raise this distinction only to be clear that I will leave

THE PREFERENCE-POLICY LINK AND REPRESENTATION

aside considerations of descriptive representation per se, focusing instead on elected representatives as policymakers (Professor Beitz similarly focuses on substantive rather than descriptive representation in his lectures).

A final distinction related both to my empirical analyses of representation and to Professor Beitz's discussion is between "dyadic" and "systemic" representation. Dyadic representation concerns the relationship between citizens' desires and the behavior of the specific individuals they elect, while systemic representation reflects the degree to which citizens' desires are reflected in the behavior of the political system as a whole. As Professor Beitz (p. 67) notes, "Much of the political science of democratic representation is devoted to examining the 'dyadic' (actually, the one-to-many) relationship between individual elected representatives and their constituents.... But the most consequential failures of democratic representation only become visible at the level of the system. Disparities in policy responsiveness by class and race, partisan bias, and legislative dysfunction are features of the system as a whole."

As a practical matter too, dyadic studies of citizens and representatives can provide misleading impressions of the ability of voters to influence government. For one thing, even strong dyadic relationships between elected representatives and the constituents they represent may not result in fair and effective representation for the polity as a whole. Biased districting, such as that documented by Professor Karlan in this volume, means that even perfect correspondence between the desires of individual citizens and the behavior of their representatives will produce a biased outcome, since citizens in some jurisdictions (e.g., those in small states) will have more representatives per constituent than others.

Another reason to focus on policy outcomes rather than the behavior of individual representatives in assessing the fairness and effectiveness of representation is that representatives have incentives to *appear* responsive to their voters in their more easily observed behavior, even if their behind-the-scenes activity pushes policy in directions their constituents would oppose. Elected representatives may need to balance incentives to respond to their voters with the desires of campaign donors, interest groups, party leaders, or their own personal political orientations. Since voters are typically the least attentive and least well informed of these groups, representatives may choose to act in accord with voters' wishes in their most high-profile, most visible, activities, such as final roll-call votes in Congress. But they may be far less responsive to their constituents' wishes on less visible activity like procedural votes or amendments offered during committee markup. In fact, numerous studies show exactly that pattern,[1] calling into question the usefulness of dyadic analyses in assessing representatives' true responsiveness to constituent preferences.

Finally, representation must be assessed at the systemic level because a central determinant of government policymaking is agenda control. Which of the many potential issues and policies make it onto the legislative agenda is as important as the choices that are made about the issues that are addressed. While individual representatives play a part in determining which issues are addressed and which are not, party leaders play the central role, and the many factors that shape their decisions in this regard (including interest groups, campaign donors, media outlets, etc.) are largely hidden. The agenda is inherently a characteristic of the political system, an "emergent" attribute that reflects a wide range of largely invisible choices made by multiple actors within a complex structure. Empirical studies of representation that focus on congressional voting miss this important aspect of policymaking altogether.

---

1. Hall and Wayman 1990; Crespin 2010; Hutchings, McClerking, and Charles 2004.

EMPIRICAL ANALYSIS OF THE PREFERENCE-POLICY LINK

In the research I describe below, I examine the link between citizens' preferences and the policies the federal government adopts. I take this relationship, which I'll call the "preference-policy link," to be central to democratic governance and reflective of the ability of citizens to influence what their government does. I'll assess the strength of this relationship and how it varies across different kinds of citizens and argue that the glaring inequalities I document in the preference-policy link between more and less economically advantaged Americans show that representation is indeed unfair and ineffective for the majority of American citizens.

While my empirical analyses relate most obviously and directly to fairness to individual citizens, I'll argue below that it has broader implications for the other aspects of fair and effective representation that Professor Beitz highlights in his lectures. Assessments of systemic features of our political system, such as party competition, districting, or interest group lobbying, all rest in large measure on how they impact the preference-policy link.

To assess the impact of citizen preferences on government policy, I identified about two thousand proposed policy changes between the mid-1960s and the early 2000s, excluding changes that would require a change in Supreme Court jurisprudence or a constitutional amendment.[2] The proposed policy changes involved virtually every area of federal policymaking: tax policy, trade agreements, healthcare, education, foreign military engagements, abortion, same-sex

---

2. This project is described in detail in Gilens 2012 and Gilens and Page 2014. I excluded from my data set proposed changes that would have required a constitutional amendment or a change in Supreme Court jurisprudence. I also excluded policies that are typically addressed at the state or local level (such as K–12 school curricula or sales taxes).

marriage, the minimum wage, family leave policy, school prayer, and so on. I included both proposed changes that made it onto the congressional agenda or were discussed by the White House, and those that received some degree of public attention but were never taken up (at least publicly) by policymakers in Washington.[3] By including potential policy changes that never made it onto the congressional or White House agenda, my assessments of government responsiveness reflect both the role of agenda setting (that is, the influence policymakers can exert by choosing what potential policy changes to address or ignore) as well as decision-making with regard to policies that do make it onto the government's agenda.

For each of those two thousand or so proposed policy changes, I relied on representative national surveys to gauge the strength of support or opposition to that proposed change among Americans at the bottom, middle, and top of the income distribution. I then used historical records, congressional reviews, and other sources to code the positions on these same proposed policy changes among a set of the most powerful interest groups in Washington (groups such as the US Chamber of Commerce, the Pharmaceutical Manufacturers Association, the National Rifle Association, the AARP, the AFL-CIO, and so on).[4] Finally, I determined whether or not the proposed change occurred within four years of survey.

In analyses of these data that simultaneously took into account the preferences of middle-income Americans, affluent Americans, and organized interest groups, I found that proposed policy changes

---

3. To identify proposed policy changes, I examined thousands of questions from representative national surveys conducted during these years, looking for questions that were specific enough to be reliably coded as having been adopted or not within four years of the year the survey was taken. For a discussion of the suitability of the "survey agenda" for this analysis, see chapter 2 of Gilens 2012.

4. See Gilens 2012, chap. 5, for an account of how I identified the most powerful interest groups in Washington.

that were strongly favored by the well-off were much more likely to be adopted than those that they strongly opposed. The same was true for organized interest groups (about 80 percent of which represent business interests). In stark contrast, the preferences of middle-income (or poor) Americans mattered not at all: policies strongly opposed by the middle class or poor were just as likely to be adopted as those they strongly favored. It would not be surprising to find some tendency for more advantaged Americans to shape government policy to their liking. But the utter lack of responsiveness of policymakers to the preferences of middle-income, much less poor, Americans is starkly inconsistent with the most basic tenets of democracy.

This pattern of associations between preferences and policy doesn't mean that affluent Americans or organized interest groups always got what they wanted. A strong status quo bias (which is built into our system of checks and balances and exacerbated by our currently high levels of partisan polarization) can prevent policy changes favored by these groups from being adopted.[5]

Just as the well-off and interest groups didn't always get what they want, the middle class and the poor did frequently get the policies they preferred, but not because policymakers were responsive to their wishes. Rather, less affluent Americans got the policies they wanted from government when they preferred the status quo (and support for change among moneyed interests was not great enough to overcome the status quo bias) or when they happened to want the same things the affluent or interest groups preferred.[6]

The distinction between getting what you want (which ordinary citizens often did) and influencing what you get (which ordinary

---

5. Examples include the "privatization" of Social Security and federal support for school vouchers.
6. Preferences tend to be similar across low- and high-income Americans on military issues, drug policy, support for higher education, and the environment, among other issues.

citizens did not), corresponds to the distinction Professor Beitz makes between "congruence" (that is, the alignment of preferences and policies, for whatever reason) and "responsiveness" (actual influence over policy). Congruence between policy preferences and policy outcomes is important: the less such congruence exists, the less satisfied citizens are likely to be with their government. But if the majority of Americans get what they want from government only when they agree with elites or favor the status quo, that is not a functioning democracy. Congruence may be high in many autocracies and theocracies, at least across a range of issues and time periods, but that doesn't make autocratic rule any more "democratic." Nor does congruence alone give ordinary citizens any assurance that government policy will change as changing conditions lead citizens to reexamine what they want their government to do.

CITIZEN COMPETENCE AND THE LIMITS OF POLICY RESPONSIVENESS

A common objection to the notion that government policy should track the preferences of the governed is that the public at large is uninformed and ill-equipped to identify the policies that would advance their own interests and values. From this perspective, citizens are easily bamboozled into supporting policies that undermine their interests, blinded by partisan and other "tribal" allegiances, and ignorant of the basic facts required to have even a rudimentary understanding of many public policies.

Decades of survey data confirm the public's low levels of factual information about government and public policy. Moreover, in any modern nation-state, government policymaking involves many complex, technical, and unfamiliar issues that it would be foolish to expect ordinary citizens to hold meaningful preferences about.

Indeed, among the core rationales for representative government is the division of labor between constituents and elected officials: citizens need not be experts in public policy if they can delegate such expertise to their elected representatives (or to the paid staff of those representatives, who are often the ones with the greatest technical expertise).

Despite the public's low levels of information about politics and policy, I believe that citizens' policy preferences are, generally speaking, reflective of their interests and values, and are a viable basis for guiding government policymaking. As a collective, citizens manage to form meaningful policy preferences, despite limited knowledge, via three mechanisms: cue taking, specialization, and aggregation.[7]

Citizens who lack knowledge about any given policy issue often look to better-informed cue-givers to form preferences. Depending on the issue, those cue givers might be partisan elites, interest groups such as the AARP or the Sierra Club, their religious, union, or professional organization, or simply personal acquaintances who are more knowledgeable about that particular issue. Second, just like elites, citizens tend to "specialize" in a small subset of the many policy issues that face the country. Depending on an individuals' interests and profession, some citizens are more attentive to and knowledgeable about healthcare, others about education, or US policy in the Middle East, or climate change. If citizens can form reasonable preferences on the policies they care about most, and use those issues as a basis for choosing between parties or candidates, then the public can guide policymakers even if most citizens are uninformed on most policy issues most of the time.

Finally, the relatively uninformed views of many individual citizens can cancel out when they are aggregated, such that the public as a whole has more stable and more "rational" preferences than those

---

7. See chapter 1 of Gilens 2012 for an extended discussion of this topics.

of the typical individual member of that public. Studies of public opinion find that, unlike individual preferences, collective (aggregated) policy preferences tend to be quite stable over time while also responding in sensible ways to changing conditions: public support for unemployment spending increases when the unemployment rate rises, support for defense spending increases when the threat of war goes up, support for tax cuts declines when tax rates are lowered, and so on.[8]

How well do these three factors work to generate "reasonable" aggregate policy preferences (that is, preferences that resemble what individuals might hold if they had the information and motivation to form opinions on each of the many issues that policymakers address)? One insight into this question comes from "deliberative polls" that provide randomly selected members of the public with the information and opportunity to discuss and debate a wide range of issues. One such effort from the mid-1990s brought over four hundred randomly selected Americans together for four days in Austin, Texas.[9] They were presented with briefing materials, expert question-and-answer sessions, and opportunities to deliberate in small groups about a range of economic, foreign policy, and family issues. Surveys conducted before and after this experience showed some shifts in preferences among individuals on many issues, but little aggregate change.[10] In short, the public's aggregate preferences as expressed on surveys at any given point in time seem to reflect—imperfectly, but pretty well—the hypothetical "informed preferences" they might

8. Page and Shapiro 1992.
9. Fishkin and Luskin 1999.
10. That is, some individuals who supported a policy prior to the deliberative experience came to oppose it and vice versa. However, the amount of aggregate change (averaged across all participants) was only about five percentage points on the typical issue. In comparison, a control group that was also surveyed twice but had no intervening deliberative experience or new information showed a three-percentage-point aggregate shift on the typical issue.

express if provided with the kind of information and opportunity to deliberate that experiments like these offer.

REVERSE REPRESENTATION?

A final empirical challenge to the notion that government policy should reflect the preferences of the governed is the concern that the public's preferences are in fact a reflection of the views of political elites in the first place. If citizens take cues from political leaders, as suggested above, then congruence between public preferences and government policy may reflect not public influence over policymakers but policymakers' influence over the public.[11] Political elites do, of course, exert considerable effort to shape public opinion in favor of the policies they wish to pursue. But there is good reason to believe their success in this regard is typically limited. First, there are usually competing elites attempting to move public opinion on a given issue in different directions. Second, elites are strategic in attempting to "lead" public opinion in directions that the public (or a targeted subset of the public) is willing to be lead.[12] In this way, citizens place constraints on elites that result, not in failed attempts at elite influence, but in efforts at influence that are not made to begin with. Third, the considerable gap between what middle-class Americans say they want the government to do and what the government does suggests that efforts to bring public opinion in line with elites' policy preferences are not particularly effective. Finally, the stronger connection between affluent Americans' preferences and government policy is not paralleled by a similarly strong connection among the

---

11. See, for example, Disch 2021.
12. See, for example, John Zaller 1994.

most highly educated Americans.[13] Because education is a better proxy than income for political interest and attentiveness, we would expect to find the strongest association among those with the most education. The stronger connection with high income than with high education suggests that the preference-policy link rests instead on the ability of those with money to shape policy.

THE NORMATIVE EVALUATION OF POLITICAL INSTITUTIONS

The widespread and long-standing belief that ordinary citizens' ability to shape government policymaking is central to democracy does not preclude other, sometimes countervailing, consideration. As Professor Beitz notes, there are many reasons we might not *want* perfect translation of majority views into government policy. First, minority rights must be protected, which may require constitutional constraints or supermajority requirements that obstruct a majority from imposing its will. Second, as noted above, it is often impractical to expect the public to hold meaningful preferences on obscure, technical, or complex issues (although cues from trusted experts or other elites can often provide an effective substitute for direct knowledge). And inhibiting responsiveness to the public may provide a degree of policy stability that is important for effective governance (although, as noted above, studies show that the public's policy preferences are in fact quite stable, and when they do change, it is typically for perfectly sensible reasons such as a change in social or economic conditions).

These considerations notwithstanding, I believe that many of the concerns with our political structures and institutions, including

---

13. Gilens 2012, 93ff.

gerrymandering, organized interest competition (i.e., lobbying), and partisan polarization, are rooted in their impact on the fairness and effectiveness of individual citizens' capacity to influence government decision-making. Assessing the fairness and effectiveness of representation requires the kind of analyses of political institutions and political competition that Professor Beitz offers in these lectures. But the normative judgments of those institutions as contributing to or undermining fair and effective representation rest, I will argue, largely on their impact on the preference-policy link. In short, the theories of political competition that Professor Beitz calls for are needed precisely because the forms of competition that they address underlie citizens' ability to form policy preferences consistent with their interests and values, and to see those preferences reflected in the policies their government adopts.

GERRYMANDERING

One of the structural features of American politics that Professor Beitz discusses is gerrymandering. As Professor Beitz notes, single-member districts can create "partisan asymmetries" giving one party an advantage in the translation of citizens' votes into legislative seats. (This can result either from the purposeful drawing of district boundaries to advantage or disadvantage one party or from self-sorting that results in the geographic concentration of one party's voters.)

Partisan competition is distorted, Professor Beitz argues, when one party's adherents are less able to achieve their political goals through their votes than those of the other party. In other words, the unfairness to the disadvantaged political party is problematic because it unfairly undermines the preference-policy link for that party's adherents.

Professor Beitz goes on to observe that gerrymandering undermines fair and effective representation in a second, distinct, way: by making elections less competitive. There are many reasons why less competitive elections undermine representation, but common to them all is the fundamental problem that they make government less responsive, and less equally responsive, to the preferences of its citizens. "Safe districts," which virtually guarantee a win for one party or the other, undermine the ability of the other party's voters to participate meaningfully in choosing their representative. The predictable result, as empirical studies confirm, is to induce elected representatives to attend only to the desires of their same-party constituents (and, especially, their same-party donors), thereby undermining the preference-policy link for the other party's voters.[14]

ORGANIZED INTEREST COMPETITION

Another institutional threat to fair and effective representation that Professor Beitz discusses is the pro-business tilt of lobbying and organized interest groups. As Professor Beitz notes, one function of lobbying is to provide information and other resources to policymakers in the hope that policy will better reflect the preferences of the interest organization, or coalition of organizations, involved. The unfairness that Professor Beitz emphasizes is the impact of informational imbalances on the deliberative environment in which policymakers come to understand and evaluate alternative policy choices.

From this perspective, it is not the provision of information or organizational resources that makes lobbying problematic, it is the disjunction between the distribution of policy preferences

---

14. Barber 2016.

among interest groups (and the vastly greater resources of business groups) and the distribution of policy preferences among citizens. If the interest group universe (adjusted for varying resources) reflected the interests and policy preferences of the citizenry, then we might view lobbying as a helpful mechanism that works to provide information, facilitate coordination among like-minded interests, and bring government policy more in line with citizens' preferences. In short, if lobbying worked to strengthen and equalize the preference-policy link for citizens, the objection to its distorting impact on policymakers' informational environment would be moot. But in its current form, citizens who share the policy preferences that the interest group system promotes are unfairly advantaged while the political influence of those who hold opposing preferences is undermined.

POLARIZATION AND GRIDLOCK

As Professor Beitz notes, two additional features of the political system, polarization and gridlock, can undermine fair and effective responsiveness. Polarization can push policy toward the political extremes when one party or the other manages to gain sole control of government (at the local, state, or national level). This clearly undermines the preference-policy link, as extremist policies that satisfy party activists, donors, or affiliated interest groups clash with the desires of the median voter.[15]

Under conditions of divided partisan control, on the other hand, polarization can result in gridlock as the polarized parties refuse to compromise. Gridlock clearly and directly conflicts with effective representation as policies fail to change in response to changing

15. See Bafumi and Herron 2010.

conditions. Gridlock similarly conflicts with fair representation inasmuch as it advantages citizens who benefit from the status quo while disadvantaging those on the "losing side" of changing conditions. One oft-cited example is the failure of US policy to respond to decades of growing economic inequality—a failure that reinforces the disproportionate political power of the well-to-do.

Polarization may have other deleterious consequence for our politics (or, indeed, beyond our politics, when it exacerbates social distrust and feeds violent or extremist actions). But as with gerrymandering and lobbying, the primary way in which polarization and gridlock undermine fair and effective representation is by weakening the preference-policy link for the public writ large.

JUSTIFYING PURPOSES AND PREFERENCE FORMATION

In my very brief accounts of three aspects systemic political competition I focused on their impact on the preference-policy link as the basis for normative assessments. I argued that political competition as embodied in these institutions and conditions is dysfunctional and normatively undesirable because it undermines the link between citizens' preferences and government policy.

Now I'll take a step back and briefly address the four justifying purposes that Professor Beitz identifies as the bases for his normative evaluation of political competition. My contention is that the first three of these reflect the same concerns with the preference-policy link that underlie my substantive accounts of gerrymandering, lobbying, and polarization and gridlock. The fourth justifying purpose focuses on preference formation rather than policy responsiveness and raises a different set of concerns, which are nonetheless foundational to representation as embodied in the preference-policy link.

THE PREFERENCE-POLICY LINK AND REPRESENTATION

A polity with a strong and roughly equal link between citizens' preferences and government policy would satisfy, at least in large measure, each of the first three justifying purposes Professor Beitz identifies. With a strong and equal preference-policy link, the political system would by definition be *responsive to the people* (the first justifying purpose). It would arguably also satisfy the second purpose: that the system would take a *fair account of the political interests of each citizen*. The distinction between these two criteria reflects the difference between preferences (that is, citizens' own understandings of their desired government policy) and interests (here meaning the ways in which government policy affects citizens). Without going deeply into the complex distinction between preferences and interests, I will simply stipulate that citizens must be free to define their own interests (that is, the ways in which they desire government actions to affect them) rather than have those interests defined by some third party (whether their elected representatives or university professors).[16]

With this stipulation, the difference between satisfying preferences and satisfying interests rests on the effectiveness of a desired policy in producing the outcomes that its citizen supporters want. This will always be a partial and contingent relationship. While some political systems might be better at crafting policies to achieve desired ends (while minimizing undesired consequences), the necessarily imperfect relationship between intended and realized consequences need not be understood as necessarily a failure of

---

16. Among the many complex nuances of the notion of "interests" is the question whether an individual can have an "interest" in the impact of a policy on others. For example, we might readily acknowledge that a policy that enhances the ability of individuals to support themselves is "in their interest," but it is less clear whether individuals' desire to see their social group (or another social group) prosper means that a policy that enhances the ability of members of that group to support themselves is "in the interest" of the individual who values that group's well-being.

democratic governance. (That said, to the extent that policymakers fail to do their job as well as they could, or policymakers systematically advantage some citizens over others in crafting policy, then government might fail in this second justifying purpose even if it succeeds in being "responsive to the people" in a more limited sense as reflected in a strong and equal preference-policy link.)

The third justifying purpose is that the political system should be capable of *resolving conflict over public policy*. A strong preference-policy link would be expected to satisfy this criterion on the basis of majority rule (perhaps subject to constitutional, supermajority, or other constraints). Of course, one can imagine challenging circumstances such as a very closely divided public that swings back and forth from one side of an issue or the other over time, even if few citizens actually change their preferences, or cyclical preferences where no one policy option is favored by a majority. While long a theoretical concern, these circumstances are empirically rare.[17]

Professor Beitz's fourth justifying purpose relates to citizens' preference formation: that the political environment should allow a reasonable *range of alternatives* and allow participants to *deliberate about them*. If citizens' preferences are poorly formed because the information environment is biased or fails to provide useful opportunities for citizens to benefit, either directly or indirectly, by deliberation around the alternative policy options and desired ends, then even a strong and equal preference-policy link will fail to achieve the larger goal of advancing citizens interests.

I will set aside the host of questions about how one might identify the reasonable range of alternatives that should be represented in public debate around a particular issue, or how one might assess the quality of deliberation available to citizens. From an empirical

17. See Hotelling 1929; Arrow 1951; and Van Deemen 2014.

perspective, however, it is instructive to return to the example of the deliberative poll described above. After citizens were provided with what might plausibly be considered a reasonable range of alternatives across an array of public policies, and an opportunity to discuss and deliberate about those policies, the aggregate preferences of those citizens showed little change. This suggests that, at least for those prominent issues, the informational environment was not so highly skewed nor the deliberative opportunities so lacking that citizens' views were substantially altered by the additional information and deliberative opportunities they were offered.

The results of this deliberative poll certainly do not allay all concerns about citizens' ability to form policy preferences consistent with their interests and values. But they do suggest that the America's "democratic deficit" lies more in the failure to adopt policies that the public supports than in the failure of the public to sensibly identify which policies to support.

CONCLUSION

My claim in these reflections on Professor Beitz' lectures is not that fairness to individual citizens and responsiveness to their preferences are the only normative criteria we should apply in assessing our political institutions or the nature of political competition. But I do believe that many of those assessments will point back to this one fundamental feature of democracy: that government should respond strongly and equally to all its citizens. We need analyses of political competition as it exists in our various political practices and institutions to understand how those practices and institutions impact the preference-policy link, and how competition can best be structured to facilitate the responsiveness of government to the preferences of its citizens. The importance of the project that Professor Beitz advances in his lectures is underlined by the empirical failure of our current institutions to provide anything resembling fair and effective representation for the majority of American citizens.

Systems, Dyads, and a Contingency Theory of Competition

A Citizen's View

JANE MANSBRIDGE

INTRODUCTION

Charles Beitz's subtle and multifaceted analysis of democratic representation as a system emphasizes the need to encompass multiple arenas and plural criteria for judgment. I embrace this systemic approach and hope to extend it from the perspective of a citizen interacting with the modern state.

My analysis is rooted in observing that as human interdependence inevitably increases, we will need more and more state regulation, and therefore state coercion, to solve the free-rider problems that accompany that interdependence. Our eighteenth- and nineteenth-century democratic structures cannot provide sufficient legitimacy for all the state coercion needed to regulate that ever-increasing interdependence. Because I see state coercion as inevitably increasing, I focus on how to legitimate that coercion through increases in both the perceived legitimacy of the laws and the underlying normative legitimacy based on principles justified through deliberation and reflection (Mansbridge 2014b, 2022).

A focus on perceived legitimacy, backed by normative legitimacy, provides a new lens on three issues: systems, dyads, and competition. That focus requires looking at all the contacts that citizens have with the state and the full representative system, including legislatures, administrative agencies, the judiciary, and even civil society associations, and the ways they and their interests are represented in these arenas. A legitimacy focus also requires looking closely not only at systems but at the dyadic one-on-one interactions between citizens and their representatives. Finally, a legitimacy focus suggests a contingency theory of competition, asking in which contexts which structures and practices of political competition may produce more perceived and normative legitimacy, and at what costs. Some structures long scorned in political science produce less intense competition. These include nonpartisan or single-party cities and state legislatures, districts with long incumbencies, as well as the less scorned but still controversial vehicle of ranked-choice voting. These less competitive structures arguably produce more perceived legitimacy; international comparisons suggest they might.

THE FULL REPRESENTATIVE SYSTEM

The concept of a "representative system" helps us make sense of the full panoply of ways that citizens encounter the democratic state, through which, ideally, through their representatives, they make laws for (i.e., coerce) themselves.[1]

---

1. Beitz (p. 19) reasonably restricts his analysis to electoral representation

A "system" in this analysis does not mean a mechanistic system in which each component has a defined and invariant function. Nor does it mean that the system as a whole has only one function. It means that the whole can and should be judged as a whole and not just as a sum of the parts. To make the case that a given part has a useful role in the system's overall functioning, one has to develop criteria for the system as a whole, such as the "fairness of the rules that structure" elements of the process of representation (Beitz, p. 75). As Beitz points out, however, the criteria for what I would call the normative legitimacy of the system are both plural and contested. I argue that in that plurality and contest, contingency can play a major role. In Beitz's words, "Institutions that are unproblematic in some circumstances can become problematic in others" (p. 21).

One major reason for conceiving of representation as a system is that parts of the system may have strong practical or normative flaws, but their negative aspects may be compensated for by their positive functions in the system. For example, within a deliberative system, both political protest and what I have called "enclave deliberation" (likes talking only to likes) may be extremely undeliberative in themselves. Protesters may shout slogans and demonize their opponents. Enclaves of the like-minded may shut out opposing views. But both protest and enclaves sometimes play important roles in the deliberative system— protests by drawing attention to ideas and facts that had previously been ignored, and enclaves by performing at least the three functions of allowing the like-minded to clarify the issues among themselves, create new ideas, and support one another in presenting those ideas in the larger system. So too in the representative system, political parties may create division and foster mutual hatred, but they also help articulate issues, recruit representatives, and motivate citizen participation.[2]

---

2. On "enclave deliberation," see Mansbridge 1986 for disadvantages, Mansbridge 1994 for advantages, and Sunstein 2000 primarily for disadvantages. On the "deliberative system," see

A second major reason for conceiving of representation as a system in a democracy is to understand better the myriad and interlocking ways that the parts of the system interact for good or ill. A full understanding of that system would include representation of citizens in the administrative state, the associations in civil society that have relations with the state, and the judiciary.[3] In my analysis, the overarching purpose of a democratic design of all parts of the representative system, including the electoral, administrative, societal, and judicial arenas, is to legitimate the laws that coerce the members of the policy, both normatively and in the eyes of the coerced.

Consider first the administrative realm. In an earlier era, when one could reasonably think of the executive as primarily "executing" the laws, the legitimacy of administrative decisions could derive in large part from legislative delegation.[4] As the growing need for regulation has made it clearer that administrations must make law, many administrators at the policy level and even the street level have begun to recognize that they receive their powers from below as well as above, and have accountability down as well as up. Their administrations have to be not only uncorrupt but also responsive to those whom they explicitly or implicitly coerce. As a result, to increase perceived legitimacy as well as substantive knowledge, administrations in many democratic polities have begun to be far more consultative, reaching out to stakeholders in

---

Mansbridge 1999a; Mansbridge et al. 2012; and Bächtiger et al. 2018. On the "representative system," see Pitkin 1967 (cited in Beitz, p. 68); Mansbridge 2011; Disch 2021; Rey 2023.

3. Discussion of the judiciary is omitted here for lack of space, but see Holst and Langvatn 2021 and other discussions of judicial actors as representatives.
4. Adopting a concept from medieval private law, John Locke proclaimed early in the history of democracy, "The Legislative cannot transfer the Power of Making Laws to any other hands" (Locke [1674–89] 1967, p. 380). Until the 1930s, the US Supreme Court accepted this dictum before stepping away from it under pressure from reality. Although the last few decades have seen some controversy over this point in the United States, other countries have simply accepted that in current conditions of growing interdependence and the regulation of that interdependence, administrations must make law. See fuller discussion and references in Mansbridge 2022.

what I call "recursive," two-way, communication (Mansbridge 2022). Stakeholders also reach out in force to provide crucial information to administrators and develop warm communicative relations with them. Both directions of outreach are currently highly biased to the powerful and well-funded (Beitz and Gilens, this volume).

To create more legitimate recursivity with constituents, administrations have begun to organize deliberative minipublics (forums of often 150–200 citizens, chosen randomly, preferably well paid, meeting for a weekend or more). In these forums, such as citizen assemblies or Deliberative Polls, citizens read balanced background materials, engage experts in question-and-answer sessions, deliberate together, and advise or register opinions on critical issues. For example, as a result of several Deliberative Polls on energy sources in Texas, a state whose economy depended heavily on fossil fuels nevertheless invested in more wind turbines per capita than any other state in the union (Fishkin 2009, 124). In forums like these, the citizens of the affected polity are informally represented by other citizens.[5]

Beyond the administrative realm, what we may call the "societal realm" also needs greater legitimacy. Cathy Rudder and colleagues estimate that "[t]aken together, agency rulemaking and the policy decisions of private groups account for most policy-making in advanced societies" (Rudder et al. 2016, 1). These "private groups," or nongovernmental organizations (NGOs), or "civil society" organizations, have three levels of closeness to the state: formal delegation, formal consultation, and informal influence. The closer the relation with the state, I argue, the more the public has an interest in how these groups are distributed and organized. Normative legitimacy and perhaps also perceived legitimacy depends in part on how fairly societal power is distributed among groups and how democratically they are organized internally.

---

5. See Warren 2008 on representation in minipublics, Salkin 2024 on informal representation in general, and Mansbridge 2019a on forms of non-direct accountability in minipublics.

Consider first formal delegation, that is, lawmaking by societal groups. Legislatures and administrations sometimes formally delegate power to private societal organizations. European neo-corporatist nations delegate some state decisions to business and union groups. In the United States, the formal delegation is less visible. In accrediting, for example, the federal government formally adopts the accounting standards set by one private nonprofit group, the Financial Accounting Standards Board, and gives another private nonprofit group, the Financial Industry Regulating Authority, the legal power to discipline the firms and individuals who violate those standards (Rudder et al. 2016, 61–62 and chap. 4). Next on the spectrum, short of the formal delegation of power, formal consultation may be required by law or standard procedure. Finally, informal influence is common, either through legislatures or administrations actively reaching out to societal groups or, far more frequently, through lobbying by the affected societal groups with sufficient funds and organization.

The democratic legitimacy of lawmaking, consultation, and influence by societal groups depends in part on how fairly those groups are distributed in the polity ("external equity"). A first approach to the problem would prescribe societal representation in proportion to the interests in the population. Yet the norms are not entirely clear, because the number and weight of the associations representing the citizens should also reflect degrees of affectedness as well as intensity of feeling.

The legitimacy of lawmaking, consultation, and influence by these groups also depends in part on their internal organization ("internal equity"). Here the norms of fairness in members' access to influence within the association may be clearer. The closer the ties of those organizations to the state, the more, I argue, they are normatively required to be either internally democratic or in another way representatively responsive to the constituencies that the state legislative and administrative realms take them to represent. Thus, as a baseline we may adopt Nancy Rosenblum's strictures against "government intervention in the lives of associations" on the grounds of freedom of association and freedom to organize one's association as one wants. For that baseline we may also adopt her analysis that for many groups the processes of choice and exit, of "shifting involvements," and of pluralism give us all the democracy and accountability we need (Rosenblum 2008, 6, 17, 20, 25, 27). Yet above that baseline, representational equity requires that the closer an association's formal relationship with the state, the greater is the normative justification, all things considered, for the state requiring some internal democracy in the association.

Philippe Schmitter's (1992) voucher proposal addresses both external and internal equity. It would give citizens at the voting booth the capacity to select some number of voluntary associations (e.g., ten associations) to represent them in lawmaking, consulting, and influencing the state. The state would fund these organizations depending on how many citizens chose them. The associations would therefore represent citizens' interests far more proportionally than is now the case in any democracy (external equity). State funding, however, would be conditional on internal democracy within those associations (internal equity). This proposal, although so far only notional and never taken up by any political group or movement, responds to affectedness and intensity, probably makes more information available from below, possibly increases the capacity to explain from above, and might even increase citizens' warranted perceptions of influence or potential influence over the laws that coerce them.[6]

---

6. For the complexity of associational involvement with the state and applicable norms, see Warren 2001. For the tension between requirements for democratic participation and efficient performance, and for what I would call the "contingency argument" that the requirements of internal democracy should be strongest when exit is least possible, see Smith and Teasdale 2012. For representative claims that range from the informal to the formal, see Saward 2010. For informal representational accountability through exit, see Warren 2011. For norms of informal representation through associations and in unorganized settings, see Montanaro 2017 and Salkin 2024.

From the perspective of perceived as well as normative legitimacy, all elements of the representative system—legislative, administrative, and societal—need rethinking.

DYADS

By a "dyadic" relation, I mean the relation of the representative to the individual constituent (one-to-one), not to the constituency as a whole (one-to-many). Although Beitz is correct to say that normatively it would be a mistake to focus solely on the dyadic relation, whether one-to-one or (as he frames it) one-to-many, the quality of citizens' dyadic interactions with their representatives across the representative system almost certainly affects the perceived legitimacy of the laws.

Consider the common phenomenon, in the division of labor between representatives and constituents, when representatives (in the administrative and societal as well as legislative realms) act on what they consider the constituents' interests but against their constituents' preferences. This case heightens the salience of the dyadic relation. An attractive strategy for the representative, when feasible, is simply not to make that action public (Soontjens 2021, 160). But that is a risky strategy for both perceived and normative legitimacy. When the representative's choice for the constituents' presumed interests against their preferences must be publicly known, some explaining is in order—some "giving of an account," as in the traditional meaning of accountability (Mansbridge 2014a). The representative systems in today's democracies, whether in the legislative, administrative, or societal realms, do not make this explaining easy.

In the United States, for example, when members of Congress were asked if they thought they could explain to their constituents a vote for what they considered good public policy but believed the public would not understand, many said that their attempts at explaining only made their constituents angry. One said that if he "had a chance to sit down with all of my constituents for 15 minutes and talk to them," he would have voted for what he thought was good policy. But because he "didn't have . . . a chance to explain myself," he voted against that policy.[7] Constituents also rarely get a chance to explain to their representatives how a policy affects them in the particularity of their lives, or respond to a representative's explanation with information to which the representative might otherwise not have access.

Increasing perceived and normative legitimacy requires responding to these failures with increases in the capacity to explain. The aspirational ideal of "recursive representation" goes beyond one-way explanation to a goal—unachievable in its entirety—of full two-way, mutually responsive, ongoing communication between representative and constituent—the kind that currently characterizes communications between a representative and a major donor (Mansbridge 2019b, 2022). Such an ideal takes us decisively away from the "delegate" and the "trustee" models, which both derive from a time when elected representatives were almost totally out of communication with their districts for months. Because today recursive communication is far more possible than in the eighteenth, nineteenth, or even twentieth century, the norms of good political representation are beginning to change. In France, Pierre Rosanvallon writes, "[C]itizens increasingly want to be listened to and reckoned with. They want their views to be taken into account." They want representatives who "are accessible, receptive and open" and who "react to what they hear and are willing to explain their decisions" ([2006] 2008, 171).

In the United States, a small study asking open-endedly what constituents wanted from their elected representative found they

---

7. Bianco 1994, 51; Kingdon 1981, 48.

wanted primarily communication, with the representative listening and being available to them (Grill 2007). More broadly, Richard Fenno concluded, "Responsiveness, and hence, representation, require two-way communication. Although the congressman can engage in this kind of communication with only some of his supportive constituents, he can give many more the assurance that two-way communication is possible." In sum, "Access and the assurance of access, communication and the assurance of communication—these are the *irreducible underpinnings of representation*" (1978, 239–40). In normative theory, Iris Marion Young has written, "We should evaluate the process of representation according to the character of the relationship between the representative and the constituents" (2000, 128). She concluded, "A representative process is . . . better to the extent that it establishes and renews connection between constituents and representative" (129–30).

What structures make this legitimacy-enhancing recursive communication more likely? First, long incumbencies. Maligned as long incumbencies are among political scientists, they help constituents learn their representatives' names and probably make constituents more likely to contact their representatives. When the incumbent has a reputation for promoting views congenial to the constituent, the constituent may, with warrant, experience feelings of self-authorship by proxy. Second, descriptive representation. Descriptive representation, or sharing salient background experiences with constituents, increases the likelihood of contact, especially in the case of race and probably other marginalized ethnicities (see, e.g., Gay 2002; Broockman 2014). Third, single-member districts. Despite their other disadvantages, single-member plurality (SMP or "First Past the Post") electoral systems, with one representative per district, facilitate elected representatives' two-way communication with their constituents, compared to proportional representation (PR) systems, with several members per district.

The innovations devised in the last decade to promote recursive dyadic representative-constituent interaction all require single-member districts. In the United States, the Connecting to Congress project randomly chooses constituents, then allows them to read background materials and consult virtually with their member of Congress for one hour on a major issue. If this process became routine, each citizen could expect at least one conversation with a congressional representative in a lifetime. Citizens would talk about these discussions with friends. Students might enact simulated discussions in schools. In Germany, a democracy nonprofit is funding the single-member district representatives, within in its mixed proportional representation / single-member electoral system, to convene and pay electoral district councils, randomly selected groups of about fifty citizens from their districts to deliberate together for one weekend day and advise the member on upcoming legislation.[8] Both Connecting to Congress and the electoral district councils are likely to increase responsiveness, concurrence, and equity in the representative system. Dyadically, they have a normative value to citizens independent of their systemic effects. For the citizens, they import small "shards, threads and intimations" of autonomy—giving a law to oneself—into the representative process (Mansbridge 2020). They are very likely to increase the perceived legitimacy of the laws.

A CONTINGENCY THEORY OF COMPETITION

Beitz anchors his understanding of democratic representation in competition, writing, "democratic representation ... is fundamentally

---

8. For the United States, Neblo et al. 2018 and https://connectingtocongress.org/; for the Australian parallel, https://connect2parliament.com/. For Germany, https://hallobundestag.de/en.

competitive" (p. 15).[9] He specifies that the relevant kind of competition is primarily not even the "parallel" competition of racing and golf but rather the "adversarial" competition of basketball and football, in which actors increase their "chances of success by taking steps to thwart the efforts of other agents to succeed" (p. 81).[10]

The regulation of competition that Beitz, Rosenblum, Rawls, and others advocate should, I argue, include designing structures and practices that dampen the adversarial nature of that competition in contexts where intensive competition tends to delegitimate the representative process or, in the extreme case, threatens to delegitimate the democracy itself. (Such delegitimation is my definition of competition "running off the rails.") Although I can only begin such a theory here, I urge the construction of a "contingency theory of competition" to understand when intense competition is most useful and when it is most destructive. A full contingency theory of competition would spell out the ways that different forms of competitive and cooperative structures may increase or decrease both perceived and underlying normative legitimacy. It would also investigate the democratic contributions and drawbacks of those structures and practices. It would, finally, specify the contexts in which the democratic cost-benefit ratio suggests introducing or suppressing particular practices and structures.[11]

---

9. More bluntly, "democratic representation is competitive" (p. 71). Also: "In the presence of regular disagreement about policy, political competition in a representative democracy is unavoidable; indeed, the system depends on it" (p. 71). Or, quoting Knight 1935, "*democracy is competitive politics*" (p. 76n.22). Also: "The main idea is that representative democracy consists of a set of competitive processes" (p. 85), and in conclusion, "The perspective I suggested conceives of democratic representation as a competitive system" (p. 113).
10. Beitz writes that "for the most part" his analysis is concerned with competition in the adversarial sense (p. 81n.38, citing Agmon 2022, 6–7, who himself cites Simmel [1922] 1955, 58 for the distinction.
11. For the contingency approach in other contexts, see Mansbridge 1986, 2014a, and citations in Mansbridge 2023.

SYSTEMS, DYADS, AND A CONTINGENCY THEORY

The US Founders, in abhorring faction, drew not only from their own experiences as wealthy property-owners threatened by popular protest but also from their reading of history and literature drawn from history (e.g., feuds in Italian city-states). They took the "violence of faction" as given. James Madison's *Federalist* 10 begins by warning that the "conflicts of rival parties" had produced a "prevailing and increasing distrust . . . echoed from one end of the continent to the other." Those words have increased resonance today. Arguing that passions attach themselves to the differing opinions produced by reason's fallibility, Madison concluded, in a much-quoted passage,

> [T]he latent causes of faction are thus sown in the nature of man. . . . A zeal for different opinions . . . , an attachment to different leaders ambitiously contending for pre-eminence and power; or to persons of other descriptions whose fortunes have been interesting to the human passions, have, in turn, divided mankind into parties, inflamed them with mutual animosity, and rendered them much more disposed to vex and oppress each other than to co-operate for their common good. So strong is this propensity of mankind to fall into mutual animosities, that where no substantial occasion presents itself, the most frivolous and fanciful distinctions have been sufficient to kindle their unfriendly passions and excite their most violent conflicts. ([1787] 2001a, pp. 43–44)

With the benefit of experimental evidence not available to the Founders, today many social psychologists believe that some in-group/out-group hostility is innate. Tajfel's minimal group experiments in 1970 began a line of research showing how easily people can cathect onto their group and discriminate in their group's favor even when the "group" is based on nothing more than which modern painter one prefers. People routinely think the members of the out-group are more homogeneous than they actually are and farther from one's own group than they actually are. Members of an in-group easily demonize members of an out-group. This feature of human nature, probably functional in the 98 percent of human history spent as hunter-gatherers, is almost certainly less functional now.[12] It requires structural guardrails. As Madison wrote, "[W]e well know that neither moral nor religious motives can be relied on as an adequate control."

Madison's solution, as well known as his diagnosis, was the "regulation" of conflicting interests by involving "the spirit of party and faction in the necessary and ordinary operations of the government." But how? The Founders did not envision political parties, let alone the current two-party system in the United States or the variation in electoral structures available globally today. Yet party structures can range from the potentially highly competitive, as in the United States, to the more "consensual," as in Switzerland (Lijphart 2012). In the United States the conditions that reduce internal competition are nonpartisan organization, one-party domination, and long incumbencies. The state of Nebraska in the United States and the province of Alberta in Canada are formally nonpartisan, as are about three-quarters of US cities and many Canadian cities, such as Toronto, Ontario, and Vancouver. Many US states are dominated by one party (e.g., Massachusetts, Wyoming, and twenty-two other states), and for almost forty years, between 1945 and 1982, the US Congress was under the control of one party. In many states and cities, long incumbencies provide

---

12. "Natural" does not always mean "good" or even "must be accepted." As with spontaneous defecation, training and supportive institutional structures can help humans control many innate impulses. On in-group/out-group research, see Tajfel 1970; Haslam et al. 1996; and in a possibly too laudatory overview, Van Bavel and Packer 2021.

little competition.[13] Some contexts thus have a "competitive structure," but the arena is not "situationally competitive" (Beitz, p. 92), while others have a one-party or nonpartisan structure, but considerable within-party or nonpartisan competition (Beitz, p. 73n.11). The less competitive environments have the disadvantages of not articulating political positions clearly and discouraging turnout (Schaffner et al. 2001). But these less competitive environments may also have the possible advantages of better outcomes (see Lijphart 2012 comparing nations), lower cynicism and higher perceived legitimacy among the citizens (Lijphart 2012 comparing nations), better dyadic communication between representatives and constituents, and a lower likelihood of delegitimating democracy itself. Many of these hypothesized effects are as yet unmeasured in the United States.

A contingency theory of competition on the dimension of more to less intense competition might begin with the simple strategy of avoiding the costs at the extremes of both low- and high-intensity competition. Thus in the United States in the late 1940s, the two political parties aimed so much at the "median voter" that a major committee of the American Political Science Association perceived an absence of choice and promulgated a statement urging greater internal party coherence with, by implication, clearer and more intense competition (Committee 1950). By contrast, after 1982, as the southern Democrats left the Democratic Party, partisanship in the United States became more equally balanced between Democrats and Republicans, making control of Congress more uncertain, the incentives to destroy the opposition greater (Lee

13. For national structures, see Lijphart 2012. For nonpartisan states, provinces, and cities, see Schaffner et al. 2001; for one-party domination in states, see Ballotpedia, https://ballotpedia.org/Veto_overrides_in_state_legislatures ("States with Veto-Proof Majorities"). For control of the US Congress, see Lee 2016.

2016), and the rhetoric of competition more violent. As social media helped amplify the polarization, political scientists, pundits, and ordinary citizens began to worry that the system was, in Beitz's term, "running off the rails" (p. 83). Such a context of high social division might prompt a recommendation to reduce the intensity of competition.

To elaborate such a contingency theory, one would need considerable empirical evidence, beginning with a conceptual categorization of types of competition from the more to less intense (or perhaps more to less cooperation-inducing), then some normative and empirical speculation on the pluses and minuses of intense competition, then evidence to back up those speculations, feasible suggestions for how to increase or decrease the intensity of competition, and, if possible, evidence that the institutional changes deriving from such speculations both moved the system in the predicted direction and affected citizens' warranted perceptions of the legitimacy of the laws.

Among the advantages of lowered intensity of competition, I would advance the hypothesis (currently backed by informal qualitative evidence) that long incumbencies would foster better negotiation by allowing representatives to create long-standing legislative relationships across political divides. Such relationships facilitate the kind of probing for the "interests behind the positions" that characterizes good negotiation (Mansbridge and Martin 2015). Incumbency also produces long-standing representative-constituent relationships that facilitate a representative's explaining that a negotiated outcome has major benefits as well as costs.

Another advantage of less intense competition might be attracting to the task of electoral representation more (and possibly more cooperative) individuals. Many women do not want to run for office because they dislike competition, particularly of the adversarial kind.[14] This dislike is not confined to women. In 2013 Shauna Shames interviewed a young Black man at Harvard Law School who said he loved politics, but the "tenor" of the electoral arena bothered him:

> I think if you go back to the '60s and the '70s and further back, there were parties, so there was partisan politics, but at the end of the day, people viewed it as a joint venture. You'll hear anecdotes about people debating on the floor, but after, they'd go out to dinner and smoke some cigars and slap each other on the back. They were competitors, but there wasn't the ruthlessness that I see now, and that's very unsettling.... [The current] lack of willingness to compromise just makes the whole prospect of going into politics seem potentially unfulfilling, because I'm a very results-oriented person.[15]

With more such individuals in the legislatures, representation might be more effective, fairer, and perhaps even perceived to be more legitimate.

Yet the changes in structure that would probably reduce the intensity of competition do not come without costs. Ranked-choice voting, for example, discourages negative campaigning along with promoting equity. As the "Fair Vote" website puts it, "With RCV, candidates also compete for second-choice votes from their opponents' supporters, which lessens the incentive to run negative campaigns.

---

14. Gender differences in competitiveness are well documented, for example, Niederle and Vesterlund 2007, finding 35 percent of women versus 73 percent of men choosing competition. For the effects of differences in attitudes toward competition in running for office, see Kanthak and Woon 2015; Schneider et al. 2016.
15. Shames 2017, 1. Interviews in Lee 2016 confirm the accuracy, for many representatives, of this description and the changes over time—changes probably caused in large part, as noted, by the loss of long-term hegemony by the Democratic Party and the consequent rise of razor-thin competition for control of Congress.

In RCV contests, candidates do best when they reach out positively to as many voters as possible, including those supporting their opponents."[16] Yet ranked-choice voting, like most measures that reduce the intensity of competition, also weakens political parties and probably reduces both the clarity of issues and the motivation of voters. Because of these costs, a contingency theory would suggest instituting ranked-choice voting and other intensity-reducing measures when the needs were greatest for reduced rancor in the body politic and for creative legislative negotiation to avoid gridlock. A contingency approach would also ask how easily the desired ends could be met by other means and how easily the costs of a proposed remedy could be mitigated.

Conceptualizing a continuum from more to less intense competition, and from more to less cooperation-preserving competition, might have to take into account different kinds, as well as different intensities, of competition. Beitz, Agnon, and others have resurrected Georg Simmel's useful concept of "parallel" competition. But the contrasting form they posit, of "frictional" or "adversarial" competition, needs development, including a spectrum from more to less intense confrontation. In the most intense "hardball" adversarial competition, any action short of illegality that could harm one's opponent may be justified (cf. Tushnet 2004). Moving toward less intense competition, the adversarial competition of formal debate includes strict rules of engagement that prevent, for example, ad hominem

---

16. https://fairvote.org/our-reforms/ranked-choice-voting/. Unlike many of the features of Lijphart's "consensus" democracies, ranked-choice voting can be introduced without major-scale changes in representational structures. Rosenbluth and Shapiro 2018 and Shapiro in his other writings, however, argue that single-member plurality electoral systems tend to produce two big parties, which then tend to produce moderate positions and candidates. These questions are susceptible to empirical investigation. Webber 2017, cited in Wolkenstein, forthcoming, suggests that the success of Westminster two-party model in the UK may depend in part on the strong conflict-containing norms of Her/His Majesty's Loyal Opposition.

arguments. Yet within those guidelines, the debaters never deviate from their positions; the competition is precisely over the debater's skill in defending that fixed position. In a still less intense version of competition, the adversarial competition of substantively motivated argument, one attacks the other's position and defends a position that one thinks objectively has merit, but is willing, on being presented with good evidence or logic to the contrary, to change one's mind. In such a substantively motivated argument, the audience for one's arguments is not only others but also oneself. One might even describe this kind of adversarial competition as a competition between ideas rather than between individuals. The stance of substantively motivated argument is fairly common among legislators, administrators, actors in civil society, and members of the judiciary. That form of adversarial competition can also produce arguments and facts that convince the citizenry through a process of reason-giving that has its own intrinsic legitimacy. Some of the benefits commonly ascribed to competition among individuals can arise, in some contexts, from substantively motivated adversarial engagement. That form of engagement may come with fewer costs in social cohesion and perhaps more positive perceptions of the legitimacy of the final decision.[17]

CONCLUSION

In *For the People? Democratic Representation in America*, Charles Beitz has produced a precise, careful, and subtle analysis of the norms of fairness in the competitive structures of electoral representation. Taking a cue from his embrace of myriad structures, plural criteria,

---

17. For the costs of competition in social cohesion, see, e.g., Kahn 1992; Hussain 2018, 2020; Herzog, forthcoming.

and systemic understandings, I have added the societal and administrative realms to the overall systems conception of democratic representation; brought back the normative importance of the dyadic representative constituent relation, particularly through recursive communication; and suggested a contingency analysis of the value of competition for our normative assessments of democratic representation. Throughout I have focused on the perceived, as well as the underlying normative, legitimacy of the growing number of laws that citizens will have to obey as we move into a more interdependent future.

Unrepresentative Democracy in America

PAMELA S. KARLAN[*]

Professor Beitz has offered a thoughtful and thought-provoking analysis of whether—and if so, why and how—the United States' representative institutions are failing. I take the ultimate goal of his project to be, in his words (Beitz, p. 18), "What do these diagnoses suggest about the requirements of fair and effective representation?" Those are, of course, not only Professor Beitz's words. He draws the phrase "fair and effective representation" from the US Supreme Court's decision in the pathmarking one-person, one-vote case, *Reynolds v. Sims*.[1] So consider the proposition the Supreme Court offered at the very beginning of the paragraph where it used the phrase he quotes: "Logically, in a society ostensibly grounded on representative government, it would seem reasonable that a majority of the people of

---

[*] Kenneth and Harle Montgomery Professor of Public Interest Law and Co-Director of the Supreme Court Litigation Clinic, Stanford Law School. Some of the material in this commentary is drawn from Pamela S. Karlan, *The New Countermajoritarian Difficulty*, 109 Cal. L. Rev. 2323 (2021).

1. Reynolds v. Sims, 377 U.S. 533, 564 (1964).

a State could elect a majority of that State's legislators."[2] Generalizing that point, we might posit that in a nation where federal power is ostensibly grounded on representative government, it would seem reasonable that a majority of the people of the nation could elect a majority of Congress. And it seems even more reasonable to believe that fair and effective representation requires that a majority of the people of the nation be able to elect the president. Fair and effective representation requires at least some measure of majoritarianism.[3]

In practice, though, we have a structure that falls systemically short of that ideal. This commentary builds out a point that Professor Beitz makes in his first lecture when he offers (Beitz, p. 21) "five facts drawn from the literature about democratic representation in the United States." to show that representation is failing. The "fifth and possibly the most complex intimation of failure in representation is partisan bias in districting for the House of Representatives and many state legislatures" (Beitz, p. 31). He then drops a footnote citing the work of my colleague Jonathan Rodden and observes (Beitz, p. 31n.52) that "there is also partisan bias in the definition of Senate constituencies, in that the median Senate constituency (or state) is more Republican leaning than the country as a whole. . . . Obviously this bias isn't a product of gerrymandering."

I'm not a political scientist or a political philosopher; I'm a law professor. And I focus much of my work on the Constitution, which is the ultimate "constitutive rule" governing the political competition that forms the focus of Professor Beitz's second lecture.[4] In this

---

2. *Reynolds*, 377 U.S. at 565.
3. That is not to say it requires nothing *beyond* majoritarianism. As Professor Beitz explains, a fair and effective system requires political opportunity for numerical minorities as well. And a democratic polity necessarily places some issues beyond majority control altogether—for example, certain rights of conscience or basic human rights.
4. Beitz (p. 83). In Professor Beitz's taxonomy, "Some rules are constitutive of competition, like rules defining what it means to win—for example, the rule of chess defining checkmate.

commentary, I suggest that perhaps the greatest example of representational failure in contemporary US politics is not the partisan gerrymandering of the House of Representatives—though that gerrymandering has produced all sorts of pathologies—but the composition of the Senate. That failure is precisely because, as Professor Beitz puts it so well (Beitz, p. 67), "democratic representation is primarily a jurisdiction-wide practice." Voters, and citizens, care not just about whether they can elect representatives of their choice; they care equally, perhaps even more, about the overall composition of legislative bodies because *that* is what determines whether their preferred policy outcomes have a chance of being enacted.[5] And along the way, I will suggest that, perhaps in a nonobvious way, some of the contemporary bias in the Senate is actually the product of what we could describe as *meta-gerrymandering*—partisan manipulation of

---

Others are more precisely regulative; they constrain the manner of competition—for example, the rule of chess prohibiting deliberately distracting behavior."

5. I develop this point at greater length in Karlan 1993, 1705, 1717, where I distinguish between the "aggregation" rules that determine which candidate wins a specific seat and the "governance" concerns that play out within elected bodies: "Because the voter's horizon extends beyond the moment of representative selection to various opportunities for collective decisionmaking by assembled legislators, she necessarily will be concerned both with who serves as the representative(s) of her district, and just as centrally, with the overall composition of the governing body. She will, in short, be interested in the degree of both her direct and her virtual representation." To my mind, *Reynolds* was ultimately a governance case. The Court implicitly recognized that all of the plaintiffs had an unfettered right to participate in the formal election process, and although it found that the votes of citizens in the more populous districts were diluted, this dilution did not implicate any particular voter's ability to elect the actual legislators of her choice. In my view, the real injury in *Reynolds* was that once the elected representative arrived in the legislature, her constituents' effective voting power in the legislature would be unfairly minimized because their representative could be outvoted by representatives of smaller groups of constituents. Put somewhat differently, *Reynolds* sought to protect the governance rights of the majority, which was unable to elect a legislature whose overall composition reflected its preferences. One piece of evidence for the proposition that citizens care about governance concerns is the fact that over two-thirds of the individuals who made contributions to candidates running for the House of Representatives in 2018 lived outside the district. Stevens and McCammond 2018 (providing an interactive tool showing where each candidate's contributions came from).

jurisdictional boundaries so baked into the structure of our polity that it lies outside public consciousness and beyond repair by any of the usual anti-entrenchment devices available to us (initiatives, judicial challenges, ordinary legislation, political mobilization, or the like).

The past decades have seen something new in US politics: a partisan divide between large-population and small-population states. To be sure, we've always had big states and small states: at the time of the founding, Virginia had more than twelve times the population of Delaware.[6] The Constitutional Convention "nearly dissolved amid conflict between small and large states over how to apportion representation in the national legislature."[7] Ultimately, that conflict was resolved by the "Connecticut Compromise" under which each state received equal suffrage in the Senate while seats in the House of Representatives were allocated on the basis of population.[8] Negotiating the relative political power of populous and sparsely populated states was critical to their *being* a United States. And when the Fourteenth Amendment—the foundation of much of our constitutional commitment to political equality—was ratified, things were even more skewed: New York had over one hundred times as many people as Nevada.[9]

---

6. See US Census 1791.
7. Klarman 2016, 257.
8. Given Professor Beitz's discussion of the effects of partisan gerrymandering, it is perhaps worth remembering that it was not until 1842 that federal law required the use of single-member districts to elect representatives. See Karlan 2018, 1921, 1929–30. For discussions of the partisan considerations and theories of representation that underlay the 1842 apportionment act, see Quitt 2008, 627; and Ross 2017, 408. And apropos of Professor Beitz's suggestion (p. 97) that alternative methods of aggregating votes might provide an "attractive solution[]" to some of the internal pathologies of political competition, it is worth noting that at the time Congress adopted the requirement of single-member districts, alternatives like ranked choice or cumulative voting had either not yet been invented or were relatively unknown. As Senator Charles Buckalew of Pennsylvania (a leading late nineteenth-century advocate of proportional representation) explained, at the time he had first pressed for districted elections for state and local offices, the "just, equal, almost perfect system" of cumulative voting "was unknown; it had not then been announced abroad or considered here, and we did what best we could." Quoted in Issacharoff et al. 2022, 1156.
9. See US Census 1872.

What Jonathan Rodden points out in the work that Professor Beitz cites is that we now have a "highly polarized partisan geography."[10] In contemporary America, "[M]ostly rural, less populated states [are] voting increasingly Republican."[11] More alarmingly, the population gap between large and small states is growing: within the next generation, 70 percent of Americans will live in the fifteen largest states, leaving only 30 percent of Americans in the remaining thirty-five.[12]

The impact of this on the *Reynolds v. Sims* proposition about the nature of fair and effective representation requiring that a popular majority be able to elect a majority of a jurisdiction's legislators is dramatic: 30 percent of the population, composed of individuals whose interests and partisan preferences differ in systematic ways from their compatriots, has the capacity to control, in a durable way, how one of the central organs of representative government—the Senate—operates.

And there is not much we can do about that... unless large numbers of citizens relocate themselves to states like North Dakota and Wyoming.

Perhaps the most fixed constitutive or regulatory rule in the Constitution governing representation involves the Senate. Article V provides a mechanism for amending the Constitution—a process that has been used repeatedly to change the electoral process, each time to make it formally more inclusive and democratic. But Article V ends with a proviso that "no State, without its Consent, shall be deprived of its equal Suffrage in the Senate."[13] So what we have is a system where an organ of government that is capable of creating all

---

10. See Rodden 2019.
11. Drutman 2020c.
12. Klein 2020; Anonymous 2020.
13. US Constitution Article V.

sorts of gridlock—from refusing to enact laws dealing with critical social and economic problems to refusing to confirm judicial nominees to refusing to ratify the president's choices of high-level executive officials[14]—is becoming increasingly subject to capture by a numerical minority that supports a minoritarian political party.

Before turning to the contemporary consequences, it is worth reviewing the history. We tend to think of the map of the United States as fixed beyond politics. But partisanship is actually baked into the map. The states we have, and thus the representational structure they instantiate, is the product of a series of highly partisan, and sometimes directly race-conscious, decisions about the admission—or nonadmission—of new states.

Prior to the Civil War, "[D]isputes over state admissions were primarily proxy fights in the sectional battle over slavery."[15] In order to maintain the balance of power between the North and the South, Congress adopted a practice of pairing the admission of new free states and new slave states.[16] So racial considerations directly inflected the decision of how to constitute the upper chamber of Congress.

Then, during the Civil War and Reconstruction, Republicans in Congress pushed through the admission of four new states in order to shore up their control of the national government, despite the readmission of the southern states. Most strikingly, in 1864, Congress granted statehood to Republican Nevada, despite its having less than half the population of Oregon (then the least populous state) and thus not meeting the traditional constitutive norm for creating a new state—that admission should wait until the proposed state's population roughly equaled the population of at least one existing state.

---

14. See Beitz pp. 22–28, 35–42, discussing gridlock. For an empirical, legal, and normative discussion of the phenomenon of nonconfirmed, temporary executive branch officials, see O'Connell 2020, 613.
15. Levinson and Sachs 2015, 400, 443.
16. Stewart and Weingast 1992, 223, 226.

At the same time, Congress denied statehood to Utah, which was far more populous but dominated by Democrats.[17]

After the Civil War ended, Republicans continued their "use of statehood politics to secure their hold on the presidency and the Senate."[18] In 1889, Congress split the Dakota Territory and admitted North Dakota, South Dakota, and Washington, each of them then heavily Republican and dramatically underpopulated (which the two most Republican remain to this day). Although it admitted one state that leaned Democratic (Montana), it declined to confer statehood on two other Democratic-leaning territories (Utah and New Mexico), despite the fact that all these areas had similar populations.[19] And with respect to New Mexico, "The Spanish heritage of most New Mexico residents and the prevalence of the Spanish language in the region frequently prompted Republican statements wondering whether such people were even capable of independent self-government."[20] Overall, of the eleven states admitted between 1861 and 1890 (excluding West Virginia, which really was simply a partition of a preexisting state), five had populations smaller than the average existing congressional district.[21] Wyoming has never reached that size.

Putting that history together with the demography, within the next generation, less than a third of the US population, living in states that lean heavily toward the Republican Party, will select nearly three-quarters of the Senate.

The skew is already evident. The current Senate has forty-eight Democrats, forty-nine Republicans, and three independents (who each currently caucus with the Democrats). But the Democratic

17. Stewart and Weingast 1992, 227.
18. Stewart and Weingast 1992, 226.
19. Stewart and Weingast 1992, 236–37.
20. Stewart and Weingast 1992, 240.
21. Stewart and Weingast 1992, 255.

senators represent tens of millions more people than the Republican senators do.[22] Moreover, because the Republican Party can gain a Senate majority without having to appeal to the nationwide median voter, the party has less incentive to move its policies toward the center. And thus our current system fails to fulfill a basic purpose that Professor Beitz identifies (Beitz, p. 86): that the system be "responsive to the people in the sense that policy would change when durable electoral majorities favor change." We risk a pervasive and persistent disconnection between durable *popular* majorities and durable *electoral* majorities. As *Reynolds* (1964) insists, that disconnect cannot produce "fair and effective representation."

Turning from elections to multimember bodies to the presidential election, we find yet another set of constitutive or regulative rules with their own form of pathology. The pathology here stems from the fact that our presidential election is decided not by popular vote but by the vote of the Electoral College. This system creates a second potential for disconnection between the formal majority of electors and the popular majority of voters.

And that potential has been realized, to striking effect. In two of the six most recent presidential elections—in 2000 and 2016—a candidate who lost the national popular vote won the presidency.[23] This is something quite new in our history.[24]

Recent work by a trio of University of Texas economists has suggested that the United States' experience since 2000 with what they call "electoral inversions" has not been a fluke. They have estimated

---

22. Millhiser 2020, reporting that in the then equally divided Senate, Democratic senators represented forty-one million more people than Republican senators did.
23. See Ballotpedia, "Splits between the Electoral College and Popular Vote," https://ballotpedia.org/Splits_between_the_Electoral_College_and_popular_vote (https://perma.cc/379S-UL4A).
24. While there are at least five other elections where at least some scholars have suggested the winning candidate received fewer popular votes than a competitor, only the two twenty-first century examples are straightforward. I describe why in Karlan 2021, 2323, 2341–42.

that in elections where the candidates' popular votes are closely matched, the probability of inversions in which the candidate with fewer votes gets elected is quite real: "In elections decided by a margin of 1 percentage point or less (equal to 1.3 million votes by 2016 turnout), the probability of inversion is about 40 percent."[25] Even at a three-percentage-point margin in favor of the Democratic candidate—which would be a four-million-vote margin in a turnout like 2016's—the likelihood of a Republican inversion would be 15 percent.[26] And consider this: in 2020, Joe Biden received 7,059,547 more votes nationwide than Donald Trump. But he won Arizona, Georgia, and Wisconsin by razor-thin margins: 0.3 percent, 0.2 percent, and 0.6 percent, respectively.[27] If just a relative handful of votes had gone the other way—remember Donald Trump's "I just want to find 11,780 votes"?[28]—Trump would have carried those states, the electoral vote would have been tied 269 to 269, the choice for president would have been thrown into the House of Representatives, and Donald Trump would have been reelected.[29]

Turning next to Professor Beitz's point about fair and effective representation and racial equality, it is worth noting how presidential elections, even more than congressional elections, minimize Black political power. In the original Constitution, enslaved people were infamously counted as three-fifths of a person for purpose

25. Geruso, Spears, and Talesara 2022, 329, offering empirical support for this view.
26. Geruso, Spears, and Talesara 2022, 340. "Our results indicate that a 3.0 point margin favoring a generic modern Democrat—i.e., 48.5 percent Republican vote share, or a gap of about 4 million votes by 2016 turnout—is associated with a 15 percent inversion probability."
27. See Cook Political Report 2020.
28. For the full transcript of the call see Gardner and Firozi 2021.
29. The Twelfth Amendment provides that if no candidate for president receives a majority of the electoral vote, "the House of Representatives shall choose immediately, by ballot, the President," but that "the votes shall be taken by states, the representation from each state having one vote." Although there were 222 Democrats and 213 Republicans in the House, Republicans formed a majority of twenty-seven states' delegations, and presumably would have voted for Trump.

of allocating seats in Congress and votes in the Electoral College. While the popular focus sees the three-fifth clause as a devaluation of their personhood, the original effect of the clause of the allocation of political power was doubly perverse. People who were enslaved counted not at all in elections for those seats (or for a state's electors) given that they were not permitted to vote.[30] Their presence in the apportionment base served only to reinforce slaveholders' political power in both Congress and the presidency.[31] After the Civil War, the political power of white southerners ironically *increased*, because the Fourteenth Amendment gave southern states full credit for their Black population, but after the end of Reconstruction, those states completely disenfranchised their Black citizens. This "undeclared 'five-fifth's clause'"[32] gave southern white supremacists disproportionate power both in the House of Representatives and in picking the president and thereby in setting federal policy.[33] For example, in 1904, voters in Ohio cast the same number of votes for president as were cast in nine southern states put together, but Ohio had only twenty-three electoral votes, compared to those states' ninety-nine.[34] This disparity persisted through the presidential elections of the 1960s, as "there were many fewer ballots cast per electoral vote in the South than elsewhere."[35]

Even today, the presidential election system undermines the voting strength of Black citizens. Nearly half the nation's Black population lives in the eleven states of the former confederacy. And they vote overwhelmingly for the Democratic presidential candidate. But in this century, of all those states, only Georgia, North Carolina, and

---

30. See Karlan 2018, 1926.
31. See Wegman 2020, 82, 95, 105–7.
32. Keyssar 2020, 9.
33. Wegman 2020, 107.
34. Keyssar 2020, 190 n. 38.
35. Keyssar 2020, 190 n. 38.

Virginia have *ever* cast their electoral votes for a Democrat. By contrast, "in Texas, a state with thirty-eight electoral votes and a population that was 40 percent Black or Hispanic, since 1980 not a single electoral vote" has been cast for the presidential candidate Black and Hispanic voters prefer.[36] This disadvantage lies atop the disadvantage that Professor Beitz (p. 59) identifies: that because Black voters tend to live in larger states, "the small-state bias of the Senate may contribute" to the system's failure to respond equally to their concerns.

So political competition in the United States is skewed in deeply structural ways. And that skew has become self-reenforcing. In the last ten presidential elections, Democratic candidates have been elected five times and Republican candidates have been elected five times—twice, though, while receiving fewer popular votes than their Democratic rival. But Republican presidents have been able to successfully nominate ten justices to the United States Supreme Court (six of whom are currently sitting),[37] while Democratic presidents have successfully nominated only five (only three of whom now sit).[38] And that has produced a Court whose decisions have permitted what I think Professor Beitz (p. 83) would characterize as "'unhealthy' competition" in which the Republican Party tries to move Democratic voters off the playing field entirely through laws that make it harder to vote—that deny them any chance to be, in Professor Beitz's phrase (p. 88), "agents of democratic self-government," or Hobbesian "makers," rather than merely the "matter," of government. Moreover, the Court has deregulated political spending in ways that exacerbate the advantages the wealthy, who are disproportionately white, already

36. Keyssar 2020, 360.
37. Chief Justices Rehnquist and Roberts and Justices Thomas, Scalia, Kennedy, Souter, Alito, Gorsuch, Kavanaugh, and Barrett.
38. Justices Ginsburg, Breyer, Sotomayor, Kagan, and Jackson.

enjoy. As Professor Beitz (p. 114) so powerfully frames it, "[O]ur institutions, including their associated norms, seem ill-suited to meet the contemporary challenges of a changing polity."

For Professor Beitz, political parties are the key, in our contemporary system, to achieving any kind of fair and effective representation. So it is a special irony that the framers of our Constitution assumed they had created a system that would *prevent* the emergence of parties (what they called "faction").[39] In fact, as James Madison [1787] (2001a, 45) explained, they assumed that the "republican principle" would "suppl[y]" relief against any "faction [that] consists of less than a majority," because it would "enable[] the majority to defeat its sinister views by regular vote. It may clog the administration, it may convulse the society; but it will be unable to execute and mask its violence under the forms of the Constitution." Today, we face exactly that risk. And it is a risk tied directly to our current partisan politics. Put simply, the current Republican Party undermines the constitutional republican principle.

There's thus a wonderful double entendre in the penultimate sentence of Professor Beitz's lecture (p. 115), where he states that "restoring healthy party competition is among the most critical challenges facing representative democracy in the United States today." In the context of the lecture, he is using the word "healthy" to modify the phrase "party competition." And he's certainly right about that. Political parties are critical to effective, responsive, and responsible governance. But we can't ignore the need to restore healthy *parties* as well. As long as one of our major parties is in thrall to election deniers and coup plotters and vote suppressors and Orban fanboys, representative democracy is under a serious threat.

---

39. See generally Levinson and Pildes 2006, 2311, 2313.

RESPONSE

Reply to Commentators

Preferences and Policy, Legitimacy, and Countermajoritarianism

CHARLES R. BEITZ

Let me begin by thanking Martin Gilens, Pamela Karlan, and Jane Mansbridge for their commentaries. Over the years I have learned from all of them in ways that will be obvious to readers of their work. So it was an honor that they joined the discussion of the lectures in Berkeley and, all the more, that they contributed to this volume.

Although there are points of tangency, the three commentaries do not overlap very much in substance. They do, however, have at least two features in common. Each builds out and critically elaborates one or another theme in the lectures. Each also supplies empirical and theoretical details that deepen, qualify, and refine the main themes. In both respects these contributions will make this volume more valuable for readers. But both features complicate my task in crafting a response. The first means that the most obvious strategy—to organize a reply according to common themes in the commentaries—is not available. The second means, as a practical matter, that I cannot hope to respond to all three commentaries in their richness. Instead,

I proceed by identifying a substantive theme in each commentary and responding to it as best I can.

PREFERENCES AND POLICY

Martin Gilens's illuminating commentary begins by offering some distinctions that help to clarify the concept of representation and explain how the tendency to concentrate on dyadic representation can produce a misleading impression of the functioning of the system. He calls attention to the importance for policymaking of control over the legislative agenda, an element of the system of representation that would be invisible if one limited one's attention to dyadic relationships. But the main concern of his contribution is the relationship that he calls the "preference-policy link" (hereafter, PPL). This is the central idea that structures his pathbreaking research, and it is also central to his normative conception of fair and effective representation.

An uncareful reader might suppose that Gilens's ultimate interest is in what I described in the lectures as the "congruence" between the policy preferences of the people and the policy outputs of government: the greater the (aggregate) congruence, the higher the quality (or fairness, or effectiveness...) of representation. But he makes clear in his commentary (and in his book) that high congruence is not his central normative interest or the basis of his view of good representation. His primary interest is in what I called "responsiveness" as distinct from congruence, which is to say, in influence as distinct from satisfaction.

The "preference-policy" links his research sought to identify are links between policy changes that are preferred by majorities and adoption of those changes in public policy. A system is responsive, in Gilens's sense, to the extent that an increase in public support for a policy change is associated with an increase in the chances that the change will be adopted in public policy.[1] Gilens's innovation was to notice that the "link" can be estimated not only for the public as a whole but also for different income groups, so that the extent of their influence on policy can be compared. The most eye-catching of his findings involve comparisons of the strength of the "link" for the wealthy and for the middle class:

> I found that proposed policy changes that were strongly favored by the well-off were much more likely to be adopted than those that they strongly opposed.... In stark contrast, the preferences of middle-income (or poor) Americans mattered not at all: policies strongly opposed by the middle class or poor were just as likely to be adopted as those they strongly favored. ... [T]he utter lack of responsiveness ... to the preferences of middle-income, much less poor, Americans is starkly inconsistent with the most basic tenets of democracy.[2]

It is compatible with this to observe that there is relatively high congruence of preferences and policy for middle-income citizens. This could be the case if middle-income and wealthy citizens agree about many policies. But in that case high congruence is, so to speak, coincidental. It is not evidence of responsiveness. Gilens writes: "[I]f the majority of Americans get what they want from government only when they agree with elites or favor the status quo, that is not a functioning democracy."[3]

This is not only a descriptive claim: "[T]he normative judgments of [competitive] institutions as contributing to or undermining fair

---

1. Gilens 2012, 70.
2. Gilens, this volume, pp. 124–25.
3. Ibid., p. 126. For "democracy by coincidence," Gilens and Page 2014, 573 and Gilens 2015.

and effective representation rest[] ... largely on their impact on the preference-policy link." Gilens argues that the forms of competition described in the lectures are important insofar as they enable citizens to achieve two objectives: "to form policy preferences consistent with their interests and values, and to see those preferences reflected in the policies their government adopts."[4] I point this out because the first objective (to form what we might call "informed preferences") is quite a different matter than enabling citizens to exert influence over the policymaking process by voting, lobbying, contributing to campaigns, and so forth. There is, of course, a large, and largely skeptical, literature devoted to the competence of ordinary citizens to judge which policy alternatives are likely to contribute the most to the satisfaction of their interests, particularly once one looks beyond the relatively small number of policy issues that are made salient in public political contestation. But Gilens argues here, as he argues at greater length in his book, that citizens "as a collective" are able to form "meaningful policy preferences."[5] This is famously controversial within political science.[6] I did not engage the empirical controversy in the lectures and will leave it aside here. But it is important to observe that taking seriously the concern to enable citizens to form informed policy preferences puts considerable weight on the fourth of the justifying purposes I listed in the second lecture, which relates to the interest in maintaining healthy deliberative environments in the various arenas of competition. If we accept that there is such an interest, then the PPL, taken in its own terms, is not all there is to fair and effective representation.[7]

---

4. Gilens, this volume, p. 131.
5. Ibid., p. 127 and Gilens 2012, chap. 1.
6. Perhaps most famously, in the recent literature, in Achen and Bartels 2017. See also the discussion in Disch 2021, chap. 3.
7. Gilens recognizes this point: see this volume, p. 134, noting that preference formation raises distinct normative concerns. These concerns direct our attention to the structure of

Gilens goes on to argue that, properly understood, the main objections to gerrymandering, distortions in interest competition, and the impact of polarization and gridlock can be interpreted as failures of the PPL. So, for example, in interest representation, the problem is that the distribution of preferences among organized interests does not accurately reflect their distribution among the public. It thus contributes to distortion of the PPL.[8] Gilens then considers the four "justifying purposes" identified in the second lecture and argues that three of them can be interpreted in terms of the PPL. If this is true, then it might not have been necessary to articulate these purposes separately; I might simply have argued that a (or *the*) basic norm for a system of fair and effective representation is that the system translate the distribution of policy preferences in the public into public policies that reflect a fair aggregation of those preferences. A "fair aggregation" is, presumably, one in which a preference shared by a majority of the people, when there is one, would be translated into public policy. Failures of representation are failures to enact majority preferences into policy.

From Gilens's perspective this is an ideal; there may be both practical and principled reasons why we should not evaluate the quality of representation exclusively according to the PPL criterion. The latter include familiar considerations of minority rights and policy stability. Still, these considerations operate as constraints on the underlying normative idea, which he takes to be basic: "the widespread and long-standing belief that ordinary citizens' ability to shape government policymaking is central to democracy."[9]

---

contestation in the public sphere, a subject that needs more extended attention than was possible in the lectures.
8. Ibid., pp. 132–33.
9. Ibid., p. 130.

Gilens's presentation might be read to suggest that we have a disagreement about the normative basis of evaluative judgments about the institutional structure of democratic political competition. I am not certain that this reads him correctly. Officially my view is more pluralist than his. The lectures do not, as he does, identify any single basic norm that can be said to underly the requirements of fair and effective representation. I do not rule out the possibility, though I am skeptical that there is any single value with enough substance to be informative about those requirements. Officially his view is fundamentally majoritarian (more exactly, we might call it "preference-majoritarian"); but he allows that a majoritarian aggregation rule applied to preferences might need to be constrained for reasons of the kind I have just mentioned.

Whether we agree or not about the best way to interpret the justifying purposes, let me offer a brief remark about preference-majoritarianism in the context of democratic representation. In sum: the idea that representative institutions should deliver policy responsive to the preferences of a majority of the electorate can be interpreted in either of two ways. It might be seen as a first-order normative requirement for institutions. Or it might be seen as a heuristic, useful for identifying malfunctions of the system that are objectionable for reasons other than that they fall short of whatever is the optimal level of preference-policy responsiveness. The first interpretation seems to me to be at odds with basic features of a representative order. The second interpretation seems to me highly plausible.

To explain the difficulty with the first interpretation we might look back to my remarks, in the second lecture, about the shortcomings of the "democracy scaled up" view, with which this interpretation of the PPL has something in common. The PPL criterion might be seen to require that the system of representation select the policies that the people (or a majority of them) would select if they could somehow make the choice themselves. But a system of representation, as I said, is a division of labor. The system divides the role of citizen from the role of representative, assigning different expectations to each. With the exception of the most publicly salient of policy issues, it does not expect individual citizens to form views about most problems of public policy. Moreover, in a well-designed representative system, there will be a variety of deliberative forums in which groups of various kinds can contest proposals for policy change. Epistemically effective forms of contestation can be expected to bring about changes in views about desirable policy change. This means that it matters when, in the course of these deliberative processes, preferences are taken to be significant; for purposes of assessment, not all preferences are created equal. For both reasons, the idea that there should be a systematic and strong across-the-board connection between majority preferences and policy outcomes, as the PPL theorizes that connection, asks both too much and too little of the system of representation. It is neither realistically attainable as a matter of fact nor obviously desirable as a matter of democratic principle.

These considerations do not count against the heuristic interpretation of the PPL. We might reasonably regard Gilens's documentation of failures of the PPL as highlighting a democratic malfunction that requires further analysis, and that the further analysis need not rest in an appeal to the relationship between preferences and policy outcomes. This seems to me particularly clear with regard to the eye-catching empirical regularity I mentioned earlier: that "ordinary Americans" (say, middle-income citizens) tend to get the policies they want only when their preferences align with those of the wealthy (or favor the status quo). Otherwise the wealthy's preferences win. I agree that this is an objectionable feature of the system of representation. The inference from my view of justifying purposes is that at least part of the objection lies in the presumption that the interests that tend to lose out when these preferences do not align are more urgent than the preferences that dominate. Admittedly, it takes a longer chain of reasoning to justify this "substantive" objection than the chain of reasoning that sees the failure as a "procedural" matter of minority dominance. And the longer chain will involve generalizations from a theory of the political economy of democratic politics that have no analog in the objection from minority rule.

One way to make the substantive objection plausible is to consider a fanciful thought experiment. Imagine that the empirical regularity were different. Suppose that middle-income citizens get the outcomes they want when their preferences align with those of the poor, which (again suppose) they usually do. Otherwise—say, when middle-income preferences align with those of the wealthy—the poor's preferences win. (Perhaps the representation system gives extra weight to the votes of the poor, in a progressive variant of Mill's famous scheme for plural voting.) This does not seem to me obviously objectionable, yet it would also be a case of minority rule. What this suggests—though it would take a longer argument to defend the point—is that substantive considerations may play a role in judgments about the quality of the system of representation that is not reflected in the straightforward application of the PPL criterion.

To generalize: the absence of influence over the outcomes of a decision-making process is not necessarily problematic morally. Nobody has any influence over the outcome of a fair lottery, yet in some circumstances we are not troubled by this. What Gilens presents as troubling is a comparison: of the influence of the wealthy and of the non-wealthy. The trouble is one of inequality or more generally of unfairness. It is not fair that the wealthy have more influence than the non-wealthy. Why not? One response is that there are more non-wealthy than wealthy; a minority's preference is, in effect, allowed to outweigh the majority's. Another response is that there is no good justification for institutions that systematically enable the wealthy to prevail when preferences conflict—no claim, that is, that the interests that tend to prevail in such conflicts are more important from a moral point of view than the interests that do not prevail.[10] The violation here is of substantive, perhaps distributive, justice.

Gilens does not press the theoretical question I have just raised, about the reasons why we should regard it as unfair for the wealthy to prevail in cases in which they are in a minority. But it would be natural to advance some form of the first response. My own view is that this would not be incorrect, but that it would be difficult to sustain as a normative view about the basis of majority rule without relying on some form of the second view as its foundation. The principle of majority rule is notoriously difficult to defend as a foundational requirement of pure procedural justice. For example, as Niko Kolodny has argued, it is not obviously (or perhaps at all) entailed by plausible conceptions of political equality.[11] In the cases of interest to Gilens and me, it seems more plausible to hold that the violation is one of substantive justice—of systematically allowing the wealthy to advance their interests to an extent that is unlikely to be justifiable. It is a predictable and to some extent remediable form of injustice to which systems of election and representation are vulnerable.

DEMOCRATIC LEGITIMACY AND THE COSTS OF COMPETITION

Jane Mansbridge's commentary offers a rich set of reflections unified by a concern for the legitimacy of representative democratic institutions. I concentrate here on the concern for legitimacy, both

---

10. This response is compatible with Gilens and Page's conclusion in a widely cited article: "[I]f policymaking is dominated by powerful business organizations and a small number of affluent Americans, then America's claims to being a democratic society are seriously threatened" (2014, 577).
11. Kolodny 2023, sec. 29.2. Compare Rawls 1999, sec. 54; Beitz 1989, 58–67; Estlund 2008, chap. 4.

because it motivates the proposals for enhancing dyadic representation and because it explains the apprehension about political competition becoming counterproductively intense. A concern for institutional legitimacy is notably lacking in my original lectures, and Mansbridge's commentary might suggest (although she does not put it this way) that in this respect my sketch of the justifying purposes of representation is incomplete.[12]

As a beginning, it will help to place this concern in context. Mansbridge notes that as human interdependence increases, there is an increasing need for state regulation, backed by coercive threats, "to solve the free-rider problems that accompany . . . interdependence."[13] Political institutions will need to be widely regarded as legitimate in order to minimize resistance to the extension of the state's regulatory reach.

Mansbridge distinguishes between the "perceived legitimacy of the laws" (some would say their "sociological" legitimacy) and "an underlying normative legitimacy based on principles justified through deliberation and reflection."[14] I think we must take the primary concern to be the "perceived" legitimacy of the laws. The motivating worry is that a growing regulatory burden might undermine people's willingness to accept and support the state's use of coercion to enforce its regulations. That would be a bad thing because the resulting instability would reduce the effectiveness of the state's

---

12. Henry Brady made a similar suggestion in comments on the lectures. Martin Gilens agrees that the perceived legitimacy of representative institutions might be an independent source of reasons bearing on matters of institutional design and reform (such as measures to increase descriptive representation), but does not pursue the point (this volume, p. 120).
13. Mansbridge, this volume, p. 139. This is a long-standing concern for her; see, for example, Mansbridge 2012. We might add that the concern arises at the global level as well, where it is even more challenging.
14. Mansbridge, this volume, p. 140. Elsewhere she distinguishes between "empirical" and "normative" legitimacy and writes, "Empirical legitimacy does all the work in backing the coercion that solves collective action problems" (2014b, 11).

attempts to solve the collective action problems that give rise to the need for regulation. Thus, for example, Rawls argues that the stability of a well-ordered society, as he understands it, depends on the existence of a widely shared sense of justice together with a belief that institutions conform to its requirements. These serve to restore the social system to equilibrium when it suffers destabilizing shocks, as all institutions do from time to time.[15] The value of legitimacy in this view is at least partly that it is a condition of the capacity of institutions to satisfy their justifying purposes effectively. The political problem is instability, and it is enough for the kind of instability that concerns Mansbridge that institutions come to be perceived as illegitimate.

Let me turn now to the connection between the concern for institutional legitimacy and the distinction between dyadic and systemic representation. Although she shares the view that the systemic perspective is essential, Mansbridge holds that the dyadic relationship between a representative and her constituents has independent normative significance.[16] She agrees with Pitkin that when an individual representative departs from constituency preferences, she owes her constituents an explanation.[17] On a purely systemic view, of course, it would be difficult to explain why this should be, since on such a view the dyadic relationships of individual representatives to their constituents melt away. If one were to follow Robert Weissberg's seminal analysis of "collective" representation, for example, what would matter is simply the relationship between the jurisdiction-wide electorate

---

15. Rawls 1999, sec. 69.
16. Mansbridge distinguishes this relationship from the one-to-many relationship of a representative to her constituency as a whole (this volume, p. 146), which is how I characterized dyadic representation in the lectures. But since she is ultimately interested in the set of one-to-one relationships of a representative to each of the members of her constituency, I am not sure that there is a significant disagreement.
17. Pitkin 1967, 209.

and the legislature. As he observes, it is possible for the legislative majority to agree with the jurisdiction-wide electoral majority even if the quality of dyadic representation is very low (as measured by the amount of agreement between individual representatives and their own constituencies). Perhaps there is a high level of virtual representation. We can see this from a simple example. Say that constituency C1 returns representative R1 and constituency C2 returns representative R2 and that the majority policy preferences in C1 and C2 differ. If R1 consistently votes with the majority preference in C2 and R2 consistently votes with the majority preference in C1, the quality of collective or systemic representation would be high even though that of dyadic representation is obviously low.[18]

There is no reason to disparage virtual representation of this kind. Indeed, in any system of territorial representation its possibility is crucial. (Think of the representation of dispersed minorities.) But the claim that the dyadic relationship has independent normative importance suggests that our simple example is too simple: it is based on too thin an idea of representation. What, exactly, is missing? One possibility, compatible with the Weissberg view, is that consistently weak representation at the dyadic level makes elections less effective as mechanisms of accountability; over time, the quality of collective representation may be likely to suffer. The system of collective representation is sustained by individual choices made in individual constituencies among candidates for office, and those choices are likely to be better informed when the dyadic relationship is stronger. This may be true, and Mansbridge would probably agree. However, her account of "recursive representation" suggests an additional possibility: that under good collective but bad dyadic representation, constituents are likely to feel alienated from their representatives. To borrow a phrase from Iris Marion Young, they may feel that their

18. Weissberg 1978.

representatives "have lost connection" with them.[19] The communicative relationship between represented and representative has atrophied, or perhaps it never existed. When feelings of alienation from the representative system become widespread, it is a short step to concern about institutional legitimacy.

Given the framework within which this concern arises for Mansbridge, it is hard to disagree that standards of successful democratic representation ought to incorporate the value of institutional legitimacy as a desideratum. Perhaps it is implicit in the third justifying purpose, about decisiveness, which calls attention to the importance of effectiveness in resolving dispute about policy. Without repeating the lectures, there are at least two dimensions to effectiveness as a value in competitive democratic processes. Of course those processes should be effective in resolving disputes. But effectiveness in resolving disputes has value only if the disputed policy, once adopted, is actually implemented. A loss of legitimacy, as Mansbridge understands it, could be an obstacle to both dimensions of effectiveness.

That much seems clear. But it is a further question how our thinking about institutional design might be influenced by taking legitimacy seriously. Mansbridge suggests that one response might be to promote more "recursive representation": to facilitate more extensive "interactive relationships" in which representatives and constituents can participate in "two-way, mutually responsive" communication under circumstances that discourage grandstanding and encourage the honest exchange of views.[20] She cites as an illustration the experimental study of Michael Neblo and colleagues in which one-off, town meeting-style gatherings were arranged among individual members of the US House and small, randomly chosen groups of

---

19. Young 2000, 128; Mansbridge cites the paper on p. 148.
20. Mansbridge, this volume, p. 147.

their constituents. The hope was that representatives would become more aware of their constituents' interests and constituents would become better informed about their representatives' policy priorities and their relationship to constituency needs.[21] The illustration is instructive and its aspirations attractive, although the design of the experiment fell short of them in various ways (for example, sessions were short and representatives did not actually exchange views with constituents; they responded to written questions). And it is far from clear that the model can be scaled sufficiently to have a discernible impact on the perceived legitimacy of representative institutions nationally.[22] On the other hand, even occasional attempts to facilitate effective two-way communication among representatives and randomly chosen groups of constituents could have other beneficial effects for the quality of representation. For example, they might provide opportunities for those marginalized in the ordinary structure of political competition to engage and be heard.

The other way the concern for legitimacy arises in Mansbridge's commentary involves the role and regulation of political competition in democratic representation. The motivating worry seems to be that in circumstances in which growing interdependence increases the state's need to resort to coercion to solve free-rider problems, intensifying forms of political competition may tend "to delegitimate the representative process." That prospect may be a reason to introduce elements into the process that "dampen the adversarial nature" of competition.[23] This line of thought leads to what is, in effect, the research program that Mansbridge calls a "contingency theory of competition." It would "spell out the ways that different forms of

---

21. Neblo, Esterling, and Lazer 2018.
22. This may be why Mansbridge classifies recursive representation as an "aspirational ideal" (p. 147). For discussion of the issue of scale in the Neblo study, see Fishkin 2019.
23. Mansbridge, this volume, p. 150.

competitive and cooperative structures may increase or decrease both perceived and underlying normative legitimacy[,] ... investigate the democratic contributions and drawbacks of those structures [, and] ... specify the contexts in which the democratic cost-benefit ratio suggests introducing or suppressing particular practices and structures."[24]

It is hard not to be defensive in a response to commentaries, so—in my defense, and without meaning to say that Mansbridge suggests otherwise—let me add a note of clarification. In calling attention to the competitive nature of various aspects of democratic representation, it was not my aim to argue that it is better—fairer, more effective—to organize decision-making processes as competitive rather than noncompetitive or cooperative, and certainly not to set forth any general position about the extent of competitiveness desirable in arenas with competitive structures. The aim was to correct the relative lack of attention in recent democratic theory to the competitive character of the politics of democratic representation as it is structured by law and practice in the system of representation as we have it. Competitive processes generally, and competitive political processes in particular, characteristically raise distinctive questions of fairness. The lectures aim to identify these questions and propose a way to respond to them. Part of the argument is that to respond to these questions adequately we must take account of the institutional and political contexts in which the processes operate and the (potentially) valuable functions that competition serves within them. If doing so would be part of a "contingency theory of competition," then I am happy to endorse the proposal. Perhaps I've sketched some elements of such a theory. The view entails that competition can "run off the rails" in a competitive arena when competitors seeking an advantage are motivated to act in ways that undermine the social

24. Ibid.

value that justifies the use of the competitive process. As I noted in the second lecture, the optimal level of competitiveness is ordinarily not the maximum. This is obviously true when the concern is the perceived legitimacy of these processes.

If the level of competitiveness that would be optimal for purposes of legitimacy is not the maximum, then the question arises in what ways institutions might be structured and regulated so as to moderate competition. Mansbridge suggests various possibilities: for example, allowing for long incumbencies, organizing competition on some other basis than between parties (e.g., by making elections nonpartisan), tolerating one-party domination at local and state levels, and exploiting the advantages of single-member districts. She suggests that any of these measures could reduce the intensity of political competition and increase voter satisfaction, and thus yield higher perceived legitimacy.[25]

To reach a considered view about the desirability of any of these measures one would need to take account of a host of contingencies—perhaps to develop "a contingency theory of competition"?—and this is obviously beyond us here. As a matter of principle, the important point, as Mansbridge recognizes, is that whatever increase in voter satisfaction would be brought about by reducing the intensity of electoral competition might come at a cost in democratic values. To return to the distinction between congruence and responsiveness, I argued in the first lecture that, of the two, responsiveness is the more important democratic value: it is a sign that the people can control the government. Features like long incumbencies and one-party domination achieve voter satisfaction by reducing the diachronic capacity for control. On my view that can be a democratic cost. In some circumstances there might also be another kind of cost. If, say, long incumbencies have the effect of leaving a cohesive minority

25. Ibid., pp. 153–155.

with no effective prospect of representation, that minority will lack grounds for assurance that its interests will be taken into account in policymaking. Its members are likely not only to be dissatisfied with individual policy outcomes but also alienated from the system, with adverse consequences for legitimacy. Whether the benefits of these measures justify the costs will of course depend on contextual considerations as well as a judgment about the impact on the functioning of the representative system as a whole. The point here is simply to underscore the potential democratic costs of efforts to reduce the intensity of political competition. Putting the point differently, it is to reiterate that competitive processes rely on competition to produce various social values. Measures that attenuate competitive conduct might put those values at risk.

Measures that would remove or attenuate the role of parties in organizing electoral competition may also have costs. Healthy competition between parties serves not only to identify alternatives for policy but also to incentivize informed communication about the alternatives in the public sphere. To put it in terms familiar from Schattschneider, they make it possible for voters to play an informed role in democratic decision-making. While it may be true that non-party competition, for example, will produce more citizen satisfaction, it may also be less effective in eliciting forms of public political deliberation that enable voters to influence the political agenda and hold public officials to account. Those, again, are significant democratic costs to be weighed against whatever benefit might be derived from increasing citizen satisfaction. What this shows, to put it in Mansbridge's terms, is that the value of legitimacy may compete with the value of democratic control. She is right to observe that the extent of the potential conflict depends on the contingencies of political and social circumstance, and certainly right to insist that considerations of institutional legitimacy should have some place in assessing the quality of representation. The main consideration I have urged in response is that measures aimed at increasing the perceived legitimacy of representative institutions can have costs in democratic values, particularly in the extent to which these institutions realize the value of popular control of government.

THE SENATE, ELECTORAL COLLEGE, AND UNFAIRNESS TO PARTISANS

Pamela Karlan writes that she "builds out" a point about partisan bias made in the first lecture, but in fact she does much more. She begins with the "countermajoritarian difficulty" that emerges when changes in political geography are layered onto the constitutional provisions for representation in the Senate; offers an illuminating historical digression showing how partisanship was "baked into" the process of admission of new states and the drawing of jurisdictional boundaries; considers the consequences of this for selection of the president in the Electoral College (and, not incidentally, selection of justices of the Supreme Court); and attends throughout to the adverse impact of these aspects of the constitutional structure on the representation of Black citizens. This is a large agenda. I will concentrate on the problem of the Senate, which Karlan describes as "perhaps the greatest example of representational failure in contemporary US politics."[26] The problem is enormously—even surpassingly—important politically. The problem is also puzzling theoretically for reasons I try to articulate. I will also comment more briefly about the Electoral College.

Karlan's starting point is that states (rather than persons) are represented equally in the Senate. She recalls a critical passage in the

---

26. Karlan, this volume, p. 161. For the problem as a "countermajoritarian difficulty" and more extensive historical discussion, see also Karlan 2021.

landmark case of *Reynolds v. Sims* in which the Court writes: "Logically, in a society ostensibly grounded on representative government, it would seem reasonable that a majority of the people of a State could elect a majority of that State's legislators."[27] Generalizing, she writes that "it would seem reasonable that a majority of the people of the nation could elect a majority of Congress." She adds: "And it seems even more reasonable to believe that fair and effective representation requires that a majority of the people of the nation be able to elect the president. Fair and effective representation requires at least some measure of majoritarianism."[28]

The Senate, of course, conspicuously violates this principle (and by design). This has been famously controversial from the time of the framing, when advocates of a national government failed to persuade the Constitutional Convention of its superiority to a federal system.[29] Federalism made it arguable that states as such had interests in representation at the federal level (though, in fact, it is hardly clear that this justifies equal representation for states). The traditional objection is that the failure to accord representation to states in proportion to population is an offense to political equality; it means that voters in small states are in a position to exercise greater influence over outcomes in the Senate than voters in large states.[30]

---

27. *Reynolds v. Sims*, 377 U.S. 533 (1964), 565.
28. Karlan, this volume, p. 160. In a footnote (p. 160n. 3) she adds that this "is not to say it requires nothing *beyond* majoritarianism."
29. Although, writing as Publius, James Madison defended the proposed constitution in the *Federalist*, he had promoted a national veto of state legislation and opposed equal representation of states in the Senate in the Constitutional Convention, ultimately accepting it as the price of agreement to any constitution at all. For discussion see, for example, Kernell 2003.
30. There are other objections. As Kolodny points out, unequal representation in the Senate means that citizens of small states stand to gain a disproportionate share of federal resources, and empirical research shows that they do (e.g., Lee and Oppenheimer 1999, chap. 6). And the fact that unequal representation is embedded in the Constitution might be taken to undermine the foundations of equal citizenship (Kolodny 2023, 360–62). Wilson offers a more comprehensive critical discussion (2019, chap. 6).

Karlan subscribes to this objection. But her concern runs further. As her colleague Jonathan Rodden has pointed out, in the last several decades a "highly polarized partisan geography" has emerged in the United States, with smaller states tending to lean Republican and larger states tending to lean Democratic. Karlan observes that, in the near future, "30 percent of the population, *composed of individuals whose interests and partisan preferences differ in systematic ways from their compatriots*, have the capacity to control, in a durable way, how one of the central organs of representative government—the Senate—operates."[31] The passage I have emphasized suggests that the normative problem is not only that, under the constitutional rules, small-state voters have greater opportunities for influence in the Senate. It is also that the combination of the rules and changes in political geography have produced a situation in which Republican voters as a group have systematically greater opportunities for influence in the Senate than Democratic voters as a group. (It is worth noting that the partisan geography has not always been as polarized as it is today. We would not have the problem in the form that concerns Karlan if large and small states were more nearly comparable in their partisan division, even though the inequality would remain.) The theoretical question is whether this "baked in" partisan asymmetry constitutes an additional kind of unfairness and, if so, in what the unfairness consists.

I'll return to this question shortly, but first let me recall the other problem that concerns Karlan. As she notes, the rules governing representation in the Electoral College (the "aggregation rules") together with the changes in political geography already mentioned produce a

---

31. Karlan, this volume, p. 163 (emphasis added); see Rodden 2019, 9. Karlan observes: "The skew is already evident. The current Senate has forty-eight Democrats, forty-nine Republicans, and three independents (who each currently caucus with the Democrats). But the Democratic senators represent tens of millions more people than the Republican senators do" (pp. 165–66).

parallel possibility of partisan distortion in presidential elections. It is revealed in the phenomenon of "electoral inversions"—presidential elections in which the winner of the nationwide popular vote loses in the Electoral College. When we take account of political geography, we see that the likelihood of Republicans benefiting from electoral inversions, as they did in 2000 and 2016, is greater than that of Democrats.[32] Institutional rules that allow electoral inversions might be seen as objectionable simply because inversions are, by definition, countermajoritarian. But, as in the case of the Senate, the fact that they are more likely to benefit Republican than Democratic candidates means that they are another instance of partisan asymmetry. And, again, the theoretical question is whether this makes matters worse as a matter of democratic principle.

How might someone respond to that question? Let us focus on the Senate. One intuitive response is that the Republican advantage may be becoming entrenched (a national Republican minority will be able to control the Senate "in a durable way" for many years). If a national minority of Republicans gain majorities in the Senate in a succession of election cycles, then the prospect of rotation in office on which the legitimacy of the system depends would be endangered. Here the ambiguity of "legitimacy" we noticed earlier suggests that the objection has two dimensions. One reason we might think that majoritarian systems are justified in spite of the possibility of neglect of minority interests is that they can ordinarily be expected to produce policy over time that satisfies the interests of a broad swath of the population. But if one group—one party, or a long coalition that supports it—cannot look forward to taking its turn in policymaking, particularly when it attracts the votes of national majorities, then the system would fail to be sufficiently responsive. This is a complaint about the normative legitimacy of the system—the first dimension.

---

32. Karlan cites a study now published as Geruso, Spears, and Talesara 2022.

And this, in turn, might plausibly undermine the perceived legitimacy of the system, at least among the majority, with ominous consequences for institutional stability—the second dimension.

Another intuitive response arises when we notice the incentive effects of partisan asymmetry in elections to the Senate. The choice of electoral strategies by parties and candidates is endogenous to the electoral system. So, for example, a Republican Party that feels confident of winning a Senate majority with a nationwide popular vote minority has less incentive to select candidates and craft policies that appeal to the nationwide median voter. As Karlan notes, this could reduce the responsiveness of the system and incentivize the taking of more extreme positions, contributing to the cycle that produces gridlock, undermining effectiveness.[33]

A third response would look more directly at the likely policy consequences of Republican entrenchment in the Senate. The consequences for representation of minorities are particularly significant for this response. Karlan explains how the apportionment of the Senate tends to disadvantage Black voters as a group, who overwhelmingly vote Democratic. Institutional rules enabling Republican entrenchment might be seen as objectionable threats to the urgent political interests of Blacks.[34] The objection depends on the contingent assumption that, as a group, they share some important political interests. This, of course, is not straightforwardly a matter of unequal representation or of responsiveness to majority preferences; Blacks are paradigmatically a "discrete minority." The force of the objection

---

33. Karlan, this volume, p. 166.
34. For example, Gould, Shepsle, and Stephenson argue that, because large states tend to be more racially diverse, Senate malapportionment exacerbates systemic racial inequality (2021, 513–14). They allow that the argument rests on a contingency but hold, plausibly, that "more diverse large states and less diverse small states are a stable feature of American politics" (514 n. 22). For empirical evidence that Senate malapportionment disadvantages the political interests of Blacks, see Griffin 2006b.

derives from the normative requirement that the system should be structured so as to protect citizens from systematic neglect of their urgent interests.

These responses are speculative; I do not mean to offer a theory that explains the impression that "the new countermajoritarian difficulty" is more problematic than the bare fact of unequal representation might suggest. But they do indicate several ways that objections to the phenomenon Karlan describes might be framed within the view of fair and effective representation sketched in the lectures.

Much of what I have said also applies to partisan distortion in the Electoral College. There is, however, a confounding factor that ought to be acknowledged. Electoral inversions in presidential elections are usually identified by comparing the partisan division in the national popular vote with the division in the Electoral College. As I noted, however, the conduct of campaigns is endogenous to the prevailing electoral rules. A rational candidate will aim to win the popular vote in enough states to provide at least the number of electoral votes required to win the election. Because the representation of states in the Electoral College is not proportional to their populations, because almost all states award electors on a winner-takes-all basis, and for other reasons (e.g., average turnout varies by state), winning in the Electoral College may not require winning the national popular vote. Indeed, a strategy that aimed to win the national popular vote could be a losing strategy in the Electoral College. This means that we should not infer from the national popular vote share that a candidate who actually wins under the existing rules would win the same vote share in a counterfactual campaign that aimed to maximize the candidate's national popular vote share.[35] This, of course, does not

---

35. Geruso et al. briefly recognize the endogeneity problem but do not attempt to evaluate the kind of counterfactual case that I suggest in the text (2022, 349). It is worth noting their conclusion that "there is no guarantee that any change to the Electoral College system,

deny that we should be troubled by the possibility that the Electoral College system can deny the presidency to the candidate who would (counterfactually) be preferred by the largest number of voters in a national campaign, or that such a "counterfactual inversion" might be more likely when a national majority would favor the Democrat than when a national majority would favor the Republican. But it underscores the fact that a normatively meaningful conception of an inversion in the Electoral College is a more complicated idea than the idea of an inversion that is ubiquitous in the literature.

We should not lose sight of the larger concern that is only intimated in Karlan's commentary. The concern is made explicit in the longer paper from which it draws.[36] She observes there that the American polity is changing due principally to the impact of changes in immigration policy dating to the 1960s. Today the share of immigrants in the total population is near a historic high. Immigration will soon account for more of the net growth in population than new births. At the same time, as I noted in the first lecture, voters have sorted into more ideologically distinct parties. Partisan identities have become increasingly aligned with other forms of identity, particularly among Republicans. That process seems to have been exacerbated by the strategic decisions of many Republican politicians to seek electoral majorities by appealing to the racial resentment that is in some measure a consequence of demographic change. In that context, partisan distortion in the Senate and the Electoral College that entrenches the power of a national Republican minority may be especially troubling. Summarizing the political result, Karlan writes:

---

short of implementing a national popular vote, will reduce the probability of inversion or of asymmetry" (2022, 354). Compare Cervas and Grofman 2019.

36. Karlan 2021.

> The worsening disjuncture between where Americans live and how the Constitution allocates political power is a major source of a new countermajoritarian difficulty, which lies not only in the courts, but in the Senate and the Electoral College as well. Put squarely, our political system may be incapable of reflecting the new majority.[37]

That prospect is ominous indeed. Karlan is not optimistic that the constitutional institutions can be reformed in ways that would enable the new majority to gain control of them. Others (like Gilens, in recent work) are more hopeful.[38]

The lectures stop short of examining practical prospects for reform, and we cannot adjudicate the disagreements here. But the conclusions converge with those of all three commentators in underscoring the urgency of the reform project. In today's political environment, representative government in America falls short of accomplishing the purposes that justify it. The urgent question is whether it can be saved by means of reforms that are actually available to us today.

---

37. Karlan 2021, 2334.
38. Page and Gilens 2020. For alternative reform proposals see, among many others, Drutman 2020a; Lessig 2019.

REFERENCES

Abramowitz, Alan I. 2010. *The Disappearing Center: Engaged Citizens, Polarization, and American Democracy*. New Haven: Yale University Press.

Abramowitz, Alan I. 2018. *The Great Alignment: Race, Party Transformation, and the Rise of Donald Trump*. New Haven: Yale University Press.

Abramowitz, Alan I., and Steven W. Webster. 2018. "Negative Partisanship: Why Americans Dislike Parties but Behave Like Rabid Partisans." *Political Psychology* 39(S1): 119–35.

Achen, Christopher H. 1978. "Measuring Representation." *American Journal of Political Science* 22(3): 475–510.

Achen, Christopher H., and Larry M. Bartels. 2017. *Democracy for Realists: Why Elections Do Not Produce Responsive Government*. Princeton: Princeton University Press.

Agmon, Shai. 2022. "Two Concepts of Competition." *Ethics* 133(1): 5–37.

Ahler, Douglas J., and David E. Broockman. 2018. "The Delegate Paradox: Why Polarized Politicians Can Represent Citizens Best." *Journal of Politics* 80(4): 1117–33.

Aldrich, John H. 2011. *Why Parties? A Second Look*. Chicago: University of Chicago Press.

Aldrich, John H. 2015. "Did Hamilton, Jefferson, and Madison 'Cause' the U.S. Government Shutdown? The Institutional Path from an Eighteenth Century Republic to a Twenty-First Century Democracy." *Perspectives on Politics* 13(1): 7–23.

Aldrich, John H., and John D. Griffin. 2018. *Why Parties Matter: Political Competition and Democracy in the American South*. Chicago: University of Chicago Press.

REFERENCES

Anderson, Elizabeth. 2010. *The Imperative of Integration*. Princeton: Princeton University Press.

Anderson, Sarah E., Daniel M. Butler, and Laurel Harbridge-Yong. 2020. *Rejecting Compromise: Legislators' Fear of Primary Voters*. Cambridge: Cambridge University Press.

Anonymous. 2020. "Note: Pack the Union." *Harvard Law Review* 133: 1049–70.

Ansolabehere, Stephen, and Shiro Kuriwaki. 2022. "Congressional Representation: Accountability from the Constituent's Perspective." *American Journal of Political Science* 66(1): 123–39.

Ansolabehere, Stephen, Maxwell Palmer, and Benjamin Schneer. 2018. "Divided Government and Significant Legislation: A History of Congress from 1789 to 2010." *Social Science History* 42(1): 81–108.

Arrow, Kenneth J. 1951. *Social Choice and Individual Values*. New York: Wiley.

Bachrach, Peter, and Morton S. Baratz. 1962. "Two Faces of Power." *American Political Science Review* 56(4): 947–52.

Bächtiger, André, John Dryzek, Jane Mansbridge, and Mark Warren. 2018. "Introduction." In *The Oxford Handbook of Deliberative Democracy*, edited by André Bächtiger, John Dryzek, Jane Mansbridge, and Mark Warren, 1–32. Oxford: Oxford University Press.

Bafumi, J., and Michael Herron. 2010. "Leapfrog Representation and Extremism: A Study of American Voters and Their Members in Congress." *American Political Science Review* 104(3): 519–42.

Bagg, Samuel, and Udit Bhatia. 2022. "Intra-party Democracy: A Functionalist Account." *Journal of Political Philosophy* 30(3): 347–69.

Balkin, Jack M. 2021. "How to Regulate (and Not Regulate) Social Media Symposium: Free Speech and Social Media Platform Regulation." *Journal of Free Speech Law* 1(1): 71–96.

Barber, Michael J. 2016. "Representing the Preferences of Donors, Partisans, and Voters in the US Senate." *Public Opinion Quarterly* 80(S1): 225–49.

Barry, Brian. 1965. *Political Argument*. London: Routledge.

Bartels, Larry M. 2016. *Unequal Democracy*. 2nd ed. Princeton: Princeton University Press.

Bartolini, Stefano. 1999. "Collusion, Competition and Democracy: Part I." *Journal of Theoretical Politics* 11(4): 435–70.

Bartolini, Stefano. 2000. "Collusion, Competition and Democracy: Part II." *Journal of Theoretical Politics* 12(1): 33–65.

Bashir, Omar S. 2015. "Testing Inferences about American Politics: A Review of the 'Oligarchy' Result." *Research & Politics* 2(4): 1–7.

Bauer, Raymond, Ithiel de Sola Poole, and Lewis Anthony Dexter. 1963. *American Business and Public Policy: The Politics of Foreign Trade*. New York: Atherton Press.

REFERENCES

Baumgartner, Frank R., Jeffrey M. Berry, Marie Hojnacki, Beth L. Leech, and David C. Kimball. 2009. *Lobbying and Policy Change: Who Wins, Who Loses, and Why.* Chicago: University of Chicago Press.

Beerbohm, Eric. 2012. *In Our Name: The Ethics of Democracy.* Princeton: Princeton University Press.

Beitz, Charles R. 1989. *Political Equality: An Essay in Democratic Theory.* Princeton: Princeton University Press.

Beitz, Charles R. 2018. "How Is Partisan Gerrymandering Unfair?" *Philosophy & Public Affairs* 46(3): 323–58.

Benkler, Yochai, Robert Faris, and Hal Roberts. 2018. *Network Propaganda: Manipulation, Disinformation, and Radicalization in American Politics.* New York: Oxford University Press.

Bentley, Arthur F. 1908. *The Process of Government: A Study of Social Pressures.* Chicago: University of Chicago Press.

Bianco, William T. 1994. *Trust: Representatives and Constituents.* Ann Arbor: University of Michigan Press.

Binder, Sarah A. 2003. *Stalemate: Causes and Consequences of Legislative Gridlock.* Washington, DC: Brookings Institution Press.

Binder, Sarah A. 2015. "The Dysfunctional Congress." *Annual Review of Political Science* 18(1): 85–101.

Binder, Sarah A. 2021. "Legislative Stalemate in Postwar America, 1947–2018." In *Dynamics of American Democracy*, edited by Eric M. Patashnik and Wendy J. Schiller, 65–86. Lawrence: University Press of Kansas.

Birch, Anthony Harold. 1971. *Representation.* London: Pall Mall Press.

Black, Oliver. 2005. *Conceptual Foundations of Antitrust.* Cambridge: Cambridge University Press.

Bonica, Adam, and Gary W. Cox. 2018. "Ideological Extremists in the U.S. Congress: Out of Step but Still in Office." *Quarterly Journal of Political Science* 13(2): 207–36.

Bonica, Adam, Nolan McCarty, Keith T. Poole, and Howard Rosenthal. 2013. "Why Hasn't Democracy Slowed Rising Inequality?" *Journal of Economic Perspectives* 27(3): 103–23.

Brady, David W., and Craig Volden. 2006. *Revolving Gridlock: Politics and Policy from Jimmy Carter to George W. Bush.* 2nd ed. New York: Avalon Publishing.

Brady, Henry E., and Thomas B. Kent. 2022. "Fifty Years of Declining Confidence & Increasing Polarization in Trust in American Institutions." *Daedalus* 151(4): 43–66.

Branham, J. Alexander, Stuart N. Soroka, and Christopher Wlezien. 2017. "When Do the Rich Win?" *Political Science Quarterly* 132(1): 43–62.

Brennan, Geoffrey, and Alan P. Hamlin. 2000. *Democratic Devices and Desires.* Cambridge: Cambridge University Press.

REFERENCES

Broockman, David E. 2014. "Distorted Communication, Unequal Representation: Constituents Communicate Less to Representatives Not of Their Race." *American Journal of Political Science* 58(2): 307–21.

Broockman, David E., Joshua L. Kalla, and Sean J. Westwood. 2023. "Does Affective Polarization Undermine Democratic Norms or Accountability? Maybe Not." *American Journal of Political Science* 67(3): 808–28.

Brunell, Thomas. 2008. *Redistricting and Representation: Why Competitive Elections Are Bad for America*. New York: Routledge.

Bryce, James. 1888. *The American Commonwealth*. 3 vols. New York: Macmillan.

Buchler, Justin. 2011. *Hiring and Firing Public Officials: Rethinking the Purpose of Elections*. New York: Oxford University Press.

Burns, James MacGregor. 1963. *The Deadlock of Democracy: Four-Party Politics in America*. Englewood Cliffs, NJ: Prentice-Hall.

Butler, D. E. 1947. "Appendix III: The Relation of Seats to Votes." In *The British General Election of 1945*, by R. B. McCallum and Alison Violet Readham, 277–92. London: Oxford University Press.

Butler, Daniel M. 2014. *Representing the Advantaged: How Politicians Reinforce Inequality*. Cambridge: Cambridge University Press.

Butler, Daniel M., and David E. Broockman. 2011. "Do Politicians Racially Discriminate Against Constituents? A Field Experiment on State Legislators." *American Journal of Political Science* 55(3): 463–77.

Cain, Bruce E. 2015. *Democracy More or Less*. New York: Cambridge University Press.

Canes-Wrone, Brandice. 2015. "From Mass Preferences to Policy." *Annual Review of Political Science* 18(1): 147–65.

Canes-Wrone, Brandice, and Nathan Gibson. 2019. "Developments in Congressional Responsiveness to Donor Opinion." In *Can America Govern Itself?*, edited by Frances E. Lee and Nolan McCarty, 69–92. Cambridge: Cambridge University Press.

Canes-Wrone, Brandice, and Kenneth M. Miller. 2022. "Out-of-District Donors and Representation in the US House." *Legislative Studies Quarterly* 47(2): 361–95.

Carnes, Nicholas. 2013. *White-Collar Government: The Hidden Role of Class in Economic Policy Making*. Chicago: University of Chicago Press.

Carnes, Nicholas, and Noam Lupu. 2021. "The White Working Class and the 2016 Election." *Perspectives on Politics* 19(1): 55–72.

Castle, Jeremiah J., and Kyla K. Stepp. 2021. "Partisanship, Religion, and Issue Polarization in the United States: A Reassessment." *Political Behavior* 43(3): 1311–35.

Caughey, Devin. 2018. *The Unsolid South: Mass Politics and National Representation in a One-Party Enclave*. Princeton: Princeton University Press.

Caughey, Devin, and Christopher Warshaw. 2018. "Policy Preferences and Policy Change: Dynamic Responsiveness in the American States, 1936–2014." *American Political Science Review* 112(2): 49–66.

REFERENCES

Cervas, Jonathan R., and Bernard Grofman. 2019. "Are Presidential Inversions Inevitable? Comparing Eight Counterfactual Rules for Electing the U.S. President." *Social Science Quarterly* 100(4): 1322–42.

Charnock, Emily J. 2020. *The Rise of Political Action Committees: Interest Group Electioneering and the Transformation of American Politics.* New York: Oxford University Press.

Chen, Jowei, and Jonathan Rodden. 2013. "Unintentional Gerrymandering: Political Geography and Electoral Bias in Legislatures." *Quarterly Journal of Political Science* 8(3): 239–69.

Christiano, Thomas. 1996. *The Rule of the Many: Fundamental Issues in Democratic Theory.* New York: Routledge.

Cobb, Roger W., and Charles D. Elder. 1983. *Participation in American Politics: The Dynamics of Agenda-Building.* 2nd ed. Baltimore: Johns Hopkins University Press.

Cohen, Joshua. 2003. "For a Democratic Society." In *The Cambridge Companion to Rawls*, edited by Samuel Freeman, 86–138. Cambridge: Cambridge University Press.

Cohen, Joshua. 2009. "Money, Politics, Political Equality." *Philosophy, Politics, Democracy: Selected Essays*, 268–302. Cambridge, MA: Harvard University Press.

Committee on Political Parties, American Political Science Association. 1950. "Toward a More Responsible Two-Party System." *American Political Science Review* 44(3; Supplement): 1–96.

Conti, Gregory. 2019. *Parliament the Mirror of the Nation: Representation, Deliberation, and Democracy in Victorian Britain.* Cambridge: Cambridge University Press.

Cook Political Report. 2020. *National Popular Vote Tracker.* https://www.cookpolitical.com/2020-national-popular-vote-tracker.

Crespin, Michael H. 2010. "Serving Two Masters: Redistricting and Voting in the U.S. House of Representatives." *Political Research Quarterly* 63(4): 850–59.

Curiel, John A., and Tyler Steelman. 2018. "Redistricting Out Representation: Democratic Harms in Splitting Zip Codes." *Election Law Journal: Rules, Politics, and Policy* 17(4): 328–53.

Curry, James M., and Frances E. Lee. 2020. *The Limits of Party: Congress and Lawmaking in a Polarized Era.* Chicago: University of Chicago Press.

Dahl, Robert A. 1956. *A Preface to Democratic Theory.* Chicago: University of Chicago Press.

Dahl, Robert A. 1961. *Who Governs? Democracy and Power in an American City.* New Haven: Yale University Press.

Dahl, Robert A. 1967. *Pluralist Democracy in the United States: Conflict and Consent.* Chicago: Rand McNally.

Dahl, Robert A. 1982. *Dilemmas of Pluralist Democracy: Autonomy vs. Control.* New Haven: Yale University Press.

REFERENCES

Dahl, Robert A., and Charles E. Lindblom. 1953. *Politics, Economic and Welfare: Planning and Politico-Economic Systems Resolved into Basic Social Processes.* New York: Harper and Brothers.

DeFord, Daryl R., Nicholas Eubank, and Jonathan Rodden. 2021. "Partisan Dislocation: A Precinct-Level Measure of Representation and Gerrymandering." *Political Analysis* 30(3): 403–25.

Dias, Nicholas, and Yphtach Lelkes. 2021. "The Nature of Affective Polarization: Disentangling Policy Disagreement from Partisan Identity." *American Journal of Political Science* 66(3): 775–90.

Disch, Lisa Jane. 2002. *The Tyranny of the Two-Party System.* New York: Columbia University Press.

Disch, Lisa Jane. 2021. *Making Constituencies: Representation as Mobilization in Mass Democracy.* Chicago: University of Chicago Press.

Dowding, Keith M. 1991. *Rational Choice and Political Power.* Aldershot, Hants: E. Elgar.

Downs, Anthony. 1957. *An Economic Theory of Democracy.* New York: Harper.

Druckman, James N., and Lawrence R. Jacobs. 2015. *Who Governs? Presidents, Public Opinion, and Manipulation.* Chicago: University of Chicago Press.

Drutman, Lee. 2015. *The Business of America Is Lobbying: How Corporations Became Politicized and Politics Became More Corporate.* New York: Oxford University Press.

Drutman, Lee. 2020a. *Breaking the Two-Party Doom Loop: The Case for Multiparty Democracy in America.* New York: Oxford University Press.

Drutman, Lee. 2020b. "The Republican and Democratic Parties Are Heading for Collapse." *Foreign Policy*, September 22, 2020. https://foreignpolicy.com/2020/09/22/two-party-collapse-republican-democrat-doom-loop/.

Drutman, Lee. 2020c. "The Senate Has Always Favored Smaller States. It Just Didn't Help Republicans until Now." *Five-Thirty-Eight.* July 29, 2020. https://perma.cc/GN4B-FTJ6.

Drutman, Lee. 2021. "Elections, Political Parties, and Multiracial, Multiethnic Democracy: How the United States Gets It Wrong Symposium." *New York University Law Review* 96(4): 985–1020.

Drutman, Lee, and Timothy M. LaPira. 2020. "Capacity for What? Legislative Capacity Regimes in Congress and the Possibilities for Reform." In *Congress Overwhelmed: The Decline in Congressional Capacity and Prospects for Reform*, edited by Timothy M. LaPira, Lee Drutman, and Kevin R. Kosar, 11–33. Chicago: University of Chicago Press.

Drutman, Lee, and Christine Mahoney. 2017. "On the Advantages of a Well-Constructed Lobbying System: Toward a More Democratic, Modern Lobbying Process." *Interest Groups & Advocacy* 6(3): 290–310.

Dryzek, John S. 2010. *Foundations and Frontiers of Deliberative Governance.* Oxford: Oxford University Press.

REFERENCES

Dryzek, John S., André Bächtiger, Simone Chambers, Joshua Cohen, James N. Druckman, Andrea Felicetti, James S. Fishkin, et al. 2019. "The Crisis of Democracy and the Science of Deliberation." *Science* 363(6432): 1144–46.

Dunn, John. 2019. *Setting the People Free: The Story of Democracy*. 2nd ed. Princeton: Princeton University Press.

Duverger, Maurice. 1954. *Political Parties, Their Organization and Activity in the Modern State*. Translated by Barbara and Robert North. London: Methuen.

Dworkin, Ronald. 2000. *Sovereign Virtue: The Theory and Practice of Equality*. Cambridge, MA: Harvard University Press.

Edmundson, William A. 2020. "What Is the Argument for the Fair Value of Political Liberty?" *Social Theory and Practice* 46(3): 497–514.

Eisgruber, Christopher L. 2001. *Constitutional Self-Government*. Cambridge, MA: Harvard University Press.

Elgin, Catherine Z. 2017. *True Enough*. Cambridge, MA: MIT Press.

Elkjær, Mads Andreas, and Michael Baggesen Klitgaard. 2021. "Economic Inequality and Political Responsiveness: A Systematic Review." *Perspectives on Politics* 2021: 1–20. https://doi.org/10.1017/S1537592721002188.

Ellis, Christopher. 2017. *Putting Inequality in Context: Class, Public Opinion, and Representation in the United States*. Ann Arbor: University of Michigan Press.

Emerson, Blake. 2019. *The Public's Law: Origins and Architecture of Progressive Democracy*. New York: Oxford University Press.

Emmett, Ross B. 2009. *Frank Knight and the Chicago School in American Economics*. London: Routledge.

Enns, Peter K. 2015. "Relative Policy Support and Coincidental Representation." *Perspectives on Politics* 13(4): 1053–64.

Erikson, Robert S. 1972. "Malapportionment, Gerrymandering, and Party Fortunes in Congressional Elections." *American Political Science Review* 66(4): 1234–45.

Estlund, David. 2008. *Democratic Authority: A Philosophical Framework*. Princeton: Princeton University Press.

Eulau, Heinz, and Paul D. Karps. 1977. "The Puzzle of Representation: Specifying Components of Responsiveness." *Legislative Studies Quarterly* 2(3): 233–54.

Fenno, Richard E., Jr. 1978. *Home Style: House Members in Their Districts*. Boston: Little, Brown.

Finkel, Eli J., Christopher A. Bail, Mina Cikara, Peter H. Ditto, Shanto Iyengar, Samara Klar, Lilliana Mason, et al. 2020. "Political Sectarianism in America." *Science* 370(6516): 533–36.

Fiorina, Morris P. 1996. *Divided Government*. 2nd ed. Boston: Allyn and Bacon.

Fiorina, Morris P. 2017. *Unstable Majorities: Polarization, Party Sorting, and Political Stalemate*. Stanford: Hoover Institution Press.

Fiorina, Morris P. 2021. "How to Cure the Ills of Contemporary American Democracy? A Review Essay." *Political Science Quarterly* 136(4): 741–50.

REFERENCES

Fiorina, Morris P., and Samuel J. Abrams. 2009. *Disconnect: The Breakdown of Representation in American Politics*. Norman: University of Oklahoma Press.

Fishkin, James S. 1995. *The Voice of the People: Public Opinion and Democracy*. New Haven: Yale University Press.

Fishkin, James S. 2009. *When the People Speak*. Oxford: Oxford University Press.

Fishkin, James S. 2019. "Critical Dialogue." Review of *Politics with the People: Building a Directly Representative Democracy*, by Michael A. Neblo, Kevin M. Esterling, and David M. J. Lazer (New York: Cambridge University Press, 2018). *Perspectives on Politics* 17(2): 527–28.

Fishkin, James S., and Robert C. Luskin. 1999. "Bringing Deliberation to the Democratic Dialogue." In *A Poll with a Human Face*, edited by Max McCombs and Amy Reynolds, 3–38. Mahwah, NJ: Lawrence Erlbaum Associates.

Follett, Mary Parker. 1918. *The New State: Group Organization the Solution of Popular Government*. New York: Longmans, Green.

Forrester, Katrina. 2019. *In the Shadow of Justice: Postwar Liberalism and the Remaking of Political Philosophy*. Princeton: Princeton University Press.

Fowler, Anthony, Seth Hill, Jeff Lewis, Chris Tausanovitch, Lynn Vavreck, and Christopher Warshaw. 2023. "Moderates." *American Political Science Review* 117(2): 643–60.

Fraga, Bernard L. 2018. *The Turnout Gap: Race, Ethnicity, and Political Inequality in a Diversifying America*. Cambridge: Cambridge University Press.

Frymer, Paul. 1999. *Uneasy Alliances: Race and Party Competition in America*. Princeton: Princeton University Press.

Gallup. 2023. "Confidence in Institutions Down." https://news.gallup.com/poll/1597/confidence-institutions.aspx.

Gardner, Amy, and Paulina Firozi. 2021. "Here's the Full Transcript and Audio of the Call between Trump and Raffensperger." *Washington Post*, January 5, 2021. https://www.washingtonpost.com/politics/trump-raffensperger-call-transcript-georgia-vote/2021/01/03/2768e0cc-4ddd-11eb-83e3-322644d82356_story.html.

Garson, G. David. 1974. "On the Origins of Interest-Group Theory: A Critique of a Process." *American Political Science Review* 68(4): 1505–19.

Gay, Claudine. 2002. "Spirals of Trust? The Effect of Descriptive Representation on the Relationship between Citizens and Their Government." *American Journal of Political Science* 46(4): 717–32.

Geruso, Michael, Dean Spears, and Ishaana Talesara. 2022. "Inversions in US Presidential Elections: 1836–2016." *American Economic Journal: Applied Economics* 14(1): 327–57.

Gilens, Martin. 2012. *Affluence and Influence: Economic Inequality and Political Power in America*. New York: Russell Sage Foundation.

Gilens, Martin. 2015. "The Insufficiency of 'Democracy by Coincidence': A Response to Peter K. Enns." *Perspectives on Politics* 13(4): 1065–71.

REFERENCES

Gilens, Martin, and Benjamin I. Page. 2014. "Testing Theories of American Politics: Elites, Interest Groups, and Average Citizens." *Perspectives on Politics* 12(3): 564–81.

Gilens, Martin, Shawn Patterson, and Pavielle Haines. 2021. "Campaign Finance Regulations and Public Policy." *American Political Science Review* 115(3): 1074–81.

Glock, Judge. 2022. "The Mismeasurement of Polarization." *National Affairs*, no. 50: 16–26.

Golder, Matt, and Jacek Stramski. 2010. "Ideological Congruence and Electoral Institutions." *American Journal of Political Science* 54(1): 90–106.

Goldman, Alvin I. 1999. "Why Citizens Should Vote: A Causal Responsibility Approach." *Social Philosophy and Policy* 16(2): 201–17.

Goodin, Robert E. 2008. *Innovating Democracy: Democratic Theory and Practice after the Deliberative Turn*. Oxford: Oxford University Press.

Gould, Jonathan, Kenneth Shepsle, and Matthew Stephenson. 2021. "Democratizing the Senate from Within." *Journal of Legal Analysis* 13(1): 502–57.

Graham, Matthew H., and Lilla V. Orr. 2020. "What Would Delegates Do? When and How the Delegate Paradox Affects Estimates of Ideological Congruence." *Electoral Studies* 63: 102–9.

Green, Jeffrey Edward. 2010. "Three Theses on Schumpeter: Response to Mackie." *Political Theory* 38(2): 268–75.

Griffin, John D. 2006a. "Electoral Competition and Democratic Responsiveness: A Defense of the Marginality Hypothesis." *Journal of Politics* 68(4): 911–21.

Griffin, John D. 2006b. "Senate Apportionment as a Source of Political Inequality." *Legislative Studies Quarterly* 31(3): 405–32.

Griffin, John D., and Brian Newman. 2008. *Minority Report: Evaluating Political Equality in America*. Chicago: University of Chicago Press.

Grill, Christopher J. 2007. *The Public Side of Representation: A Study of Citizens' Views about Representation and the Representative Process*. Albany: State University of New York Press.

Grossmann, Matt, and David A. Hopkins. 2016. *Asymmetric Politics: Ideological Republicans and Group Interest Democrats*. New York: Oxford University Press.

Grossmann, Matt, Zuhaib Mahmood, and William Isaac. 2021. "Political Parties, Interest Groups, and Unequal Class Influence in American Policy." *Journal of Politics* 83(4): 1706–20.

Grumbach, Jacob M. 2022. *Laboratories against Democracy: How National Parties Transformed State Politics*. Princeton: Princeton University Press.

Grumbach, Jacob M., and Alexander Sahn. 2020. "Race and Representation in Campaign Finance." *American Political Science Review* 114(1): 206–21.

Gudgin, Graham, and Peter John Taylor. 1979. *Seats, Votes, and the Spatial Organisation of Elections*. London: Pion.

REFERENCES

Guerrero, Alexander A. 2014. "Against Elections: The Lottocratic Alternative." *Philosophy & Public Affairs* 42(2): 135–78.

Guinier, Lani. 1994. *The Tyranny of the Majority: Fundamental Fairness in Representative Democracy*. New York: Free Press.

Habermas, Jürgen. 1974. "The Public Sphere: An Encyclopedia Article [1964]." Translated by Sara Lennox and Frank Lennox. *New German Critique*, no. 3: 49–55.

Habermas, Jürgen. 1996. *Between Facts and Norms: Contributions to a Discourse Theory of Law and Democracy*. Translated by William Rehg. Cambridge, MA: MIT Press.

Hacker, Jacob S. 2004. "Privatizing Risk without Privatizing the Welfare State: The Hidden Politics of Social Policy Retrenchment in the United States." *American Political Science Review* 98(2): 243–60.

Hacker, Jacob S., and Paul Pierson. 2010. *Winner-Take-All Politics: How Washington Made the Rich Richer—and Turned Its Back on the Middle Class*. New York: Simon and Schuster.

Hacker, Jacob S., and Paul Pierson. 2014. "After the 'Master Theory': Downs, Schattschneider, and the Rebirth of Policy-Focused Analysis." *Perspectives on Politics* 12(3): 643–62.

Hacker, Jacob S., and Paul Pierson. 2015. "Confronting Asymmetric Polarization." In *Solutions to Political Polarization in America*, edited by Nathaniel Persily, 59–70. Cambridge: Cambridge University Press.

Hacker, Jacob S., and Paul Pierson. 2016. *American Amnesia: How the War on Government Led Us to Forget What Made America Prosper*. New York: Simon & Schuster.

Hacker, Jacob S., and Paul Pierson. 2020. *Let Them Eat Tweets: How the Right Rules in an Age of Extreme Inequality*. New York: Liveright.

Hajnal, Zoltan L. 2020. *Dangerously Divided: How Race and Class Shape Winning and Losing in American Politics*. Cambridge: Cambridge University Press.

Hall, Richard L., and Alan V. Deardorff. 2006. "Lobbying as Legislative Subsidy." *American Political Science Review* 100(1): 69–84.

Hall, Richard L., and Frank W. Wayman. 1990. "Buying Time: Moneyed Interests and the Mobilization of Bias in Congressional Committees." *American Political Science Review* 84(3): 797–820.

Harris, Fredrick C., and Viviana Rivera-Burgos. 2021. "The Continuing Dilemma of Race and Class in the Study of American Political Behavior." *Annual Review of Political Science* 24(1): 175–91.

Hasen, Richard L. 1998. "The 'Political Market' Metaphor and Election Law: A Comment on Issacharoff and Pildes." *Stanford Law Review* 50(3): 719–30.

Hasen, Richard L. 2012. "Lobbying, Rent-Seeking, and the Constitution." *Stanford Law Review* 64(1): 191–254.

Hasen, Richard L. 2016. *Plutocrats United: Campaign Money, the Supreme Court, and the Distortion of American Elections*. New Haven: Yale University Press.

REFERENCES

Haslam, Alex, Penny Oakes, John Turner, and Craig McGarty. 1996. "Social Identity, Self-Categorization, and the Perceived Homogeneity of Ingroups and Outgroups: The Interaction between Social Motivation and Cognition." In *Handbook of Motivation and Cognition: Foundations of Social Behavior*, edited by Richard Sorrentino and Edward Higgins, vol. 3, 182–222. New York: Guilford Press.

Heath, Joseph. 2014. *Morality, Competition, and the Firm: The Market Failures Approach to Business Ethics*. New York: Oxford University Press.

Hertel-Fernandez, Alexander. 2019. *State Capture: How Conservative Activists, Big Businesses, and Wealthy Donors Reshaped the American States—and the Nation*. New York: Oxford University Press.

Herzog, Lisa. Forthcoming. "How Much (and What Kind of) Economic Competition Is Compatible with Democratic Competition?" In *Democracy and Competition: Rethinking the Forms, Purposes, and Values of Competition in Democracy*, edited by Alfred Moore and Samuel Bragg. Oxford: Oxford University Press.

Hill, Seth J., and Gregory A. Huber. 2017. "Representativeness and Motivations of the Contemporary Donorate: Results from Merged Survey and Administrative Records." *Political Behavior* 39(1): 3–29.

Hill, Seth J., and Chris Tausanovitch. 2015. "A Disconnect in Representation? Comparison of Trends in Congressional and Public Polarization." *Journal of Politics* 77(4): 1058–75.

Hobbes, Thomas. [1651] 1994. *Leviathan*. Edited by Edwin Curley. Indianapolis: Hackett.

Hofstadter, Richard. 1948. *The American Political Tradition and the Men Who Made It*. New York: Knopf.

Holst, Catherine, and Silje Aambø Langvatn. 2021. "Descriptive Representation of Women in International Courts." *Journal of Social Philosophy* 52(4): 473–90.

Hotelling, Harold. 1929. "Stability in Competition." *Economic Journal* 39: 41–57.

Howell, William G., and Terry M. Moe. 2016. *Relic: How Our Constitution Undermines Effective Government, and Why We Need a More Powerful Presidency*. New York: Basic Books.

Hussain, Waheed. 2018. "Why Should We Care about Competition?" *Critical Review of International Social and Political Philosophy* 21(5): 570–85.

Hussain, Waheed. 2020. "Pitting People against Each Other." *Philosophy & Public Affairs* 48(1): 79–113.

Hutchings, Vincent L., Harwood K. McClerking, and Guy-Uriel Charles. 2004. "Congressional Representation of Black Interests: Recognizing the Importance of Stability." *Journal of Politics* 66(2): 450–68.

Ingham, Sean. 2016. "Popular Rule in Schumpeter's Democracy." *Political Studies* 64(4): 1071–87.

REFERENCES

Issacharoff, Samuel. 2001. "Private Parties with Public Purposes: Political Parties, Associational Freedoms, and Partisan Competition." *Columbia Law Review* 101(2): 274–313.

Issacharoff, Samuel. 2018. "Democracy's Deficits." *University of Chicago Law Review* 85(2): 485–520.

Issacharoff, Samuel, and Pamela S. Karlan. 1998a. "Standing and Misunderstanding in Voting Rights Law Commentary." *Harvard Law Review* 111(8): 2276–93.

Issacharoff, Samuel, and Pamela S. Karlan. 1998b. "Hydraulics of Campaign Finance Reform." *Texas Law Review* 77(7): 1705–38.

Issacharoff, Samuel, and Pamela S. Karlan. 2004. "Where to Draw the Line: Judicial Review of Political Gerrymanders." *University of Pennsylvania Law Review* 153(1): 541–78.

Issacharoff, Samuel, Pamela S. Karlan, Richard H. Pildes, Nathaniel Persily, and Franita Tolson. 2022. *The Law of Democracy: Legal Structure of the Political Process*. 6th ed. St. Paul, MN: Foundation Press, West Academic.

Issacharoff, Samuel, and Richard H. Pildes. 1998. "Politics as Markets: Partisan Lockups of the Democratic Process." *Stanford Law Review* 50(3): 643–717.

Iyengar, Shanto, Yphtach Lelkes, Matthew Levendusky, Neil Malhotra, and Sean J. Westwood. 2019. "The Origins and Consequences of Affective Polarization in the United States." *Annual Review of Political Science* 22: 129–46.

Jacobson, Gary C. 2015. "How Do Campaigns Matter?" *Annual Review of Political Science* 18: 31–47.

Jacobson, Gary C., and Jamie L. Carson. 2020. *The Politics of Congressional Elections*. 10th ed. Lanham, MD: Rowman & Littlefield.

Jones, Philip Edward. 2013. "The Effect of Political Competition on Democratic Accountability." *Political Behavior* 35(3): 481–515.

Kahn, Alfie. 1992. *No Contest: The Case against Competition*. Boston: Houghton Mifflin.

Kaldor, Nicholas. 1961. "Capital Accumulation and Economic Growth." In *The Theory of Capital*, edited by F. A. Lutz and D. C. Hague, 177–222. London: Macmillan.

Kalla, Joshua L., and David E. Broockman. 2016. "Campaign Contributions Facilitate Access to Congressional Officials: A Randomized Field Experiment." *American Journal of Political Science* 60(3): 545–58.

Kalla, Joshua L., and David E. Broockman. 2018. "The Minimal Persuasive Effects of Campaign Contact in General Elections: Evidence from 49 Field Experiments." *American Political Science Review* 112(1): 148–66.

Kanthak, Kristin, and Jonathan Woon. 2015. "Women Don't Run? Election Aversion and Candidate Entry." *American Journal of Political Science* 59(3): 595–612.

Karlan, Pamela S. 1993. "The Rights to Vote: Some Pessimism about Formalism." *Texas Law Review* 71: 1705–40.

Karlan, Pamela S. 2018. "Reapportionment, Nonapportionment, and Recovering Some Lost History of One Person, One Vote." *William and Mary Law Review* 59: 1921–59.

REFERENCES

Karlan, Pamela S. 2021. "The New Countermajoritarian Difficulty." *California Law Review* 109(6): 2323–55.

Kateb, George. 1981. "The Moral Distinctiveness of Representative Democracy." *Ethics* 91: 357–74.

Katz, Jonathan N., Gary King, and Elizabeth Rosenblatt. 2020. "Theoretical Foundations and Empirical Evaluations of Partisan Fairness in District-Based Democracies." *American Political Science Review* 114(1): 164–78.

Keena, Alex, Michael Latner, Anthony J. McGann, and Charles Anthony Smith. 2021. *Gerrymandering the States: Partisanship, Race, and the Transformation of American Federalism.* Cambridge: Cambridge University Press.

Kelly, Nathan J. 2019. *America's Inequality Trap.* Chicago: University of Chicago Press.

Kennedy, Caleb. 2012. "Scalia Defends Gay Rights Position." *Daily Princetonian*, December 11, 2012, 1.

Kenny, Christopher T., Cory McCartan, Tyler Simko, Shiro Kuriwaki, and Kosuke Imai. 2022. "Widespread Partisan Gerrymandering Mostly Cancels Nationally, but Reduces Electoral Competition." *arXiv.* http://arxiv.org/abs/2208.06968, accessed August 17, 2022.

Kernell, Samuel. 2003. "'True Principles of Republican Government': Reassessing James Madison's Political Science." In *James Madison: The Theory and Practice of Republican Government*, edited by Samuel Kernell, 92–125. Stanford: Stanford University Press.

Key, V. O. 1942. *Politics, Parties and Pressure Groups.* New York: Thomas Y. Crowell.

Key, V. O. 1949. *Southern Politics in State and Nation.* New York: Knopf.

Key, V. O. 1952. *Politics, Parties, and Pressure Groups.* 3rd ed. New York: Crowell.

Key, V. O. 1961. *Public Opinion and American Democracy.* New York: Knopf.

Keyssar, Alexander. 2020. *Why Do We Still Have the Electoral College?* Cambridge, MA: Harvard University Press.

Kinder, Donald R., and Nathan P. Kalmoe. 2017. *Neither Liberal Nor Conservative: Ideological Innocence in the American Public.* Chicago: University of Chicago Press.

King, Gary, and Robert X. Browning. 1987. "Democratic Representation and Partisan Bias in Congressional Elections." *American Political Science Review* 81(4): 1251–73.

Kingdon, John W. 1981. *Congressmen's Voting Decisions.* New York: Harper and Row.

Klarman, Michael J. 2016. *The Framers' Coup: The Making of the United States Constitution.* New York: Oxford University Press.

Klein, Ezra. 2020. *Why We're Polarized.* New York: Simon & Schuster.

Kloppenberg, James T. 2016. *Toward Democracy: The Struggle for Self-Rule in European and American Thought.* New York: Oxford University Press.

Knight, Frank H. 1921. *Risk, Uncertainty and Profit.* Boston: Houghton Mifflin.

Knight, Frank H. 1935. *The Ethics of Competition and Other Essays.* New York: Harper & Brothers.

REFERENCES

Kolodny, Niko. 2019. "What, If Anything, Is Wrong with Gerrymandering?" *San Diego Law Review* 56(4): 1013-38.

Kolodny, Niko. 2023. *The Pecking Order: Social Hierarchy as a Philosophical Problem.* Cambridge, MA: Harvard University Press.

Krehbiel, Keith. 1998. *Pivotal Politics: A Theory of U.S. Lawmaking.* Chicago: University of Chicago Press.

Kristol, Irving. 1978. *Two Cheers for Capitalism.* New York: Basic Books.

Krouse, Richard W. 1982. "Two Concepts of Democratic Representation: James and John Stuart Mill." *Journal of Politics* 44(2): 509-37.

La Raja, Raymond, and Brian Schaffner. 2015. *Campaign Finance and Political Polarization: When Purists Prevail.* Ann Arbor: University of Michigan Press.

Landemore, Hélène. 2020. *Open Democracy: Reinventing Popular Rule for the Twenty-First Century.* Princeton University Press.

LaPira, Timothy M., Lee Drutman, and Kevin R. Kosar. 2020. "Overwhelmed: An Introduction to Congress's Capacity Problem." In *Congress Overwhelmed: The Decline in Congressional Capacity and Prospects for Reform* edited by Timothy M. LaPira, Lee Drutman, and Kevin R. Kosar, 1-7. Chicago: University of Chicago Press.

Laruelle, Annick, and Federico Valenciano. 2008. *Voting and Collective Decision-Making: Bargaining and Power.* Cambridge: Cambridge University Press.

LaVaque-Manty, Mika. 2006. "Bentley, Truman, and the Study of Groups." *Annual Review of Political Science* 9: 1-18.

Lax, Jeffrey R., and Justin H. Phillips. 2012. "The Democratic Deficit in the States." *American Journal of Political Science* 56(1): 148-66.

Lax, Jeffrey R., Justin H. Phillips, and Adam Zelizer. 2019. "The Party or the Purse? Unequal Representation in the US Senate." *American Political Science Review* 113(4): 917-40.

Lee, Frances E. 2009. *Beyond Ideology: Politics, Principles, and Partisanship in the U.S. Senate.* Chicago: University of Chicago Press.

Lee, Frances E. 2016. *Insecure Majorities: Congress and the Perpetual Campaign.* Chicago: University of Chicago Press.

Lee, Frances E., and Bruce I. Oppenheimer. 1999. *Sizing up the Senate: The Unequal Consequences of Equal Representation.* Chicago: University of Chicago Press.

Leighley, Jan E., and Jonathan Nagler. 2013. *Who Votes Now? Demographics, Issues, Inequality, and Turnout in the United States.* Princeton: Princeton University Press.

Lessig, Lawrence. 2015. *Republic Lost: The Corruption of Equality and the Steps to End It.* Rev. ed. New York: Twelve.

Lessig, Lawrence. 2019. *They Don't Represent Us: Reclaiming Our Democracy.* New York: Dey Street.

Levendusky, Matthew. 2009. *The Partisan Sort: How Liberals Became Democrats and Conservatives Became Republicans.* Chicago: University of Chicago Press.

REFERENCES

Levinson, Daryl J., and Richard H. Pildes. 2006. "Separation of Parties, Not Powers." *Harvard Law Review* 119(8): 2311–86.

Levinson, Daryl J., and Benjamin I. Sachs. 2015. "Political Entrenchment and Public Law." *Yale Law Journal* 125(2): 400–482.

Levitsky, Steven, and Daniel Ziblatt. 2018. *How Democracies Die*. New York: Crown.

Lijphart, Arend. 2012. *Patterns of Democracy: Government Forms and Performance in Thirty-Six Countries*. New Haven: Yale University Press.

Lindsay, A. D. 1935. *The Essentials of Democracy*. 2nd ed. London: Oxford University Press.

Lipsitz, Keena. 2011. *Competitive Elections and the American Voter*. Philadelphia: University of Pennsylvania Press.

Locke, John. [1679–89] 1967. *Two Treatises of Government*. Edited by Peter Laslett, 2nd edn. Cambridge: Cambridge University Press.

MacCallum, Gerald C. 1993. "Competition and Moral Philosophy." In *Legislative Intent and Other Essays on Law, Politics, and Morality*, edited by Marcus G. Singer and Rex Martin, 203–223. Madison: University of Wisconsin Press.

Macedo, Stephen. 2010. "Against Majoritarianism: Democratic Values and Institutional Design." *Boston University Law Review* 90(2): 1029–42.

Madison, James. 1966. *Notes of Debates in the Federal Convention of 1787*. Edited by Adrienne Koch. Athens: Ohio University Press.

Madison, James. [1787] 2001a. "No. 10." In *The Federalist*, by Alexander Hamilton, James Madison, and John Jay, 42–49. Gideon edition. Indianapolis: Liberty Fund.

Madison, James. [1788] 2001b. "No. 62." In *The Federalist*, by Alexander Hamilton, James Madison, and John Jay, 319–24. Gideon edition. Indianapolis: Liberty Fund.

Madison, James. [1788] 2001c. "No. 63." In *The Federalist*, by Alexander Hamilton, James Madison, and John Jay. Gideon ed., 325–32. Indianapolis: Liberty Fund.

Maks-Solomon, Cory, and Elizabeth Rigby. 2020. "Are Democrats Really the Party of the Poor? Partisanship, Class, and Representation in the U.S. Senate." *Political Research Quarterly* 73(4): 848–65.

Manin, Bernard. 1997. *The Principles of Representative Government*. Cambridge: Cambridge University Press.

Manley, John F. 1983. "Neo-pluralism: A Class Analysis of Pluralism I and Pluralism II." *American Political Science Review* 77(2): 368–83.

Mann, Thomas E., and E. J. Dionne. 2015. *"The Futility of Nostalgia and the Romanticism of the New Political Realists."* Washington, DC: Brookings Institution Press.

Mansbridge, Jane. 1980. *Beyond Adversary Democracy*. Chicago: University of Chicago Press.

Mansbridge, Jane. 1986. *Why We Lost the ERA*. Chicago: University of Chicago Press.

REFERENCES

Mansbridge, Jane. 1992. "A Deliberative Theory of Interest Representation." In *The Politics Of Interests: Interest Groups Transformed*, edited by Mark P. Petracca, 32–57. Boulder: Westview.

Mansbridge, Jane. 1994. "Using Power / Fighting Power." *Constellations* 1(1): 53–73.

Mansbridge, Jane. 1999a. "Everyday Talk in the Deliberative System." In *Deliberative Politics: Essays on Democracy and Disagreement*, edited by Stephen Macedo, 211–39. New York: Oxford University Press.

Mansbridge, Jane. 1999b. "Should Blacks Represent Blacks and Women Represent Women? A Contingent 'Yes.'" *Journal of Politics* 61(3): 628–57.

Mansbridge, Jane. 2003. "Rethinking Representation." *American Political Science Review* 97(4): 515–28.

Mansbridge, Jane. 2011. "Clarifying the Concept of Representation." *American Political Science Review* 105(3): 621–30.

Mansbridge, Jane. 2012. "On the Importance of Getting Things Done." *PS: Political Science & Politics* 45(1): 1–8.

Mansbridge, Jane. 2014a. "A Contingency Theory of Accountability." In *The Oxford Handbook of Public Accountability*, edited by Mark Bowens, Robert E. Goodin, and Thomas Schillemans, 55–68. Oxford: Oxford University Press.

Mansbridge, Jane. 2014b. "What Is Political Science For?" *Perspectives on Politics* 12(1): 8–17.

Mansbridge, Jane. 2019a. "Accountability in the Constituent-Representative Relationship." In *Legislature by Lot: Transformative Designs for Deliberative Governance*, edited by John Gasti and Erik Olin Wright, 189–203. London: Verso.

Mansbridge, Jane. 2019b. "Recursive Representation." In *Creating Political Presence*, edited by Dario Castiglione and Johannes Pollak, 298–337. Chicago: University of Chicago Press.

Mansbridge, Jane. 2020. "Representation Failure." In *Democratic Failure*, edited by Melissa Schwartzberg and Daniel Viehoff, 101–40. New York: New York University Press.

Mansbridge, Jane. 2022. "Recursive Representation: The Basic Idea." In *Constitutionalism and a Right to Effective Government?*, edited by Vicki C. Jackson and Yasmin Dawood, 206–20. New York: Cambridge University Press.

Mansbridge, Jane. 2023. "The Future of Political Theory." *Contemporary Political Theory* 22: 251–65.

Mansbridge, Jane, James Bohman, Simone Chambers, Thomas Christiano, Archon Fung, John Parkinson, Dennis F. Thompson, and Mark E. Warren. 2012. "A Systemic Approach to Deliberative Democracy." In *Deliberative Systems*, edited by John Parkinson and Jane Mansbridge, 1–26. Cambridge: Cambridge University Press.

Mansbridge, Jane, and Cathie Jo Martin, eds. 2015. *Political Negotiation*. Washington, DC: Brookings Institution Press.

REFERENCES

Masket, Seth. 2019. "What Is, and Isn't, Causing Polarization in Modern State Legislatures." *PS: Political Science & Politics* 52(3): 430–35.

Mason, Lilliana. 2018. *Uncivil Agreement: How Politics Became Our Identity.* Chicago: University of Chicago Press.

Matsusaka, John G. 2022. "'Congruence' and 'Responsiveness' in the Study of Representation." USC CLASS Research Paper No. CLASS15-19. https://papers.ssrn.com/abstract=2613312, accessed February 22, 2023.

Mayhew, David R. 2005. *Divided We Govern: Party Control, Lawmaking and Investigations, 1946–2002.* 2nd ed. New Haven: Yale University Press.

Mayhew, David R. 2011. *Partisan Balance: Why Political Parties Don't Kill the U.S. Constitutional System.* Princeton: Princeton University Press.

McCarty, Nolan. 2015. "Reducing Polarization by Making Parties Stronger." In *Solutions to Political Polarization in America,* edited by Nathaniel Persily, 136–45. Cambridge: Cambridge University Press.

McCarty, Nolan. 2019. *Polarization: What Everyone Needs to Know.* New York: Oxford University Press.

McCarty, Nolan, Keith T. Poole, and Howard Rosenthal. 2016. *Polarized America: The Dance of Ideology and Unequal Riches.* 2nd ed. Cambridge, MA: MIT Press.

McCarty, Nolan, Jonathan Rodden, Boris Shor, Chris Tausanovitch, and Christopher Warshaw. 2018. "Geography, Uncertainty, and Polarization." *Political Science Research and Methods* 7(4): 775–94.

McCormick, John P. 2011. *Machiavellian Democracy.* Cambridge: Cambridge University Press.

McGann, Anthony J., Charles Anthony Smith, Michael Latner, and Alex Keena. 2016. *Gerrymandering in America: The House of Representatives, the Supreme Court, and the Future of Popular Sovereignty.* Cambridge: Cambridge University Press.

Meiklejohn, Alexander. 1948. *Free Speech and Its Relation to Self-Government.* New York: Harper.

Mettler, Suzanne, and Claire Leavitt. 2019. "Public Policy and Political Dysfunction: The Policyscape, Policy Maintenance, and Oversight." In *Can America Govern Itself?,* edited by Frances E. Lee and Nolan McCarty, 239–70. Cambridge: Cambridge University Press.

Milbank, Dana. 2022. *The Destructionists: The Twenty-Five Year Crack-Up of the Republican Party.* New York: Doubleday.

Mill, John Stuart. [1861] 1977a. "Considerations on Representative Government." In *Collected Works of John Stuart Mill, vol. 19,* edited by J. M. Robson, 371–577. Toronto: University of Toronto Press.

Mill, John Stuart. [1859] 1977b. "On Liberty." In *Collected Works of John Stuart Mill, vol. 18,* edited by J. M. Robson, 213–310. Toronto: University of Toronto Press.

Miller, David. 1983. "The Competitive Model of Democracy." In *Democratic Theory and Practice,* edited by Graeme Duncan, 133–55. Cambridge: Cambridge University Press.

REFERENCES

Miller, Erin L. 2021. "Amplified Speech." *Cardozo Law Review* 43(1): 1–70.

Miller, Nicholas R. 1983. "Pluralism and Social Choice." *American Political Science Review* 77(3): 734–47.

Miller, Warren E., and Donald E. Stokes. 1963. "Constituency Influence in Congress." *American Political Science Review* 57(1): 45–56.

Millhiser, Ian. 2020. "America's Anti-democratic Senate, by the Numbers." *Vox*, November 6, 2020. https://www.vox.com/2020/11/6/21550979/senate-malapportionment-20-million-democrats-republicans-supreme-court.

Montanaro, Laura. 2017. *Who Elected Oxfam? A Democratic Defense of Self-Appointed Representatives*. Cambridge: Cambridge University Press.

Morriss, Peter. 2002. *Power: A Philosophical Analysis*. 2nd ed. Manchester: Manchester University Press.

Muirhead, Russell. 2014. *The Promise of Party in a Polarized Age*. Cambridge, MA: Harvard University Press.

Muirhead, Russell, and Nancy L. Rosenblum. 2006. "Political Liberalism vs. 'The Great Game of Politics': The Politics of Political Liberalism." *Perspectives on Politics* 4(1): 99–108.

Muirhead, Russell, and Nancy L. Rosenblum. 2016. "Speaking Truth to Conspiracy: Partisanship and Trust." *Critical Review* 28(1): 63–88.

Nagle, John F. 2017. "How Competitive Should a Fair Single Member Districting Plan Be?" *Election Law Journal: Rules, Politics, and Policy* 16(1): 196–209.

Neblo, Michael, Kevin M. Esterling, and David M. J. Lazer. 2018. *Politics with the People: Building a Directly Representative Democracy*. Cambridge: Cambridge University Press.

Nguyen, C. Thi. 2020. "Layers of Agency." In *Games: Agency as Art*, edited by C. Thi Nguyen, 52–73. New York: Oxford University Press.

Niederle, Muriel, and Lise Vesterlund. 2007. "Do Women Shy Away from Competition? Do Men Compete Too Much?" *Quarterly Journal of Economics* 122(3): 1067–101.

Nielsen, Rasmus Kleis, and Richard Fletcher. 2020. "Democratic Creative Destruction? The Effect of a Changing Media Landscape on Democracy." In *Social Media and Democracy: The State of the Field, Prospects for Reform*, edited by Nathaniel Persily and Joshua A. Tucker, 139–62. Cambridge: Cambridge University Press.

Niemi, Richard G., and John Deegan. 1978. "A Theory of Political Districting." *American Political Science Review* 72(4): 1304–23.

O'Connell, Anne Joseph. 2020. "Actings." *Columbia Law Review* 120(3): 613–728.

Odegard, Peter H. 1928. *Pressure Politics: The Story of the Anti-Saloon League*. New York: Columbia University Press.

Osmundsen, Mathias, Alexander Bor, Peter Bjerregaard Vahlstrup, Anja Bechmann, and Michael Bang Petersen. 2021. "Partisan Polarization Is the Primary

REFERENCES

Psychological Motivation behind Political Fake News Sharing on Twitter." *American Political Science Review* 115(3): 999–1015.

Ostrogorski, Moisei. 1902. *Democracy and the Organization of Political Parties*. 2 vols. New York: Macmillan.

Owen, David, and Graham Smith. 2015. "Survey Article: Deliberation, Democracy, and the Systemic Turn." *Journal of Political Philosophy* 23(2): 213–34.

Page, Benjamin I., and Martin Gilens. 2020. *Democracy in America? What Has Gone Wrong and What We Can Do about It*. Chicago: University of Chicago Press.

Page, Benjamin I., and Robert Shapiro. 1992. *The Rational Public: Fifty Years of Trends in Americans' Policy Preferences*. Chicago: University of Chicago Press.

Paine, Thomas. [1792] 2000. "The Rights of Man, Part II." In *Paine: Political Writings*, rev. ed., edited by Bruce Kuklick, 155–264. Cambridge: Cambridge University Press.

Parenti, Michael. 1970. "Power and Pluralism: A View from the Bottom." *Journal of Politics* 32(3): 501–30.

Parkinson, John, and Jane Mansbridge, eds. 2012. *Deliberative Systems: Deliberative Democracy at the Large Scale*. Cambridge: Cambridge University Press.

Pateman, Carole. 1970. *Participation and Democratic Theory*. Cambridge: Cambridge University Press.

Persily, Nathaniel. 2015. "Stronger Parties as a Solution to Polarization." In *Solutions to Political Polarization in America*, edited by Nathaniel Persily, 123–35. Cambridge: Cambridge University Press.

Pettit, Philip. 2000. "Democracy, Electoral and Contestatory." In *Designing Democratic Institutions*, edited by Ian Shapiro and Stephen Macedo, 105–44. New York: New York University Press.

Pettit, Philip. 2012. *On the People's Terms: A Republican Theory and Model of Democracy*. Cambridge: Cambridge University Press.

Pevnick, Ryan. 2016. "Does the Egalitarian Rationale for Campaign Finance Reform Succeed?" *Philosophy & Public Affairs* 44(1): 46–76.

Pierson, Paul, and Eric Schickler. 2020. "Madison's Constitution under Stress: A Developmental Analysis of Political Polarization." *Annual Review of Political Science* 23: 37–58.

Pildes, Richard H. 1999. "The Theory of Political Competition." *Virginia Law Review* 85(8): 1605–26.

Pildes, Richard H. 2005. "The Constitution and Political Competition." *Nova Law Review* 30(2): 253–78.

Pildes, Richard H. 2014. "Romanticizing Democracy, Political Fragmentation, and the Decline of American Government." *Yale Law Journal* 124(3): 804–52.

Pildes, Richard H. 2018. "The Past and Future of Voting Rights." *Proceedings of the American Philosophical Society* 162(3): 221–30.

Pitkin, Hanna Fenichel. 1967. *The Concept of Representation*. Berkeley: University of California Press.

REFERENCES

Polsby, Nelson. 1983. *Consequences of Party Reform*. New York: Oxford University Press.

Powell, G. Bingham. 2000. *Elections as Instruments of Democracy: Majoritarian and Proportional Visions*. New Haven: Yale University Press.

Powell, G. Bingham. 2013. "Representation in Context: Election Laws and Ideological Congruence Between Citizens and Governments." *Perspectives on Politics* 11(1): 9–21.

Quitt, Martin H. 2008. "Congressional (Partisan) Constitutionalism: The Apportionment Act Debates of 1842 and 1844." *Journal of the Early Republic* 28(4): 627–51.

Rawls, John. 1999. *A Theory of Justice*. Rev. ed. Cambridge, MA: Harvard University Press.

Rawls, John. 2001. *Justice as Fairness: A Restatement*. Edited by Erin Kelly. Cambridge, MA: Harvard University Press.

Rawls, John. 2005. *Political Liberalism*. Expanded ed. New York: Columbia University Press.

Rehfeld, Andrew. 2005. *The Concept of Constituency: Political Representation, Democratic Legitimacy, and Institutional Design*. Cambridge: Cambridge University Press.

Rehfeld, Andrew. 2009. "Representation Rethought: On Trustees, Delegates, and Gyroscopes in the Study of Political Representation and Democracy." *American Political Science Review* 103(2): 214–30.

Rehfeld, Andrew. 2018. "On Representing." *Journal of Political Philosophy* 26(2): 216–39.

Rey, Felipe. 2023. *El sistema representativo: Las representaciones políticas y la transformación de la democracia parlamentaria*. Barcelona: Gedisa.

Reynolds, Molly E. 2020. "The Decline in Congressional Capacity." In *Congress Overwhelmed: The Decline in Congressional Capacity and Prospects for Reform*, edited by Timothy M. LaPira, Lee Drutman, and Kevin R. Kosar, 34–50. Chicago: University of Chicago Press.

Rhodes, Jesse H., and Brian F. Schaffner. 2017. "Testing Models of Unequal Representation: Democratic Populists and Republican Oligarchs?" *Quarterly Journal of Political Science* 12(2): 185–204.

Richardson, Henry S. 2002. *Democratic Autonomy: Public Reasoning about the Ends of Policy*. New York: Oxford University Press.

Riley, Dylan. 2020. "Faultlines: Political Logics of the US Party System." *New Left Review*, no. 126: 35–50.

Rodden, Jonathan. 2015. "Geography and Gridlock in the United States." In *Solutions to Political Polarization in America*, edited by Nathaniel Persily, 104–20. Cambridge: Cambridge University Press.

Rodden, Jonathan. 2019. *Why Cities Lose: The Deep Roots of the Urban-Rural Political Divide*. New York: Basic Books.

REFERENCES

Rosanvallon, Pierre. [2006] 2008. *Counter-democracy: Politics in an Age of Distrust.* Translated by Arthur Goldhammer. Cambridge: Cambridge University Press.

Rosenblum, Nancy L. 2008. *On the Side of the Angels: An Appreciation of Parties and Partisanship.* Princeton: Princeton University Press.

Rosenblum, Nancy L. 2014. "Governing beyond Imagination: The World Historical Sources of Democratic Dysfunction." *Boston University Law Review* 94(3): 649–68.

Rosenbluth, Frances McCall, and Ian Shapiro. 2018. *Responsible Parties: Saving Democracy from Itself.* New Haven: Yale University Press.

Ross, Robert E. 2017. "Recreating the House: The 1842 Apportionment Act and the Whig Party's Reconstruction of Representation." *Polity* 49(3): 408–33.

Rudder, Catherine E., A. Lee Fritschuler, and Yon Jung Choi. 2016. *Public Policy-Making by Private Organizations.* Washington, DC: Brookings Institution Press.

Sabl, Andrew. 2015. "The Two Cultures of Democratic Theory: Responsiveness, Democratic Quality, and the Empirical-Normative Divide." *Perspectives on Politics* 13(2): 345–65.

Safire, William. 1993. *Safire's New Political Dictionary: The Definitive Guide to the New Language of Politics.* New York: Random House.

Salkin, Wendy. 2024. *Speaking for Others: The Ethics of Informal Political Representation.* Cambridge, MA: Harvard University Press.

Sartori, Giovanni. 1976. *Parties and Party Systems: A Framework for Analysis.* Cambridge: Cambridge University Press.

Saward, Michael. 2010. *The Representative Claim.* Oxford: Oxford University Press.

Scanlon, T. M. 2018. *Why Does Inequality Matter?* Oxford: Oxford University Press.

Schaffner, Brian F., Matthew Streb, and Gerald Wright. 2001. "Teams without Uniforms: The Nonpartisan Ballot in State and Local Elections." *Political Research Quarterly* 54(1): 7–30.

Schattschneider, E. E. 1935. *Politics, Pressures and the Tariff.* New York: Prentice-Hall.

Schattschneider, E. E. 1942. *Party Government.* New York: Holt, Rinehart and Winston.

Schattschneider, E. E. 1960. *The Semisovereign People: A Realist's View of Democracy in America.* New York: Holt, Rinehart and Winston.

Schickler, Eric. 2016. *Racial Realignment: The Transformation of American Liberalism, 1932–1965.* Princeton: Princeton University Press.

Schlozman, Daniel, and Sam Rosenfeld. 2019. "The Hollow Parties." In *Can America Govern Itself?*, edited by Frances E. Lee and Nolan McCarty, 120–50. Cambridge: Cambridge University Press.

Schlozman, Kay Lehman. 1984. "What Accent the Heavenly Chorus? Political Equality and the American Pressure System." *Journal of Politics* 46(4): 1006–32.

Schlozman, Kay Lehman, Henry E. Brady, and Sidney Verba. 2018. *Unequal and Unrepresented: Political Inequality and the People's Voice in the New Gilded Age.* Princeton: Princeton University Press.

REFERENCES

Schlozman, Kay Lehman, Philip Edward Jones, Hye Young You, Traci Burch, Sidney Verba, and Henry E. Brady. 2015. "Organizations and the Democratic Representation of Interests: What Does It Mean When Those Organizations Have No Members?" *Perspectives on Politics* 13(4): 1017–29.

Schlozman, Kay Lehman, Sidney Verba, and Henry E. Brady. 2012. *The Unheavenly Chorus: Unequal Political Voice and the Broken Promise of American Democracy*. Princeton: Princeton University Press.

Schmitter, Philippe. 1992. "The Irony of Modern Democracy." *Politics and Society* 20(4): 507–12.

Schneider, Monica C., Mirya R. Holman, Amanda B. Diekman, and Thomas McAndrew. 2016. "Power, Conflict, and Community: How Gendered Views of Political Power Influence Women's Political Ambition." *Political Psychology* 37(4): 515–31.

Schumpeter, Joseph A. 1942. *Capitalism, Socialism and Democracy*. New York: Harper & Brothers.

Seabrook, Nick. 2017. *Drawing the Lines: Constraints on Partisan Gerrymandering in U.S. Politics*. Ithaca: Cornell University Press.

Shames, Shauna. 2017. *Out of the Running*. New York: New York University Press.

Shapiro, Ian. 2003. *The State of Democratic Theory*. Princeton: Princeton University Press.

Shapiro, Ian. 2017. "Collusion in Restraint of Democracy: Against Political Deliberation." *Daedalus* 146(3): 77–84.

Sharpe, L. J. 1973. "American Democracy Reconsidered: Part II and Conclusions." *British Journal of Political Science* 3(2): 129–67.

Sides, John, Chris Tausanovitch, and Lynn Vavreck. 2022. *The Bitter End: The 2020 Presidential Campaign and the Challenge to American Democracy*. Princeton: Princeton University Press.

Simmel, Georg. [1922] 1955. *Conflict and The Web of Group-Affiliations*. Edited by Kurt H. Wolff. Translated by Kurt H. Wolff and Reinhard Bendix. New York: Free Press.

Sinclair, Barbara. 2016. *Unorthodox Lawmaking: New Legislative Processes in the U.S. Congress*. Washington, DC: Sage CQ Press.

Singer, Peter. 1974. *Democracy and Disobedience*. Oxford: Oxford University Press.

Smith, Graham, and Simon Teasdale. 2012. "Associative Democracy and the Social Economy: Exploring the Regulatory Challenge." *Economy and Society* 41(2): 151–76.

Soontjens, Karolin. 2021. "Chronicle of an Election Foretold: Politicians' Beliefs about Electoral Accountability and its Effects." PhD dissertation, University of Antwerp.

Spence, David B. 2019. "The Effects of Partisan Polarization on the Bureaucracy." In *Can America Govern Itself?*, edited by Frances E. Lee and Nolan McCarty, 271–300. Cambridge: Cambridge University Press.

REFERENCES

Stephanopoulos, Nicholas O., and Christopher Warshaw. 2020. "The Impact of Partisan Gerrymandering on Political Parties." *Legislative Studies Quarterly* 45(4): 609–43.

Stevens, Harry, and Alexi McCammond. 2018. "Most Campaign Contributions Come from outside Candidates' Districts." *Axios*, August 28, 2018.

Stewart, Charles, III, and Barry R. Weingast. 1992. "Stacking the Senate, Changing the Nation: Republican Rotten Boroughs, Statehood Politics, and American Political Development." 1992. *Studies in American Political Development* 6(2): 223–71.

Stewart, Richard B. 1975. "The Reformation of American Administrative Law." *Harvard Law Review* 88(8): 1667–813.

Stigler, George J. 1957. "Perfect Competition, Historically Contemplated." *Journal of Political Economy* 65(1): 1–17.

Stimson, James A., Michael B. MacKuen, and Robert S. Erikson. 1995. "Dynamic Representation." *American Political Science Review* 89(3): 543–65.

Stratmann, Thomas. 2019. "Campaign Finance." In *The Oxford Handbook of Public Choice*, edited by Roger D. Congleton, Bernard Grofman, and Stefan Voigt, vol. 1, 415–32. New York: Oxford University Press.

Strom, Kaare. 1992. "Democracy as Political Competition." *American Behavioral Scientist* 35(4–5): 375–96.

Sundquist, James L. 1980. "The Crisis of Competence in Our National Government." *Political Science Quarterly* 95(2): 183–208.

Sundquist, James L. 1988. "Needed: A Political Theory for the New Era of Coalition Government in the United States." *Political Science Quarterly* 103(4): 613–35.

Sundquist, James L. 1992. *Constitutional Reform and Effective Government*. Washington, DC: Brookings Institution Press.

Sunstein, Cass R. 1991. "Preferences and Politics." *Philosophy & Public Affairs* 20(1): 3–34.

Sunstein, Cass R. 2000. "Deliberative Trouble: Why Groups Go to Extremes." *Yale Law Journal* 110(1): 71–120.

Tabb, Kathryn. 2015. "Psychiatric Progress and the Assumption of Diagnostic Discrimination." *Philosophy of Science* 82(5): 1047–58.

Tajfel, Henri. 1970. "Experiments in Intergroup Discrimination." *Scientific American* 223(5): 96–102.

Tausanovitch, Chris. 2016. "Income, Ideology, and Representation." *RSF: The Russell Sage Foundation Journal of the Social Sciences* 2(7): 33–50.

Tesler, Michael. 2016. *Post-racial or Most-Racial? Race and Politics in the Obama Era*. Chicago: University of Chicago Press.

Thompson, Dennis F. 1976. *John Stuart Mill and Representative Government*. Princeton: Princeton University Press.

Thompson, Dennis F. 1993. "Mediated Corruption: The Case of the Keating Five." *American Political Science Review* 87(2): 369–81.

REFERENCES

Thompson, Dennis F. 2002. *Just Elections: Creating a Fair Electoral Process in the United States*. Chicago: University of Chicago Press.

Thomsen, Danielle M. 2023. "Competition in Congressional Elections: Money versus Votes." *American Political Science Review* 117(2): 675–91.

Truman, David B. 1951. *The Governmental Process: Political Interests and Public Opinion*. New York: Alfred A. Knopf.

Tufte, Edward R. 1973. "The Relationship between Seats and Votes in Two-Party Systems." *American Political Science Review* 67(2): 540–54.

Tushnet, Mark. 2004. "Constitutional Hardball." *John Marshall Law Review* 37(2): 523–53.

US Census. 1791. "Report on Census, 24 October 1791: Schedule of the Whole Number of Persons within the Several Districts of the United States." https://founders.archives.gov/documents/Jefferson/01-22-02-0216.

US Census. 1872. "1870 Census: Volume 1. The Statistics of the Population of the United States." https://www2.census.gov/library/publications/decennial/1870/population/1870a-04.pdf.

Urbinati, Nadia. 2006. *Representative Democracy: Principles and Genealogy*. Chicago: University of Chicago Press.

Urbinati, Nadia. 2014. *Democracy Disfigured: Opinion, Truth, and the People*. Cambridge, MA: Harvard University Press.

Urbinati, Nadia. 2015. "A Revolt against Intermediary Bodies." *Constellations* 22(4): 477–86.

Urbinati, Nadia, and Mark E. Warren. 2008. "The Concept of Representation in Contemporary Democratic Theory." *Annual Review of Political Science* 11(1): 387–412.

Van Deemen, A. 2014. "On the Empirical Relevance of Condorcet's Paradox." *Public Choice* 158(3–4): 311–30.

Van Bavel, Jay J., and Dominic J. Paker. 2021. *The Power of Us: Harnessing Our Shared Identities to Improve Performance, Increase Cooperation, and Promote Social Harmony*. New York: Little, Brown, Spark.

Waldron, Jeremy. 2008. "Deliberation, Disagreement, and Voting." In *Deliberative Democracy and Human Rights*, edited by Harold Koh and Ronald C. Slye, 210–26. New Haven: Yale University Press.

Waldron, Jeremy. 2016. "The Loyal Opposition." In *Political Political Theory: Essays on Institutions*, 93–124. Cambridge, MA: Harvard University Press.

Wallner, James I. 2019. *The Death of Deliberation: Gridlock and the Politics of Effort in the United States Senate*. Lanham, MD: Rowman & Littlefield.

Warren, Mark E. 2001. *Democracy and Association*. Princeton: Princeton University Press.

Warren, Mark E. 2008. "Citizen Representatives." In *Designing Deliberative Democracy: The British Columbia Citizens' Assembly*, edited by Mark E. Warren and Hilary Pearse, 50–69. Cambridge: Cambridge University Press.

REFERENCES

Warren, Mark E. 2011. "Voting with Your Feet: Exit-Based Empowerment in Democratic Theory." *American Political Science Review* 105(4): 683–701.

Warren, Mark E. 2014. "Accountability and Democracy." In *The Oxford Handbook of Public Accountability*, edited by Mark Bovens, Robert E. Goodin, and Thomas Schillemans, 39–54. Oxford: Oxford University Press.

Webber, Grégoire. 2017. "Loyal Opposition and the Political Constitution." *Oxford Journal of Legal Studies* 37(2): 357–82.

Wegman, Jesse. 2020. *Let the People Pick the President: The Case for Abolishing the Electoral College*. New York City: St. Martin's Press.

Weissberg, Robert. 1978. "Collective vs. Dyadic Representation in Congress." *American Political Science Review* 72(2): 535–47.

White, Jonathan, and Lea Ypi. 2016. *The Meaning of Partisanship*. Oxford: Oxford University Press.

Williams, Melissa S. 1998. *Voice, Trust, and Memory: Marginalized Groups and the Failings of Liberal Representation*. Princeton: Princeton University Press.

Wilson, James Lindley. 2019. *Democratic Equality*. Princeton: Princeton University Press.

Wlezien, Christopher, and Stuart N. Soroka. 2011. "Inequality in Policy Responsiveness?" In *Who Gets Represented?*, edited by Christopher Wlezien and Peter K. Enns, 285–310. New York: Russell Sage Foundation.

Wolkenstein, Fabio. Forthcoming. "Equalizing Political Competition." In *Democracy and Competition: Rethinking the Forms, Purposes, and Values of Competition in Democracy*, edited by Alfred Moore and Samuel Bragg. Oxford: Oxford University Press.

Young, Iris Marion. 2000. *Inclusion and Democracy*. New York: Oxford University Press.

Zaller, John. 1994. "Strategic Politicians, Public Opinion, and the Gulf Crisis." In *Taken by Storm*, edited by W. Lance Bennet and David L. Paletz, 250–76. Chicago: University of Chicago Press.

INDEX

For the benefit of digital users, indexed terms that span two pages (e.g., 52–53) may, on occasion, appear on only one of those pages.

Abramowitz, Alan, 25n.26
administrative state, 20, 120, 142–43
admission of new states to the United States, 164–65, 190
adversarial competition, 15–16, 80–81, 149–50, 154–55, 156–57, 186–87
African Americans. *See* Blacks
Aldrich, John, 74
Anderson, Elizabeth, 60n.134
Anderson, Sarah E., 39–40n.79
Aristotle, 8–9
Article V (US Constitution), 163–64

Balkin, Jack M., 112n.110
Baumgartner, Frank R., 109n.102, 110n.105
Bentley, Arthur F., 6
Biden, Joe, 166–67
Binder, Sarah, 22, 36n.68, 37n.70, 37
Blacks
    Democratic Party and, 30–31, 103, 194–95
    Fourteenth Amendment and, 167–68
    legislative districting and, 58–59, 103
    policy responsiveness and, 30–31, 42–43, 58
    presidential elections and, 167–69
    Senate and, 194–95
    Three-Fifths Clause and, 167–68
    voting rights and, 22, 167–68
Brady, Henry, 39n.76, 51–52, 53n.115, 106n.89, 181n.10, 182n.12
Bryce, Lord, 5–6
Buckalew, Charles, 162n.8
Burns, James Macgregor, 22
Butler, D. E., 31n.51, 31n.52
Butler, D. M., 52n.110

campaign financing
    agenda setting and, 122
    electoral competition and, 13–14, 54–55, 55n.121, 91–92
    failures of representation and, 57–58, 83–84, 104
    fairness and, 53–54, 75
    incumbents *versus* challengers and, 54–55, 54n.117, 54n.118, 54–55n.119
    parties and, 57
    party competition and, 100
    polarization and, 40n.80, 57, 57n.125
    public financing and, 55n.121
    race and, 59–60n.132

INDEX

campaign financing (*cont.*)
  responsiveness and, 57–58
  wealthy individuals' influence via, 53–54, 53n.115, 53–54n.116, 83–84
Canes-Wrone, Brandice, 43n.88, 53–54n.116
capitalism, 2, 7–9
Castle, Jeremiah J., 25n.26
Caughey, Devin, 45n.95, 73n.11, 93n.61
Chen, Jowei, 63n.141
Christiano, Thomas, 57n.124
Cicero, 1–2
citizen competence, 126
civil society organizations, 74–75, 140, 142, 143–45, 156–57
Cohen, Joshua, 50
collective representation, 183–85
competition
  adversarial competition and, 15–16, 80–81, 149–50, 154–55, 156–57, 186–87
  campaign resources and, 98–99
  competitive structure, competitiveness, and contestability distinguished, 92
  contingency theory of, 149, 186–89
  deliberative environments and, 78–79
  economic competition and, 6–7, 8, 9–10, 76, 78
  fairness and, 15–16, 79–80, 85n.47, 187–88
  incumbency and, 140, 152–53, 188–89
  legitimacy in representation and, 140, 150, 186–88
  monopolies and, 8–9
  negotiation and, 154, 155–56
  in nonpartisan or single-party polities, 140, 152–53, 188–89
  parallel competition and, 149–50, 156–57
  performative forms of, 8–10
  Progressives and, 3–4
  public communicative environment and, 2, 15–16
  regulation of, 15–16, 75–76, 77–80, 83–86, 150, 186–87, 188–89
  representation and, 15–16, 71, 85–86, 149–50, 187–88
  situational competition and, 38–94, 96–97, 98, 152–53
  social norms and, 78–79, 80, 83–86, 89, 90–91

social value of, 81–82, 83
See also electoral competition; interest competition; party competition
Congress
  admission of new states to United States and, 164–65
  committees' influence in, 23
  Connecticut Compromise and, 162
  Connecting to Congress project and, 149
  crisis governance and, 36, 36n.68
  divided government and, 35–36, 38–39
  gridlock and, 13–14, 22, 33, 35, 36–40, 41–42
  oversight responsibilities of, 23–24, 41–42
  party caucuses in, 99–100
  polarization and, 25–26
  productivity of, 22, 35–36, 37–38, 40
  public levels of trust in, 7–8
  wealth of members of, 51–52
  See also House of Representatives, Senate
congruence
  affluent voters' policy preferences and, 175
  autocratic governments and, 125–26
  constitutional government and, 47
  definition of, 43
  failures of representation and, 7–8, 14–15, 42–43, 66, 113
  minorities' political interests and, 48
  preference-policy link and, 125–26
  representation measured by, 45–47, 48, 174
  responsiveness compared to, 43–45, 44n.92, 47–49, 174, 188–89
  status quo bias and, 175
Connecticut Compromise, 162
Connecting to Congress project, 149
Constitution of the United States
  Article V and, 163–64
  Connecticut Compromise and, 162
  Constitutional Convention (1787) and, 69n.3, 162, 191
  counter-majoritarian features of, 40–41
  Fourteenth Amendment and, 167–68
  Three-Fifths Compromise and, 167–68
  Twelfth Amendment and, 167n.29
contingency theory of competition, 149, 186–89
Curry, James, 23, 23n.16

INDEX

Dahl, Robert, 6–7, 107–9, 107–8n.95
deliberative minipublics, 143
democracy
  Ancient Greece and, 1–2
  competition and, 8, 93
  populist democracy and, 3–4
  Trump as threat to, 13–14, 17
  wealth inequality as potential threat to, 105–6
  See also representation
Democratic Party
  Blacks and, 30–31, 103, 194–95
  Democratic National Convention (1968) and, 4
  McGovern-Fraser Commission, 4
  partisan bias in legislative districting and, 31–32
  polarization and, 24, 26, 27
  primary elections and, 4
  Senate and, 165–66, 192
  Southern United States and, 73n.11, 92–93, 153–54
democratic representation. *See* representation
descriptive representation, 58–59, 90, 120–21, 148
Dias, Nicholas, 27n.36
Dole, Bob, 37, 39
Downs, Anthony, 8, 72, 95
Drutman, Lee, 105–6, 107–8n.95, 110n.104
Dworkin, Ronald, 87–88n.52

Eisgruber, Christopher, 47
Electoral College, 2–3, 166–68, 167n.29, 190, 192–93, 195–97
electoral competition
  aggregate dissatisfaction with incumbent's job performance and, 95
  ballot access restrictions and, 91–92, 96–98
  campaign financing and, 13–14, 54–55, 55n.121, 91–92
  contestability and, 96–98
  deliberative environments and, 94
  democracy and, 93
  distribution of campaign resources and, 92, 98–99
  economic inequality and, 13–14
  epistemic competition and, 56–57
  fairness and, 77, 98–99
  first-past-the-post plurality decision rules and, 97
  gerrymandering and, 13–14, 33, 63, 71–72, 103–4, 132
  legislative districting and, 63, 91–92
  legitimacy and, 152–53, 156–57
  polarization and, 13–14, 71–72, 94n.66
  policy articulation and, 94, 152–53, 155–56
  primary elections and, 95n.69, 97–98
  ranked choice voting and, 97, 140, 155–56
  recruitment of candidates, 154–55
  representation and, 20, 71, 132
  responsiveness and, 93–94, 95–96, 97–98, 132
  single-member districts and, 188
  voter turnout and, 152–53
electoral inversions in presidential elections, 166–67, 169–70, 192–93, 195–96
enclave deliberation, 141
Estlund, David, 57n.124

failures of representation
  campaign financing and, 57–58, 83–84, 104
  communications environment and, 33–34
  congruence and, 7–8, 14–15, 42–43, 66, 113
  electoral inversions and, 166–67, 169–70, 192–93, 195–96
  failures of effectiveness and, 7–8, 14–15, 35, 66, 113
  fairness and, 14–15, 50–64, 66, 113
  gerrymandering and, 7–8, 22, 32–33
  gridlock and, 7–8, 13–14, 22, 35, 36–41, 133–34
  partisan bias in legislative districting and, 31
  polarization and, 7–8, 24, 42–43, 192
  political geography and, 31–32
  responsiveness and, 7–8, 14–15, 28–30, 42–43, 49, 51–60, 66, 113
  Senate and, 190–92, 194
  systemic bias and, 52–53, 121

INDEX

fairness
  ballot access regime and, 75
  campaign financing and, 53–54, 75
  class and, 51
  Congressional rules of procedure and, 75
  electoral competition and, 77, 98–99
  failures of representation and, 14–15, 50–64, 66, 113
  gridlock and, 133–34
  interest competition and, 106, 107–8, 109–11, 130–31, 132
  legislative districting, 50–51, 60, 100–1, 130–31
  political equality and, 50, 86–87
  political party competition and, 75, 101, 131
  preference-policy link and, 119, 123, 135, 175–76
  race and, 58, 103
  representation and, 15–16, 18, 86, 89, 100–4, 121–22, 141, 159–60, 163, 166–67, 174, 175–77, 190–91
  single-member districting and, 63
  systemic bias and, 52–53
federalism, 191
Federalist no. 10, 151
Fenno, Richard, 147–48
Fiorina, Morris, 25–26
Follett, Mary Parker, 6
The Founders, 2–3, 73–74, 151, 152–53, 170
  See also Madison, James
Fourteenth Amendment, 167–68
France, 147

Georgia, 168–69
Germany, 149
gerrymandering
  electoral competition and, 13–14, 33, 63, 71–72, 103–4, 132
  failures of representation and, 7–8, 22, 32–33
  fairness of, 100–4
  meta-gerrymandering and, 160–62
  "packing" and "cracking" techniques in, 31–33
  political redress for, 63n.143

preference-policy link and, 134, 177
safe seats and, 33, 63, 63n.142, 132
Voting Rights Act and, 31–32
See also legislative districting
Gilens, Martin, 28–29, 45n.95, 55n.121, 106–7, 174–81
good government reforms (Progressive Era), 3–4
Gould, Jonathan, 194n.34
Green, Jeffrey, 71n.8
Gresham's Law, 9–10
gridlock
  collective action problems and, 36–37
  congressional oversight undermined by, 23–24, 41–42
  divided government and, 38–39, 133–34
  economic inequality and, 133–34
  failure of representation and, 7–8, 13–14, 22, 35, 36–41, 133–34
  fairness and, 133–34
  government shutdowns in debt limit debates and, 22, 38
  increase since 1970s in levels of, 22
  legitimacy and, 41–42
  minority party aspirations regarding next election and, 39
  partisan sorting and, 26
  polarization and, 23, 27–28, 39, 41, 114–15, 133
  policy drift and, 24
  preference-policy link and, 134, 177
  responsiveness threatened by, 22, 37
  Senate and, 39, 40, 163–64
  status quo bias and, 23–24, 133–34
Griffin, John D., 93n.63
Grossman, Matt, 29n.45

Hacker, Jacob, 23–24
Hajnal, Zoltan, 30–31, 58–60, 59n.129, 59–60n.132
Hasen, Richard, 94n.65, 111–12
Heath, Joseph, 80n.35, 82n.39, 82, 83n.43
Hill, Seth, 25–26, 26n.28
Hispanics, 168–69
House of Representatives
  Connecticut Compromise and, 162

INDEX

Electoral College ties and, 166–67, 167n.29
legislative districting and, 31, 100, 160–62
Mayorkas impeachment (2024) and, 9
recursive representation and, 185–86
Three-Fifths Clause and, 167–68
See also Congress
Howell, William, 37n.70

immigration policy, 9, 196
incumbency
    campaign financing and, 54–55, 54n.117, 54n.118, 54–55n.119
    competition and, 140, 152–53, 188–89
    legislative negotiation and, 154
    minority representation and, 188–89
    responsiveness and, 148
informed preferences, 175–76
Ingham, Sean, 49n.103
interdependence, 139–40, 157–58, 182, 186–87
interest competition
    agenda setting and, 111, 122
    business interest overrepresentation in, 132
    democratic theory and, 105
    epistemic environment of policymaking and, 110–11
    fairness and, 106, 107–8, 109–11, 130–31, 132
    information and expertise conveyed via, 106–7, 110–11
    parties and, 74–75
    political equality ideal and, 107
    preference-policy link and, 123, 124–25, 177
    regulation of, 106–8, 113–14
    representation and, 6, 8, 132
    See also lobbying
Issacharoff, Samuel, 63n.141, 63n.143, 77n.26, 94n.65, 96n.71

Jacobson, Gary C., 54n.117

Kaldor, Nicholas, 21n.11
Kalmoe, Nathan P., 25n.26
Karlan, Pamela, 63n.141, 63n.143, 77n.26, 190–97

Katz, Jonathan N., 32n.55
Key, V. O., 5–6, 35–36, 48–49
Kinder, Donald R, 25n.26
King, Gary, 32n.55
Knight, Frank, 76–78, 76n.21, 76n.22, 78n.30, 82–83, 82n.41, 105–6
Kolodny, Niko, 86n.49, 108n.97, 181, 191n.30
Kristol, Irving, 7–8

La Pira, Timothy M., 107–8n.95
La Raja, Raymond, 57n.125
law of democracy jurisprudence, 77–78
Lax, Jeffrey, 28–29, 44n.92
Leavitt, Claire, 41–42
Lee, Frances, 23, 23n.16, 153–54
legislative districting
    apportionment act of 1842 and, 162n.8
    Blacks and, 58–59, 103
    electoral competition and, 63, 91–92
    fairness and, 50–51, 60, 100–1, 130–31
    House of Representatives and, 31, 100, 160–62
    one person, one vote precept and, 61–62, 159–60
    partisan bias in, 31, 33–34, 50–51, 60, 75, 100–4, 114–15, 121, 160
    party competition and, 100–3
    preference-policy link and, 123
    Reynolds v. Sims and, 18n.4, 159–60, 160n.2, 161n.5, 163, 190–91
    safe seats and, 33, 63, 63n.142, 132
    single-member districts and, 31, 63, 101–4, 148–49, 162n.8, 188
    state legislatures and, 31, 100, 160
    "vote dilution" and, 60
    Voting Rights Act and, 31–32, 103
    See also gerrymandering
legitimacy
    administrative state and, 142–43
    civil society organizations and, 143–45
    coercion and, 139–40, 182
    competition and, 140, 150, 186–88
    democratic control and, 189–90
    descriptive representation and, 120–21, 148
    dyadic relations between citizens and representatives and, 140, 146, 181–82, 183–84

INDEX

legitimacy (*cont.*)
  electoral competition and, 152–53, 156–57
  external equity and, 146
  gridlock and, 41–42
  institutional legitimacy and, 181–86
  internal equity and, 144–45
  normative forms of, 140, 141, 150, 157–58, 182–83, 193–94
  perceived forms of, 140, 150, 157–58, 182–83, 189–90, 193–94
  recursive representation and, 148
  Senate and, 193–94
  stability and, 182–83
  systemic representation and, 183–84
Leighley, Jan, 51n.109
Lelkes, Yphtach, 27n.36
Lessig, Lawrence, 32n.55, 50n.105, 55–56n.122
Lijphart, Arend, 152–53
lobbying
  agenda setting and, 111
  business and professional interests overrepresented in, 109, 132–33
  Dahl on, 107–9
  definition of, 105–6
  epistemic environment of policymaking and, 111–12
  fairness and, 132
  growth since 1980 of, 106–7
  information and expertise conveyed via, 108–9, 132–33
  preference-policy link and, 132–33, 134
  pressuring of policymakers and, 108–10
  regulation of, 111–12, 112n.109
  rent-seeking and, 111–12
  wealthy individuals' influence via, 53
  See also interest competition
Locke, John, 32, 142n.4

Madison, James
  counter-majoritarian features of US Constitution and, 40–41
  on factions, 151, 152–53, 170
  national veto of state legislation proposal and, 191n.29
  on religious motives and social control, 151–52
Mansbridge, Jane, 36–37, 47n.98, 71, 90n.57, 108n.98, 181–90
Mason, Lilliana, 27–28
Matsusaka, John G., 44n.92, 45n.95
Mayhew, David, 36
Mayorkas, Alejandro, 9
McGovern, George, 5
McGovern-Fraser Commission, 4
Meiklejohn, Alexander, 84n.45
meta-gerrymandering, 160–62
Mettler, Suzanne, 41–42
Mill, John Stuart, 46n.97, 69–70, 69n.3, 78–79, 180
Miller, Erin L., 55–56n.122, 79n.33
Moe, Terry, 37n.70
Montana statehood (1889), 165
Morriss, Peter, 52–53, 52–53n.114
Muirhead, Russell, 80n.37

Nagler, Jonathan, 51n.109
Neblo, Michael, 149n.8, 185–86
Nevada statehood (1864), 164–65
New Mexico statehood (1912), 165
nongovernmental organizations (NGOs). *See* civil society organizations and societal realm
North Carolina, 168–69
North Dakota statehood (1889), 165

Odegard, Peter, 5–6
Ostrogorski, Moise, 5–6

Page, Benjamin, 28–29, 55n.121, 94n.66
Paine, Thomas, 70–71
parallel competition, 149–50, 156–57
parties
  ballot access and, 99–100
  campaign financing and, 57
  divided government and, 35–36, 38–39
  endogeneity of, 74
  The Founders and, 73–74, 152–53, 170
  gatekeeping role of, 74–75
  ideological consistency of, 23
  interest competition and, 74–75

230

INDEX

as organizers of political conflict, 99–100, 104
ranked choice voting and, 155–56
See also party competition
party competition
  ballot access laws and, 100
  campaign finance laws and, 100
  candidate selection laws and, 100
  deliberative environments and, 99–100, 189–90
  democratic politics and, 77–78
  erosion since 1990 in, 115
  fairness and, 75, 101, 131
  legislative districting and, 100–3
  in legislatures, 101
  party structures and, 152–53
  policy articulation and, 189–90
  preference-policy link and, 123, 131
  primary elections and, 4–5
  Progressives and, 3–4
  regulation of, 100, 113–14, 189–90
  representation and, 6, 8, 73, 99–100, 141, 170
  single-member district systems and, 101–3
  social value of, 100
Pericles, 1–2
Pevnick, Ryan, 55n.120
Pierson, Paul, 23–24, 41
Pildes, Richard, 77n.25, 77n.26, 94n.65, 96n.71
Pitkin, Hanna, 68, 77, 183–84
polarization
  affective polarization and, 27–28, 71–72
  campaign financing and, 40n.80, 57, 57n.125
  Congress and, 25–26
  electoral competition and, 13–14, 71–72, 94n.66
  elite polarization and, 24–26, 39, 42–43, 114–15
  failures of representation and, 7–8, 24, 42–43, 192
  fairness and, 131, 133
  gridlock and, 23, 27–28, 39, 41, 114–15, 133
  ideological polarization and, 24–26, 24n.23
  norms of forbearance eroded by, 27–28

partisan sorting and, 26–27
preference-policy link and, 133–34, 177
primary elections and, 4–5, 26
social media and, 153–54
status quo bias and, 125
policy drift, 24
political equality
  fairness conditions and, 50, 86–87
  institutional design and, 83–84
  interest competition and, 107
  majoritarianism and, 86, 181
  one person, one vote precept and, 61
  Senate and, 191
political parties. *See* parties
Polsby, Nelson, 4
polyarchy, 6
Powell, Bingham, 43
preference-policy link (PPL)
  affluent voters and, 28–29, 29n.45, 123, 124–25, 129–30, 174–75, 179–81
  agenda setting and, 123–24
  congruence and, 125–26
  deliberative environments and, 136–37
  effectiveness and, 119, 123, 175–76
  fairness and, 119, 123, 135, 175–76
  gerrymandering and, 134, 177
  gridlock and, 134, 177
  highly educated voters and, 129–30
  interest competition and, 123, 124–25, 177
  legislative districting and, 123
  lobbying and, 132–33, 134
  majoritarianism and, 178–79, 180–81
  middle-income voters and, 124–25, 174–75, 179–81
  party competition and, 123, 131
  polarization and, 133–34, 177
  poor voters and, 123, 124–25, 175, 180–81
  preference formation and, 134
  resolution of public policy conflict and, 136
  status quo bias and, 125–26
  See also responsiveness
presidential election of 2000, 166, 192–93
presidential election of 2016, 5, 166–67, 192–93

INDEX

presidential election of 2020, 13, 166–67
Progressives, 3–4

ranked choice voting, 97, 140, 155–56, 162n.8
Rawls, John
  on constitutional design, 47
  on democratic representation as "regulated rivalry," 72, 75, 75–76n.19, 77n.24
  on justice, 50n.108, 182–83
  on legislative districting and fairness, 61n.135
  regulation of competition and, 15–16, 150
recursive representation, 142–43, 147–48, 184–86
Rehfeld, Andrew, 45n.95
representation
  administrative state and, 20, 142–43
  agenda setting and, 122
  citizen competence and, 126
  collective policy preferences and, 127–29, 183–85
  competition and, 15–16, 71, 85–86, 149–50, 187–88
  concept of, in Pitkin, 68
  cue taking and, 127
  delegate *versus* trustee conceptions of, 48
  deliberative environments and, 15–16, 19–20, 19n.7, 64, 70–71, 89
  "democracy scaled up" view of, 8, 15, 68, 72–73, 178–79
  descriptive representation, 58–59, 90, 120–21, 148
  division of labor involved in, 46–47, 70–71, 126–27, 178–79
  dyadic relations between citizens and representatives and, 1–2, 8, 44–45, 64–65, 67–68, 77, 121–22, 140, 146, 152–53, 154, 157–58, 174, 181–82, 183–84
  effectiveness and, 15–16, 18, 86, 88–89, 121–22, 159–60, 163, 166–67, 174, 175–77, 190–91
  electoral competition and, 20, 71, 132
  enclave deliberation, 141
  fairness and, 15–16, 18, 86, 89, 121–22, 141, 159–60, 163, 166–67, 174, 175–77, 190–91
  interest competition and, 6, 8, 132
  interest representation and, 87, 105
  majoritarianism and, 159–60, 163, 170, 177, 178–79, 180–81, 190–91
  minority rights and, 177
  party competition and, 6, 8, 73, 99–100, 141, 170
  policy stability and, 177
  protests and, 141
  racial equality and, 167–68
  recursive representation and, 142–43, 147–48, 184–86
  resolution of policy conflicts and, 15–16, 88, 185
  responsiveness and, 8–9, 15–16, 45, 121
  self-authorship by proxy and, 148
  substantive representation and, 120–21
  systemic representation and, 15, 44–45, 67, 77, 113–14, 121, 122, 139, 140, 174, 178–79, 183–84
  two-way communication and, 147–48, 185–86
  virtual representation and, 67–68, 183–85
  See also failures of representation
Republican Party
  admission of new states to union during Civil War and Reconstruction era and, 164–65
  anti-majoritarianism in contemporary politics and, 115, 165–66, 170
  changes in contemporary composition of, 21, 21n.12
  electoral inversions in presidential elections and, 192–93
  partisan bias in legislative districting and, 31–32, 103, 103n.85
  polarization and, 24–25, 26, 27
  primary elections and, 4–5
  racial resentment and, 31n.50, 196
  rural states and, 163
  Senate and, 165–66, 192, 193–95, 196–97
responsiveness
  campaign financing and, 57–58
  class and, 7–8, 28, 49–51, 121
  congruence compared to, 43–45, 44n.92, 47–49, 174, 188–89
  constitutional restrictions and, 49

INDEX

durable majorities' preferences and, 8–9, 28–29, 40, 42–43, 64, 69–70, 86, 93–94, 165–66
electoral competition and, 93–94, 95–96, 97–98, 132
failures of representation and, 7–8, 14–15, 28–30, 42–43, 49, 51–60, 66, 113
gridlock as threat to, 22, 37
incumbency and, 148
minority rights and, 130
positive responsiveness and, 44
race and, 30, 49–51, 58, 83–84, 121
representation and, 8–9, 15–16, 45, 121
stability and, 49, 130
See also preference-policy link (PPL)
Reynolds, Molly E., 165–66
Reynolds v. Sims, 18n.4, 159–60, 160n.2, 161n.5, 163, 190–91
rivalry. *See* competition
Rodden, Jonathan, 31n.52, 38n.74, 63n.141, 160, 163, 192
Rosanvallon, Pierre, 147
Rosenblatt, Elizabeth, 32n.55
Rosenblum, Nancy, 17–18, 80n.37, 99n.75, 144–45, 150
Rosenfeld, Sam, 99–100
Rudder, Cathy, 143–44

Sartori, Giovanni, 77–78
Scalia, Antonin, 38n.73
Scanlon, T. M., 50, 52n.113, 57–58
Schaffner, Brian, 57n.125
Schattschneider, E. E., 5–6, 31n.52, 72, 73–75, 73n.12, 109, 189–90
Schickler, Eric, 41
Schlozman, Daniel, 99–100
Schlozman, Kay, 51n.109, 53n.115, 106n.89, 107–8n.95
Schmitter, Philippe, 145
Schumpeter, Joseph, 71n.8, 72, 79n.31, 81–82
Senate
Article V (US Constitution) on states' equal suffrage in, 163–64
Black voters and, 194–95
Connecticut Compromise and, 162
electoral competitiveness and, 94n.64

failures of representation and, 190–92, 194
filibuster in, 39, 40
large-state representation *versus* small-state representation in, 162, 163, 191–92, 191n.30
legitimacy and, 193–94
meta-gerrymandering and, 160–62
partisan bias in constituencies of, 31n.52, 160–62, 165–66, 192, 193–95, 196–97
See also Congress
Shames, Shauna, 154–55
Shapiro, Ian, 19n.7, 156n.16
Sharpe, L. J., 35n.62
Shepsle, Kenneth, 194n.34
Simmel, Georg, 156–57
single-member districting (SMD), 31, 63, 101–4, 148–49, 162n.8, 188
Social Security, 25, 125n.5
societal realm, 143–44
South Dakota statehood (1889), 165
Stephenson, Matthew, 194n.34
Stepp, Kyla, 25n.26
Stratmann, Thomas, 54–55n.119
Strom, Kaare, 92
substantive representation, 120–21
Sundquist, James, 35–36, 38–39
Supreme Court, 142n.4, 169–70, 190

Tajfel, Henri, 151–52
Tausanovitch, Chris, 25–26, 26n.28
Texas, 143, 168–69
Thompson, Dennis, 69n.3, 95n.67, 97n.72
Three-Fifths Clause (US Constitution), 167–68
Tocqueville, Alexis de, 5–6
Truman, David, 6–7
Trump, Donald, 5, 13–14, 17–19, 115, 166–67
Tufte, Edward, 93–95, 93n.62
Twelfth Amendment, 167n.29

Urbinati, Nadia, 19–20, 33–34
Utah statehood (1896), 164–65

Verba, Sidney, 51–52, 53n.115, 106n.89, 112n.109
Virginia, 162, 168–69
virtual representation, 67–68, 183–85

INDEX

Volden, David W., 39n.76
voting rights, 22, 31–32, 103, 167–68, 169–70

Waldron, Jeremy, 88n.54, 91n.59
Warshaw, Christopher, 45n.95
Washington State, admission to union (1889) of, 165

Weissberg, Robert, 183–85
West Virginia statehood (1863), 165
Wilson, James (Founding Father), 69n.3
Wilson, James L. (political scientist), 56n.123

Young, Iris Marion, 147–48, 184–85